THE GAME OF LANGUAGE

SYNTHESE LANGUAGE LIBRARY

TEXTS AND STUDIES IN
LINGUISTICS AND PHILOSOPHY

VOLUME 22

JAAKKO HINTIKKA

in collaboration with

JACK KULAS

Department of Philosophy, Florida State University

THE GAME
OF LANGUAGE

Studies in Game-Theoretical Semantics and Its Applications

D. REIDEL PUBLISHING COMPANY

A MEMBER OF THE KLUWER ACADEMIC PUBLISHERS GROUP

DORDRECHT / BOSTON / LANCASTER

Library of Congress Cataloging in Publication Data

Hintikka, Jaakko, 1929-
 The game of language.

(Synthese language library; v. 22)

Bibliography: p.
Includes indexes.
 1. Semantics (Philosophy)–Addresses, essays, lectures.
2. Analysis (Philosophy)–Addresses, essays, lectures. 3. Game
theory–Addresses, essays, lectures. I. Kulas, Jack. II. Title. III. Series.
B840.H56   1983   149'.946   83-21102
ISBN 90-277-1687-0

Published by D. Reidel Publishing Company,
P.O. Box 17, 3300 AA Dordrecht, Holland.

Sold and distributed in the U.S.A. and Canada
by Kluwer Academic Publishers,
190 Old Derby Street, Hingham, MA 02043, U.S.A.

In all other countries, sold and distributed
by Kluwer Academic Publishers Group,
P.O. Box 322, 3300 AH Dordrecht, Holland.

Printed in The Netherlands

TABLE OF CONTENTS

PREFACE   vii

THE ORIGIN OF THE DIFFERENT CHAPTERS   xi

CHAPTER 1 / Game-Theoretical Semantics: Insights and Prospects   1

CHAPTER 2 / Semantical Games and Transcendental Arguments   33

CHAPTER 3 / Semantical Games, Subgames, and Functional Inter-
            pretations   47

CHAPTER 4 / *Any* Problems — *No* Problems   77

CHAPTER 5 / Temporal Discourse and Semantical Games   113

CHAPTER 6 / Definite Descriptions in Game-Theoretical Semantics   137

CHAPTER 7 / "Is", Semantical Games, and Semantical Relativity   161

CHAPTER 8 / Semantical Games and Aristotelian Categories   201

CHAPTER 9 / On the *Any*-Thesis and the Methodology of Linguistics 231

CHAPTER 10 / Theories of Truth and Learnable Languages   259

BIBLIOGRAPHY   293

INDEX OF NAMES   319

INDEX OF SUBJECTS   323

PREFACE

Since the first chapter of this book presents an introduction to the present state of game-theoretical semantics
(GTS), there is no point in giving a briefer survey here.
Instead, it may be helpful to indicate what this volume
attempts to do. The first chapter gives a short introduction to GTS and a survey of what is has accomplished.
Chapter 2 puts the enterprise of GTS into new philosophical perspective by relating its basic ideas to Kant's
philosophy of mathematics, space, and time. Chapters 3-6
are samples of GTS's accomplishments in understanding
different kinds of semantical phenomena, mostly in natural
languages. Beyond presenting results, some of these
chapters also have other aims. Chapter 3 relates GTS to
an interesting line of logical and foundational studies - the
so-called functional interpretations - while chapter 4 leads
to certain important methodological theses.

Chapter 7 marks an application of GTS in a more philosophical direction by criticizing the Frege-Russell thesis
that words like "is" are multiply ambiguous. This leads in
turn to a criticism of recent logical languages (logical
notation), which since Frege have been based on the ambiguity thesis, and also to certain methodological sug-
gestions. In chapter 8, GTS is shown to have important
implications for our understanding of Aristotle's doctrine of
categories, while chapter 9 continues my earlier criticism
of Chomsky's generative approach to linguistic theorizing.
Finally, chapter 10 is a systematic criticism of the principle of compositionality, another mainstay of recent logical
languages.

These extensions and applications serve to demonstrate
the potential for constructive theorizing that GTS offers.
In chapters 3-6, the emphasis is linguistic, whereas in
chapters 7-10 it is more methodological and philosophical.
The last few chapters (plus, in a way, chapter 3) amount
to a major challenge of the received logical languages of
the Frege-Russell type. If I am right, these languages
turn out to be deeply unsatisfactory for representing the
logic and semantics of natural languages. If this result

proves its mettle, it has wide-ranging implications for the entire methodology of contemporary analytic philosophy. This multiplicity of connections with different linguistic, methodological, philosophical, and logical issues is the best evidence for GTS I can think of.

There is a major development in the works, not adequately represented in the present volume, though foreshadowed in chapter 6. GTS seems to yield an extremely interesting theory of pronominal anaphora, but that theory still requires further development before it will be ready for publication.

Because of the separate origins of the different chapters, the reader will find some amount of overlap between them. We have not tried to eliminate it, partly because there is some value to the reader in the possibility of studying the different chapters independently.

Time is undoubtedly ripe for a systematic exposition of GTS. This volume is not one, unfortunately. Even though its different parts complement one another and together offer a reasonably systematic overview of GTS, they have not been merged together into a uniform exposition. However, such a systematic work is being written by Lauri Carlson and Jack Kulas. The present book serves as the best substitute for such a work that can be made available for the time being.

All the work on the new chapters, all the work on the revisions of the old ones, and most of the editing has been supported by NSF Grant no. BNS 8119033 (Principal Investigator: Jaakko Hintikka). The writing of the different essays and the production of the camera-ready copy have in many ways been facilitated by the Department of Philosophy, The Florida State University. Some of the earlier work on GTS by Jaakko Hintikka was supported by a John Simon Guggenheim Fellowship in 1979-80.

Our intellectual debts are too extensive to be exhaustively listed here. One of them is nevertheless exceptional. Chapters 4 and 10 were originally prompted by discussions with Lauri Carlson, and chapter 3 is a further continuation of earlier work done jointly with Jaakko Hintikka and Lauri Carlson, who thus deserves a great deal of credit for the ideas put forward in this volume.

Jack Kulas's contribution to the chapters he has co-authored and to the final formulation of all the book's chapters has been invaluable. He also has compiled the bibliography and the indexes that appear in this volume.

The copyediting of the book and the production of the camera-ready copy was accomplished by a team consisting of Jack Kulas, Jayne Moneysmith and Florene Ball, with assistance from John Blair, Leigh Campbell, and Constance Jakubcin. Without their dedicated efforts, this book would never have come about, and even if it had, it would have appeared much later and in a more expensive form. I owe warm thanks to them, and likewise to Ms. Kay Richardson of D. Reidel Publishing Company for her unfailing encouragement and advice.

Tallahassee, Florida   Jaakko Hintikka
April 1983

THE ORIGIN OF THE DIFFERENT CHAPTERS

Of the different chapters of this book, the following appear here for the first time:

Chapter 3, "Semantical Games, Subgames, and Functional
        Interpretations"
Chapter 4, "*Any*-Problems - *No*-Problems"
Chapter 6, "Definite Descriptions in Game-Theoretical
        Semantics"

However, chapter 6 overlaps in part with the following paper:

Jaakko Hintikka and Jack Kulas, "Russell Vindicated: Towards a General Theory of Definite Descriptions", which was presented at the Eastern Division meeting of the APA in Baltimore in December 1982, and appeared in the *Journal of Semantics* 1 (1982), 387-97.

Both these papers are based on parts of Jack Kulas's dissertation, *The Logic and Semantics of Definite Descriptions*, Department of Philosophy, Florida State University, August 1982.

Of the other essays, chapter 1 originally appeared in the *Notre Dame Journal of Formal Logic* 23 (1982), 219-41. It has been revised and expanded for this volume, however.

Chapter 2 appeared in E. M. Barth and J. L. Martens, editors, *Argumentation: Approaches to Theory Formation* John Benjamins, Amsterdam, 1982, pp. 77-91. It is reprinted here with no major changes.

Chapter 5 is reprinted, with virtually no changes, from *Linguistics and Philosophy* 5 (1982), 3-22.

Chapter 7 appeared first in the *Journal of Philosophical Logic* 8 (1979), 433-68. It is reprinted here with a number of minor changes.

Chapter 8 appeared under the title "Semantical Games, the Alleged Ambiguity of 'Is', and Aristotelian Categories" in *Synthese* 54 (1983), 443-68. This paper, especially the last few pages, has been revised for publication here. The same historical ground is also covered in my paper, "The Varieties of Being in Aristotle", forthcoming in

Jaakko Hintikka and Simo Knuuttila, editors *The Logic of Being: Historical Studies*.

Chapter 9 appeared in *Linguistics and Philosophy* 4 (1980), 101–22. It originated from the paper I read at the International Congress of Logic, Methodology, and Philosophy of Science in Hanover in 1979, and is reprinted here with only minor changes.

Chapter 10 was originally written as my contribution to a volume on Donald Davidson, but soon grew too long for that purpose. It first appeared in S. Kanger and S. Ohman, editors, *Philosophy and Grammar,* D. Reidel, Dordrecht, 1981, pp. 37–57. It has been substantially expanded for its republication here. Indeed, the last fourth of the paper is appearing here for the first time. These additions were largely prompted by discussions with Barry Richards, Barbara Partee, and Michael Arbib in 1981.

All the materials appear here with the appropriate permissions.

Chapter 1

GAME-THEORETICAL SEMANTICS:
INSIGHTS AND PROSPECTS

1. Introduction

The paradigm problem for game-theoretical semantics (GTS) is the treatment of quantifiers, primarily logicians' existential and universal quantifiers. As far as the uses of quantifiers in logic and mathematics are concerned, the basic ideas codified in GTS have long been an integral part of logicians' and mathematicians' folklore. Everybody who has taken a serious course in calculus remembers the definition of what it means for a function $y = f(x)$ to be continuous at x_0. It means that, *given* a number w, however small, *we can find* ε such that $|f(x) - f(x_0)| < \delta$ given any x such that $|x - x_0| < \varepsilon$.[1] The most natural way of making this jargon explicit is to envision each choice of the value of an existentially bound variable to be my own move in a game, and each choice of the value of a universally bound variable a move in the same game by an imaginary opponent. The former is what is covered by such locutions as "we can find", whereas the latter is what is intended by references to what is "given" to us. This is indeed what is involved in the continuity example. For what the above "ε-δ definition" of continuity says is precisely (1):

$$(1) \quad (\delta)(E\varepsilon)(x)[(|x - x_0| < \varepsilon) \rightarrow (|f(x) - f(x_0)| < \delta)].$$

Here, "we can find" corresponds to the existential quantifier "$(E\varepsilon)$", and the locution "given" to the universal quantifiers "(δ)" and "(x)". A game-theoretical treatment of the two quantifiers, for all intents and purposes, is just a systematization of the ideas involved in this example.

Logicians have even introduced a name for the functions that embody my strategy in choosing values for existentially bound variables. They are what is meant by *Skolem functions* in logic. Using $s(z)$ as such a function, we can, for instance, express what (1) says by asserting that a suitable Skolem function exists for my choice of ε, i.e., by asserting that (2):

$$(2) \quad (Es)(\delta)(x)[(|x - x_0| < s(\delta)) \rightarrow \\ (|f(x) - f(x_0)| < \delta)].$$

GTS will incorporate this role of Skolem functions.

As a matter of historical fact, however, logicians have resorted to explicitly game-theoretical conceptualizations only when there is no hope of dealing with the semantics (model theory) of a branch of logic by means of the usual Tarski-type truth definitions. The most conspicuous cases in point are the theory of partially ordered quantifiers[2] and the theory of so-called game quantifiers.[3] It is my thesis that game-theoretically inspired conceptualizations have much to offer in other parts of logical studies as well. An especially neat case in point is offered by Gödel's functional interpretation of first-order arithmetic.[4] As Dana Scott first pointed out,[5] by far the most natural way of looking at it is in game-theoretical terms. Other examples are found later in this chapter and in the relevant literature.

There is one major exception to this failure of logicians to spell out their own tacit use of game-theoretical concepts and ideas.[6] This is the important set of techniques in model theory known as back-and-forth methods. Their game-theoretical nature is fairly obvious, and their uses have occasionally been couched in game-theoretical terms, for instance, in terms of what are known as Ehrenfeucht games.

2. Simple Formal Languages

The basic ideas of GTS can be introduced most naturally by reference to formal first-order (quantificational) languages.[7] The game-theoretical treatment of such a finite, formal first-order language L can be explained in a nutshell as follows. We assume that L is an interpreted language – otherwise we cannot meaningfully speak of the truth or falsity of its sentences. Its being interpreted means that we are given some domain of individuals D on which all the nonlogical constants of L are interpreted. This in turn means that each atomic sentence (including

each identity) that can be formed from the nonlogical constants of L, plus the names of the members of D, has a
definite truth-value, true or false.   This is comparable to
what is accomplished by those clauses in a Tarski-type
truth definition that govern atomic sentences.   The function of a game-theoretical truth definition is the same as
that of the other (recursive) clauses of a Tarski-type
truth definition, viz., to extend the notions of truth and
falsity to all nonatomic sentences.

However, in GTS this is done in a way essentially different from Tarski's methods.   A two-person zero-sum
game G(S) is associated with each well-formed sentence S
of any language L', where L' is L extended by adjoining to
it a finite number of names of members of D.   We shall call
the two players *Myself* (or *I*) and *Nature*.   The definition
of G(S) is as follows:

(G. A)   If A is atomic, then I have won G(A) and Nature
has lost if A is true.   If A is false, Nature has
won and I have lost.

(G. &) $G(S_1 \mathrel{\&} S_2)$ begins by Nature's choice of S_1 or
S_2.   The rest of the game is $G(S_1)$ or $G(S_2)$,
respectively.

(G. v) $G(S_1 \vee S_2)$ begins by Myself's choice of S_1 or
S_2.   The rest of the game is $G(S_1)$ or $G(S_2)$,
respectively.

(G. U) $G((x)S[x])$ begins by Nature's choice of a member of D.   Let the name of the member chosen be
"b".   The rest of the game is then $G(S[b])$.

(G. E) $G((Ex)S[x])$ is defined likewise except that b is
chosen by Myself.

(G. ~) $G(\sim S)$ is played like G(S) except that the roles of
the two players (as defined by these rules) are
interchanged.

These rules are said to define *semantical games*.[8]

In (G. E) and (G. U), it is not assumed that the individual chosen already has a name.   Rather, it is assumed
that if it does not, the players will give it a proper name,
thus extending the given language by adjoining to it that

proper name.

But what do these games have to do with semantics? They can be brought to bear on semantics by showing how they can be used to define the crucial concept of truth. GTS is truth conditional, even though it works in a way different from Tarski-type theories of truth.

The truth of a sentence S of L can be defined as the existence of a winning strategy in G(S) for Myself, i.e., a way of choosing my moves such that I end up winning no matter what Nature does. The falsity of S means that Nature has a winning strategy in G(S).[9]

Since the output of each application of the rules formulated above is simpler than its input (in the sense of containing one logical symbol less than the input), our semantical games will always end with an atomic sentence after a finite number of moves. Hence (G. A) suffices to define winning and losing for all cases. For the same reason, the rules of semantical games can be considered rules of semantical analysis.

It is easily seen that, in the simple languages we are currently considering, the game-theoretical definition of truth just presented coincides with the usual Tarski-type definition. It can be seen almost equally easily that in many circumstances it offers interesting possibilities of modifying our usual truth definitions or otherwise putting them into a wider perspective. Suffice it here to mention only one such line of thought. In game-theoretical semantics, truth means that there is a winning strategy for Myself, and falsity means that there is such a strategy for my opponent, Nature. But who says that either one of us has a winning strategy? The law of excluded middle says so. On the basis of game theory we can now see that this law is by no means trivial or unproblematic. For, in general, it is not a foregone conclusion that there should exist a winning strategy for either one of the two players in a zero-sum two-person game.[10] When one exists, the game is said to be *determinate*. From game theory we know that the determinateness of a game is often a highly nontrivial result (or assumption). Indeed, determinateness assumptions for certain infinite games have recently played an important role as powerful potential axioms in the higher reaches of axiomatic set theory.[11] But even apart from such sophisticated situations, determinateness (and hence the law of excluded middle) can fairly easily fail. Thus the principle of excluded middle is put into an interesting general perspective by GTS.

3. Extensions and Generalizations
in Formal Languages

Several of the many interesting further developments of GTS can be discussed in reference to games connected with formal (but interpreted) first-order sentences or with sentences in various natural extensions of formal first-order languages. Here is a list of some of the further developments:

(i) The existence of a winning strategy for either player in a given G(S) can be expressed in the form of an explicit *higher-order* sentence. This sentence asserts the existence of the relevant Skolem functions. What this means is that GTS effects a translation of first-order languages into higher-order languages. For instance, (1) translates into (2), and

(3) $(x)(Ey) M(x,y)$

translates into

(4) $(Ef)(x) M(x,f(x))$,

and

(5) $(x)(Ey)(z)(Eu) M(x,y,z,u)$

translates into

(6) $(Ef)(Eg)(x)(z) M(x,f(x),z,g(x,z))$.

(I am assuming here that there are no quantifiers in M, and that propositional connectives are given the classical interpretation.)

The relation of (6) to (5) (and in general the relation of the higher-order translation of a first-order sentence that game-theoretical semantics yields to its original) can be taken to exemplify the difference between a game in normal form (game as a choice of a strategy) and the same game in extensive form.[12] Conversely, this application of familiar game-theoretical notions serves to bring their import into sharper perspective.

(ii) The interpretation of first-order languages in higher-order ones outlined in (i) above can be varied in different ways. These variations will result in so many variants of nonclassical logic. One such is to allow the game to be split into various subgames that are each played out, whereupon one of the players reveals the strategy she or he had used in the subgame.[13] The functions that embody the strategies of the players in the overall game hence depend upon the functions that incorporate players' strategies in the subgame. In other words, they are higher-order functions (functionals). Accordingly, the translations of first-order languages described in (i) above must now be in terms of sentences of even higher order than just second order. Likewise, it is seen in this way that GTS is closely related to the various functional interpretations that can be given to first-order languages and theories and have been studied in the literature.[14]

(iii) Such subgames are a natural vehicle for interpreting conditionals. A subgame is first played with the antecedent X of a conditional $(X \rightarrow Y)$ (with roles exchanged), and only if Nature manages to verify X do the players move over to the game $G(Y)$, where Nature's winning strategy in the first subgame is known to Myself. This is in excellent agreement with generally accepted ideas concerning the conditionality of conditionals: the consequent Y enters the picture only if the antecedent has turned out to be true, and does so in a way that depends on the way X has been verified.

There remain several different ways in which this game-theoretical interpretation of conditionals can be carried out. (See chapter 3.)

(iv) To preserve classical logic, the values of our function variables (Skolem functions, such as the function variables in (2), (4), and (6)) have to include quite complex (noncomputable) functions.[15] Since these functions are supposed to embody players' actual strategies, it nevertheless seems natural to restrict these functions to computable ones. This pushes our logic further away from classical logic.

Alternatively, we may think of players' strategies as being formed move by move and not chosen once and for all. In this way we may hope to be less restrictive than if we had limited the players to preselected recursive strategies. But in that case we must adopt some sort of constructivistic conception of mathematical entities, such as functions (strategy functions). Hence we are dealing here with important issues in the philosophy of mathematics.

(v) The relation of the resulting interpretations to the classical one is essentially an instance of the relation of nonstandard to standard interpretations of higher-order logic in Henkin's sense.[16] The only difference is that Henkin considers somewhat different closure conditions imposed on the values of higher-order variables than those that result from restricting the values of our function variables to computable ones. If we look away from this inessential qualification, we can say that GTS serves to extend the standard-nonstandard contrast from higher-order logics to first-order logic.

(vi) If changes (ii)-(iv) are combined with a require-ment of computability also for the moves for propositional connectives, and if a suitable rule for conditionals is chosen (see (iii) above), we obtain Gödel's famous func-tional interpretation of first-order languages.[17]

(vii) One of the first questions a game theorist is likely to ask is whether our semantical games are games with perfect information. Classical logic presupposes that se-mantical games are characterized by perfect information. This assumption is easily modified, however, especially in the case of quantifier rules. The result is then a new kind of logic that has been independently studied by a handful of logicians, viz., the logic of finite partially ordered (e.g., branching) quantifiers.[18] Several things about the theory of such quantifiers make this theory an interesting test case in logical and semantical theory. First, it is (almost) as strong as the whole of second-order logic (with standard interpretation), in the sense of having an equally difficult decision problem.[19] Second, the usual Tarski-type truth definitions do not work in the theory of partially ordered quantifiers.[20]

The simplest branching prefixes reduce to linear pre-fixes. For instance,

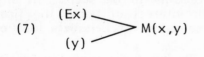

$$(7) \quad \begin{matrix} (Ex) \\ \\ (y) \end{matrix} \!\!\!\!\gtrdot M(x,y)$$

reduces to

(8)   (Ex)(y) M(x,y).

However, more complex types of prefixes are not equivalent with any linear ones. For instance, the "Henkin quantifier" illustrated by

$$
(9) \quad \begin{matrix} (x)(Ey) \\ \\ (z)(Eu) \end{matrix} \Big\rangle M(x,y,z,u)
$$

has no first-order linear equivalent.[21]

In all cases, of course, we have a second-order translation. Thus (9) is equivalent with

(10)   (Ef)(Eg)(x)(z) M(x,f(x),z,g(z)).

This illustrates how informational dependencies among quantifiers are reflected by the arguments of the corresponding Skolem functions. (Compare (9)-(10) with (5)-(6) above.)

(viii) Because of the failure of Tarski-type truth definitions for sentences containing partially ordered quantifiers (the second of the results mentioned in (vii) above), mathematical logicians have been forced to resort to game-theoretical conceptualizations in the study of partially ordered quantifiers. As was already mentioned, there is another direction in which they have sporadically done so, viz., in certain cases in which (in our terminology) a semantical game can go on to infinity.[22] Since our game rules are rules of semantical analysis, this means that one cannot define truth recursively from the bottom up, as in Tarski. For there is sometimes no bottom on which to build such a definition. This is no obstacle, however, to game-theoretical truth definitions. On the contrary, it leaves open all sorts of interesting possibilities for setting up the definition of winning and losing (or neither) in the case of infinite plays of a semantical game. The usefulness of the general theory of infinitely deep logics that can be based on this idea remains to be seen. In any case, it has the philosophical interest of being the first clear-cut, general, modern realization of Leibniz's idea of infinite analysis in logic.[23]

(ix) There is no reason why the successive choices of individuals could not be made from different subsets of D. This means modifying the received notion of a model for first-order languages. The result is Rantala's notion of urn model,[24] which has already had promising applications in Rantala's theory of definability and in Hintikka's solution of the problem of "logical omniscience" in epistemic logic.[25] We can now see that the game-theoretical truth definition can be used in the theory of urn models without any changes other than those that define urn models.

(x) Game-theoretical semantics is easily extended to intensional logics by using the well-known possible-worlds semantics for intensional logics as an interim step. The main novelty is that at each move the players are now considering not only a sentence S', but also a world w_0, which is a member of the frame with respect to which the original sentence is to be interpreted. The stronger of each pair of interrelated intensional operators (necessity, knowledge, belief, obligation, etc.) marks Nature's move, the weaker (possibility, epistemic possibility, compatibility with one's beliefs, permission, etc.) my move. A move consists of a selection of one of the worlds, say w_1, alternative to w_0. At the next move, the players will consider w_1 instead of w_0.

In brief, intensional operators are quantifiers ranging over alternative worlds. (This incidentally serves to highlight once again the fundamental importance of the alternativeness relation in intensional semantics.)

It turns out that we may then have to heed possible informational independencies between quantifier moves and moves connected with intensional operators.[26] What is more, informational dependencies need not in such cases be transitive.[27] (Any game theorist will tell you that the information sets involved in an arbitrary game are not always ordered transitively by class-inclusion.) Hence, not even branching structures suffice for the semantical representation of all the sentences that are naturally considered in this direction.

4. Transition to Natural Languages

Despite the fecundity of game-theoretical semantics in formal-language study, its most remarkable applications are to natural languages. The transition is based on the following idea: there is no prima facie counterpart in natural languages to the procedure of substituting names of individuals chosen by the players for bound variables, for there are no variables in natural languages. But what we can do is have proper names for such individuals substituted for *entire quantifier phrases*. They include, most commonly, phrases of the following forms:

(11)   some X who Y
        an X who Y
        every X who Y
        each X who Y
        any X who Y

Instead of "who" in the above phrase-forms, we could have some other wh-word.

This idea, in combination with the heuristic idea that a semantical game is an attempt on my part to verify a sentence against the schemes of recalcitrant Nature, enables us to anticipate the game rules for the main English quantifier phrases. They are illustrated by the following special cases of some of the rules:

(G. some)   If the game has reached a sentence of
[special case]   the form

                   (*)   X – some Y who Z – W,

                   then an individual may be chosen by My-
                   self from the subdomain that consists of
                   persons. If this individual does not
                   have a proper name, it is given one.
                   Let the proper name of the individual
                   chosen be "b". The game is then con-
                   tinued with respect to

                   (**)   X – b – W, b is a Y, and b Z.

For simplicity, it is assumed here, and in the next few rules, that "who" occupies the subject position in "who Z", and that the main verb in "who X" is in the singular.[28]

From (**) it is seen how the name of the individual chosen replaces the whole quantifier phrase in (*).

(G. an)   As in the corresponding case of
[special case]   (G. some), except that "a(n)" replaces
                   "some".

(G. every)   As in the corresponding case of
[special case]   (G. some), except that b is chosen by
Nature, "every" replaces "some" in (*),
and the game is continued with respect
to

$$(***) \qquad X - b - W, \text{ if } b \text{ is a } Y$$
$$\text{and } b \ Z.$$

(G. each)   As in the corresponding case of
[special case]   (G. every), except that "each" replaces
"every".

(G. any)   As in the corresponding case of
[special case]   (G. every), except that "any" replaces
"every".

In spite of their simplicity, these rules codify nontrivial theses. For instance, (G. any) incorporates the claim that "any" is univocal in English, always having basically the force of a universal quantifier. This is opposed to most of the recent literature in linguistics on "any", and puts an onus on me to square my account with the many examples in which "any" appears to have the force of an existential quantifier.[29]

Subject to explanations to be given later, the general setup and the rules for propositional connectives are still similar to those for formal languages. We are dealing with two-person zero-sum games, and a game G(S) can still be thought of, heuristically, as an attempt on the part of one of the players (namely, Myself) to verify the sentence S with which the game starts, against the opposition of Nature. At each stage of the game, some one sentence S' is being considered on which the players' next move depends. As before, some primitive vocabulary is assumed to be given, and interpreted on a given domain. But it is less clear than it is for formal languages that the game always comes to an end in a finite number of moves. It is possible, however, to show that finitude can be guaranteed by means of further amplifications of the set of our game rules, at least for the fragments of English we are here interested in.

When compared with the semantics of formal languages, one striking novelty here is that the individual chosen by one of the players at any one move is chosen from a subdomain of the total supply of individuals we can quantify over. A logician would say that we are dealing with many-sorted quantification. This fact will make more difference than perhaps is at first apparent. (Cf. below, section 10.)

Winning and losing can be defined as of old, and truth (falsity) can similarly be defined as the existence of a winning strategy for Myself (Nature).

Negation can be dealt with in terms of role swapping, just as it is in formal languages.[30] The rules for con-junction and disjunction can be carried over without major changes for the uses of "and" and "or" to connect clauses, and they can be extended in an obvious way to those uses in which they connect phrases.

5. Amplifications, Developments, and Extensions

The quantifier rules formulated above need several ex-planations, generalizations, and qualifications to be ade-quate, so the following remarks are in order here:

(a) As they are formulated above, my quantifier rules apply only to singular quantifier phrases. The corresponding rules for plural quantifier phrases can be formulated similarly in terms of a simultaneous choice of any number of individuals. This makes a tremendous difference to the logical situation, however, for what it means is that plural quantifier phrases of natural lan-guages are second-order quantifiers rather than first-order ones. For this reason, they need separate treat-ment.

(b) In the input sentence (*) of (G. some), and in the analogous input sentences for the other rules as formulated above, it is assumed that the "who" in "who Z" is in the subject position. If this assumption is dropped, we must assume that the players somehow know where "who" (or whatever wh-word we have in the quantifier phrase) is moved from in Z. (We may assume that this is shown by a trace, or that the players are otherwise aware of at least this much of the generative history of the input sentence.) Then the substituting term "b" is plugged into the output sentence in the original location of the wh-ingredient, both in the right grammatical case and with the right preposi-tional construction.

(c) Quantifier rules have to be formulated in such a way that they take care of the case where the relative clause is missing and the case where the Y part is likewise missing. In the latter case, the quantifier word, e.g., "some", has to be expanded to "someone", "somebody", "something", "somewhere", or "sometime", etc.

(d) The role of anaphoric expressions in quantifier rules requires further explanation. This topic, and the theory of anaphoric pronouns in general, will be dealt with in future publications.[31]

The basic ideas of GTS as applied to natural languages can be developed further and extended in several different directions. In some cases, there are discrepancies between semantical games played with formal languages and those played with natural languages that can be recognized and that necessitate further conceptualizations; in others, merely spelling out what is intended in our game rules prompts fascinating insights; in certain further cases, extensions of GTS as applied to formal languages have counterparts in the realm of natural-language semantics; and in still others, extensions of a game-theoretical treatment to other parts of natural languages lead to challenging problems. Here I can discuss only a selection from the just-mentioned issues.

6. Differences between Formal and Natural Languages, and Their Consequences

The following are some of the important differences between formal and natural languages, from the perspective of GTS:

(i) *Rule ordering*: In formal languages, the sentence reached at a given stage of a game always determines what happens next. The only exception mentioned above results from structures containing partially ordered quantifiers; but they are, by definition, the cases in which the order does not matter. In contrast, in natural languages several different rules may apply to the same sentence. Moreover, the order of application of the different rules has so far been left completely open. For instance, consider (*) in the special case of (G. some) formulated above. There may be structures in X, Y, Z, or W that would justify applying other game rules to (*), or justify applying (G. some) to (*) in some other way.

Is this freedom a vice or a virtue? If it is a vice, the same vice is instantiated with a vengeance by such theories as Montague semantics and Chomsky's *Aspects* theory.[32] Both allow for even more ambiguities than result from the open ordering of our game rules. Hence it is unlikely, at the very least, that the underdetermination of the order of different game rules is a serious difficulty for GTS.

However, the correct course is fairly clearly to acknowledge that too much freedom has so far been left for rule ordering in semantical games, and to try to formulate *ordering principles* that are calculated to govern this order. They constitute a new ingredient in GTS for natural languages, and they don't have any counterpart in the game-theoretical treatment of formal languages. They have already turned out to be a powerful tool in explaining a wide variety of linguistic phenomena.

There are two kinds of ordering principles for the application of game rules: general and special. The general ordering principles depend only on the general syntactical structure of the sentence to which the rules are to be applied, whereas the special ones concern the relative priority of specific rules. The crucial question in formulating general ordering principles concerns the way syntactic structure governs rule ordering. In earlier work on game-theoretical semantics, two principles of this sort were used, viz., (O. comm) and (O. LR). They say, respectively, that a rule must not be applied to a lower clause if it can be applied to a higher one, and that within a clause the rules are applied left to right.[33] It may be, however, that these two are only approximations. They can perhaps be improved in the same way as the first crude rules for backwards pronominalization were improved in Tanya Reinhart's work.[34]

These general principles can be overruled by special ones. They are exemplified by (O. any), which says that (G. any) has priority over the game rules for negation, disjunction (but not conjunction), conditionals, as well as over modal rules (in the narrow sense that excludes rules for epistemic notions and for other propositional attitudes), and by (O. each), which says that (G. each) has priority over the other quantifier rules as well as over the rules for propositional connectives.

These ordering principles, and others like them, serve to explain a wide variety of semantical phenomena. An example is the following pair of sentences:

(12) If everybody comes to the party, I'll be surprised.
(13) If anybody comes to the party, I'll be surprised.

The basis for the difference in meaning between (12) and (13) is that (G. any) has priority over (G. if), but (G. every) does not.[35] Here we are already beginning to see how sentences in which "any" appears to have the force of an existential quantifier can be analyzed in GTS.

(ii) *Scope vs. ordering*: A related difference between formal and natural languages is that in the former the scope of each quantifier is indicated explicitly. In contrast, the concept of scope does not even make sense in natural language. For in such language a quantifier phrase can in principle have pronouns or anaphoric *the*-phrases coreferential with it that are arbitrarily distant from it in the same sentence or discourse. Instead of the notion of scope, we have to deal with the notion of rule ordering, which serves many of the same purposes that scope does in formal languages but which is essentially different from it. This makes the semantics of natural languages different from the semantics of formal languages in several respects.

(iii) *Ambiguity of "is"*: In formal languages, there are, as Frege and Russell emphasized, at least four different counterparts to the one and only verb for being in many natural languages ("is" in English, "ist" in German, etc.).[36] They include the following:

(a) the "is" of identity, exemplified by "Sue's brother is Jack," and formalized by "=";
(b) the "is" of predication (the copula), exemplified by "Sue is blonde," and formalized by predicative juxtaposition;
(c) the "is" of existence, exemplified by "God is" and "There are Basques in California," and formalized by the existential quantifier;
(d) the "is" of general implication (or class inclusion), exemplified by "A whale is a mammal," and formalized in this example by "(x) $(x$ is a whale $\rightarrow$ x is a mammal)".

Does this distinction imply that natural-language words like "is" and "ist" are ambiguous, as Frege and Russell maintained? In GTS, most rules don't take into account different uses of "is". Does this mean that GTS treats "is" as unambiguous? If so, how can it do justice to the insights of Frege and Russell? These questions will be discussed below in section 9 (and in chapter 7).

(iv) *Many-sorted quantification*: As was already pointed out, in natural languages we are dealing with many-sorted quantification. In formal languages, different sortal quantifiers are distinguished from one another notationally. In contrast, in natural languages the different sorts or ranges of different quantifiers have to be gathered from sundry syntactical as well as semantical clues.[37] The nature of these clues will be examined separately.

These four new developments (i)-(iv) have remarkable consequences for the general methodology of linguistics. They are studied in the next four sections of this chapter.

(v) *Atomic sentences*: In formal languages, the natural stopping points of semantical games are atomic sentences, which normally constitute an easily recognizable class. In natural languages, the situation is different. The rules for natural-language sentences that have thus far been formulated in the literature eliminate many sentential ingredients from the sentences concerned, especially quantifiers and propositional connectives. But yet various sorts of sentential structures still remain at the point where the applicability of the rules comes to an end - for example, passive constructions, various prepositional constructions, etc. How are they to be dealt with? Here the recent functional-lexical approach to syntax[38] offers a natural complement to game-theoretical semantics as it has been developed so far. In that approach lexical rules specify the different functional structures into which a given lexical item can enter. The rules that give us the semantical interpretation of these different functional structures can serve to interpret the end-point sentences of semantical games in their various current forms. Even though this matter needs further attention, we can see here a definite convergence of two different lines of thought in the foundations of language.

7. The *Any*-Thesis and the Limitations of
Generative Grammars

It turns out that (O. any) enables us to formulate a *semantical* criterion for the admissibility of "any" in a given context "X-any-Y" in a fragment of English.[39] This criterion, called the *any*-thesis, says (in its rough unqualified form) that "any" is acceptable in this context if and only if "X-every-Y" is grammatical and different in meaning from "X-any-Y". This criterion works well in a certain fragment of English. For instance, it explains at once why "any" can occur (other things being equal) in the antecedent of a conditional (as in (13)) but not in the consequent, as illustrated by the following pair of sentences:

(14)   If Chris trained hard, she has beaten everybody by this time.
(15)   *If Chris trained hard, she has beaten anybody by this time.

Competing explanations of the admissibility and non-admissibility of "any" in different contexts mostly turn on some straightforward syntactical characteristic of those contexts, e.g., that they are governed by "if" or "not". This will not work, however. "Any" can be inadmissible in a context governed by "if", viz., when it occurs in the consequent:

(16)   *If Chris trained hard, she has by this time won any match.

"Any" can be inadmissible when governed (logically speaking) by negation:

(17)   *Not any girl has been dated by Bill.

But "any" can occur even in the consequent if there are other features of the context that create a semantical asymmetry between "any" and "every":

(18)   If Chris trained hard, she can win any match.

Thus no simple competing explanation does justice to the obvious data on which the *any*-thesis is based.

How far the *any*-thesis can be extended beyond the original fragment and what qualifications it needs are open questions. This openness does not impair its remarkable consequences, however. (For a fuller discussion of some of them, see chapter 9 below.)

First, the *any*-thesis presents to us an important instance in which the (apparently syntactical) well-formedness (acceptability) of a string (sentence) turns on semantical considerations. This wreaks havoc on Chomsky's early program of explaining well-formedness in exclusively generative (and hence syntactical) terms.

Chomsky is now willing to allow other, subsidiary factors to enter into explanations of well-formedness.[40] However, he still thinks that the generative component is the most important one for the purposes of an overall linguistic theory. But since our semantical rules apply much more widely than merely to well-formed (acceptable) strings of English words, as illustrated by the *any*-thesis, his position can be called into question. Indeed, in order to reject "X-any-Y" in those cases where "X-every-Y" is acceptable, we have to compare the meanings of the two sentences and hence to assign a meaning to the ill-formed string "X-any-Y". This illustrates a recurring phenomenon recognized by GTS, viz., that syntactical well-formedness and semantical interpretability frequently don't go together. This deprives generative syntax of much of its central theoretical interest.

This line of thought can be pushed further. Given certain further assumptions, it can be proved that the set of acceptable sentences of English is not recursively enumerable and hence not generable in any generative grammar. This shows strikingly the limitations of generative grammar as a universal explanation of acceptability. Chomsky has tried to shrug off such results as turning merely on various "imperfections" of natural languages. It can nevertheless be argued that in some cases it is transformational grammar that is dealing with fringe irregularities, while game-theoretical semantics deals with mainstream regularities. And in this direction, GTS thus suggests extremely fertile general conclusions.

8. The Failure of Compositionality

The *any*-thesis and its consequences do not indicate the only direction where further theoretical insights are forthcoming. The absence of scope indicators in natural languages implies that, among other things, natural-language discourse and natural-language sentences cannot always be analyzed into components with isolable meanings. (If there were such a component expression E and if it contained an existential quantifier, the scope of that quantifier would have to be restricted to E. But we have seen that the scopes of natural-language quantifiers cannot in principle be restricted.)

Hence we see that there is no hope for the so-called Frege Principle (the Principle of Compositionality) in the semantics of natural languages.[41] This principle says that the meaning of a complex expression is a function of the meanings of its component parts. We have just seen, however, that in natural languages there are in some cases no candidates for the role of such component expressions.

In other ways, too, it can be argued that compositionality is a lost cause in natural-language semantics. It presupposes the kind of semantical context-independence that would enable us to carry out the semantical analysis of a sentence from the inside out. We cannot hope to find such context-independence in general. Hence compositionality is bound to fail in some cases.

Since the game rules of GTS operate from the outside in, they allow us to account for those context-dependencies that violate compositionality. Cases in point are applications in which (O. any) overrules (O. comm). There are other examples where the meaning of an expression varies with the context in which it occurs. Here are some cases in point:

(19)   Anyone can beat Jimmy.
(20)   I would be surprised if anyone can beat Jimmy.
(21)   I doubt that anyone can beat Jimmy.
(22)   Bill owns a donkey.
(23)   If Bill owns a donkey, he beats it.

Among the approaches that rely on compositionality, there are those that use essentially Tarski-type truth definitions or Tarski's so-called T-schema. What GTS strongly suggests is that such approaches are unsatisfactory. This

is illustrated by the failure of Tarski-type truth definitions for branching quantifiers (cf. section 3 (vii)-(viii)
above), and by the failure of one-half of the T-schema:[42]

(24) "Anybody can become a millionaire" is true if
      anybody can become a millionaire.

This is not even true.

The transition from (9) to (10) shows that (at least in
some cases) we can restore compositionality by evoking
higher-order entities (functions that embody Myself's
strategies in semantical games). It seems to me that this
is the tacit strategy employed by Montague grammarians,
who are in fact strongly committed to compositionality.
However, the only way they can hope to abide by it is to
make liberal use of higher-order conceptualizations. There
is a price to be paid here, however. The higher-order
entities evoked in this "type-theoretical ascent" are much
less realistic philosophically and psycholinguistically than
our original individuals. Hence the ascent is bound to
detract from the psycholinguistic and methodological realism
of one's theory.

9. The Absence of the Frege-Russell Ambiguity[43]

Consider what the game played on the following sentence
looks like:

(25) Jack is a boy who plays chess.

The game rule applicable here is (G. an), with X = "Jack
is", Y = "boy", Z = "plays chess", and W = ϕ. The output sentence is then of the following form:

(26) Jack is John Jr., John Jr. is a boy, and John
      Jr. plays chess.

Nothing could be simpler. But the step from (25) to (26)
is strange when considered from the perspective of the
Frege-Russell position that "is" is multiply ambiguous.
For in (25) the first "is" is clearly an "is" of predication,
whereas in (26) the selfsame first "is" (it is part of the
very same X = "Jack is" in both sentences) has to be clas-

sified as an "is" of identity. What this means is that the Frege-Russell ambiguity claim does not apply to some occurrences of "is", i.e., that "is" cannot be said to be ambiguous between the "is" of identity and the "is" of predication if GTS is the right semantics of English.

Other examples show that the other parts of the Frege-Russell ambiguity claim cannot be upheld either in GTS. For instance, one way of dealing with a sentence like (27) is to construe it as an elliptical for (28).

(27) A whale is a mammal.
(28) If anything is a whale, it is a mammal.

Here the second "is" in (28) will be identical with the "is" of (27). In treating (28) in GTS, however, that "is" must be taken to be on a par semantically with any other typical occurrence of the "is" of predication. Therefore, we cannot maintain an ambiguity between the "is" of predication and the "is" of class inclusion, either.

These observations have important consequences. The Frege-Russell ambiguity claim is codified in the usual formalism of formal first-order languages. In this formalism, the four allegedly different senses of "is" are expressed in entirely different ways. Hence anyone who uses first-order languages (quantification theory) as his or her framework of semantical representation is committed to the Frege-Russell ambiguity claim. This makes semantical bedfellows of philosophers, logicians, and linguists as different as early Wittgenstein, Quine, Davidson, George Lakoff, and Chomsky. Hence the failure of the Frege-Russell claim in GTS has repercussions for several different approaches to logical and linguistic semantics. Even if one doesn't yet believe in the superiority of GTS compared to conventional first-order languages, as a canonical notation for semantics, it certainly offers a consistent alternative to the more traditional kinds of semantics. In any case, we thus have a remarkable situation on our hands in that some of the most central concepts of semantics – ambiguity, number of readings, etc. – turn out to be relative to one's preferred framework of semantical representation. This has important consequences for the methodology of semantics in general.

Of course, there are differences between different uses of "is" on any theory. In GTS, too, distinctions have to

be made between different kinds of primitive sentences
containing "is". Notice, however, that these differences
are not due to different meanings of this word, but to differences in the context in which it occurs. Moreover, in
certain nonatomic contexts the distinction cannot even be
made, as we have seen.

The failure of the Frege-Russell ambiguity claim should
really come as no surprise, since virtually no major
philosopher before Frege (and to some extent Mill[44] and De
Morgan)[45] relied on the ambiguity. Hence GTS should be
of interest to historians of philosophy: it promises a
framework for discussing the logic of being that is less
anachronistic than the conventional Frege-Russell logic.[46]

10. GTS and the Doctrine of Categories

This historical dimension can be pursued further.[47] It
was noted earlier that in GTS we are dealing with a many-
sorted quantification theory rather than a traditional
one-sorted one. But how is the "sort" (subdomain) determined from which the two players make their choices? To
answer this question, consider a generalization of a special
case of the rule (G. some), viz., the special case we
discussed in section 4 above. What are the clues that the
players can use to decide from which subdomain the choice
of the individual b is made? The most obvious one is the
wh-word that occurs in the quantifier phrase. (Among
them, I am here including "that", which is of course
merely the relative-clause counterpart to "what".) If it is
"who", the choice is between persons; if "where", between
locations in space; if "when", between moments (or peri-
ods) of time; and so on. Some wh-words, especially
"that" (or "what"), cover more than one subdomain, and
some domains are reached only by means of a prepositional
phrase that contains a wh-word. Apart from these irregularities, however, there is a rough equivalence between
the ranges of English quantifiers and wh-words (plus certain wh-phrases) in English.

However, the whole relative clause can be missing.
Then the meaning of Y in (*) (see (G. some)) will have to
tell the players which subdomain the choice is made from.
The need for this clue can be seen from the following: if
Y is empty (missing), the wh-word itself has to be ampli-
fied to convey the necessary information, becoming, e.g.,

"some*one*", "some*where*", "some*time*", etc. As a special case, therefore, we obtain a semantical classification of the primitive predicates of English that goes together with our earlier distinctions.

Hence we obtain a one-to-one correlation or analogy between several different distinctions. They are distinctions between

(29) (i)   different wh-words (and phrases);
      (ii)   semantically determined classes of primitive predicates;
      (iii)   the (widest) domains of quantification.

Since each application of the quantifier rules introduces an occurrence of "is", we also have a correlated distinction between

(iv)   certain different uses of "is".

The correlation of these four distinctions has a familiar ring to an historian of philosophy. The view we have arrived at is identical, mutatis mutandis, with Aristotle's doctrine of categories. Aristotle's several explanations of his doctrine correspond neatly to (i)-(iv).[48] We can now also solve the two main perennial problems that arise in interpreting Aristotle's doctrine: (1) Which distinction (i)-(iv) did Aristotle "really" mean? (2) If he meant more than one, why should they go together? Now we can see that he could have meant all of them together, and that their going together is a most natural part of the semantics of any natural language like English or ancient Greek.

It turns out, however, that the theory summed up in the parallelism of the distinctions (i)-(iv) is only an approximation. The precise ways in which it breaks down nevertheless also seem to have great systematic and historical interest.

11. Other Extensions and Applications

These dramatic developments do not exhaust the uses of GTS in logical and linguistic semantics or philosophical analysis. Among the further possibilities, which will be mentioned but not described here, there are the following:

(a) Several of the extensions mentioned in connection with formal languages have counterparts for natural languages, especially (ii)-(iii), (iv), (v), (ix), and (x).

(b) Among these, the extension of GTS to intensional and temporal language seems to be especially promising. I have argued that a game-theoretical treatment of epistemic words is needed for a semantical theory of English wh-questions, especially multiple wh-questions.[49] Furthermore, I have suggested that GTS enables us to deal better with several puzzling phenomena concerning tenses and temporal discourse in English than does any competing approach.[50]

(c) In a different direction, the subgame idea enables us to understand the mechanism of certain types of anaphora, particularly pronouns whose head is a quantifier phrase.[51] This is illustrated by the following examples due essentially to Geach and Karttunen, respectively:

(30)   If Bill owns a donkey, he beats it.
(31)   If you give every child a present for Christmas, some child will open his today.

(d) Other pronouns whose semantical behavior can be handled by means of GTS are the so-called pronouns of laziness.[52] They are pronouns that are not coreferential with their heads, and hence there is no hope of handling them in terms of variables of quantification. They are instantiated by such Karttunen-type examples as

(32)   Any man who gives his paycheck to his wife is wiser than any man who gives it to his mistress.

They can be analyzed in GTS, and the resulting explanation of the phenomenon of "laziness" can be extended to other cases, such as the following example from Geach:

(33)   John is not the only man who loves his wife.

(e) Similarly, GTS provides a new way of dealing with the anaphoric uses of *the*-phrases (definite descriptions). The main idea is to take them to represent choices from a finite set of individuals given in the beginning of a semantical game or selected by the players up to the time that the *the*-phrase in question is dealt with. This seems to yield for the first time a viable theory of such *the*-

phrases. It also suggests that looking at anaphoric pronouns in a similar way might result in a successful new
theory.

(f) Several aspects of the behavior of negation in
English can be understood better by means of GTS (see
chapter 4 below).

(g) As an analogical extension of (e), we can obtain a
new kind of treatment of anaphoric pronouns.[53] This will
differ from all treatments of anaphoric pronouns that rely
on a specific syntactical relation of an anaphoric expression to its head and also from all treatments that assimilate
the operation of anaphoric pronouns to the bound variables
of quantification theory.

(h) A large field of potential applications is constituted
by the so-called nonstandard quantifiers, such as "many",
"few", "several", "almost all", etc. Their behavior offers
some of the best examples of some of the most theoretically
significant natural-language phenomena to which GTS has
first focused our attention - for instance, informational
independence. Together with the plural uses of such
quantifier words as "some" and "any", they show convincingly how much more there is to the semantics of natural
languages like English than can be represented by means
of first-order logic.

(i) Ideas (b)-(e) can be extended to discourse (text)
semantics by means of the concept of subgame. In general, by means of GTS we can obtain a unified treatment
of important parts of sentence semantics and discourse
semantics.[54]

Not surprisingly, the principles that determine the
order in which different game rules are applied turn out to
be crucial in this enterprise. Several issues that have
been discussed in the literature can be put into a more
general perspective by considering the way in which these
ordering principles work. Furthermore, a game-theoretical
treatment of negation offers an instructive example of the
nature of the explanations that GTS can provide.[55]

In general, semantical games will, in the last analysis,
have to be combined with the other kinds of games (dialogical games) that are going on in discourse. Even
though it is useful for the purpose of philosophical clarity
to keep semantical games, which deal with a hypothetical
process of verification and falsification, apart from the
games people actually play in discourse, it is clear that
both have to be taken into account in trying to understand

fully the semantics of discourse. Lauri Carlson has made significant contributions to this enterprise in his recent book.[56]

These are only samples of what GTS can do. They also represent work that is still in progress rather than completed results. They are enough, however, to illustrate the great potential of this approach.

The main ideas of game-theoretical semantics can also be connected with the views of more than one major philosopher. Perhaps the most obvious connection is the affinity between semantical games and Wittgenstein's "language games".[57] There are also deep connections between my approach and Kant's views on logic, mathematics, and the mathematical method.[58] The latter connections are discussed in the next chapter.

NOTES

[1] Cf., e.g., G. H. Hardy, *A Course of Pure Mathematics*, seventh edition, Cambridge University Press, Cambridge, 1938, p. 186.

[2] See section II (i) of the bibliography at the end of this volume.

[3] See section II (iv) of the bibliography.

[4] See section II (v) of the bibliography.

[5] In Dana Scott, "A Game-Theoretic Interpretation of Logical Formulae", McCarthy seminar, Stanford University, July 1968 (unpublished).

[6] See section II (vi) of the bibliography.

[7] Most of the early work on GTS has been collected in Esa Saarinen, editor, *Game-Theoretical Semantics*, D. Reidel, Dordrecht, 1979. The second essay reprinted there (Jaakko Hintikka, "Quantifiers in Logic and Quantifiers in Natural Languages") comes perhaps closest to an introductory discussion.

[8] As has been explained, semantical games are played on the domain of individuals that our interpreted language can be used to convey information about. (For instance, moves connected with quantifiers are choices of members of the domain D.) Semantical games are hence essentially different from so-called dialogical games, whose moves are utterances or other kinds of propoundings of sentences. This distinguishes the semantical games of GTS from, e.g., the dialogical games of Paul Lorenzen. (For them,

see section IV (i) of the bibliography.) I will comment on the relation of Lorenzen's games to mine briefly in chapter 2 below.

[9] Even though the game-theoretical concepts used here are almost self-explanatory, a couple of brief explanations may be in order. A "strategy" of a player is a rule that tells the player in question what to do in each conceivable situation that can come up in the game. In this paper, only pure (nonprobabilistic) strategies are considered. By means of the concept of strategy, the whole game can always be reduced to a choice of strategy by each player. This is known as the "normal form" of a game. If a strategy of a player in a two-person zero-sum game wins against any strategy of one's opponent, it is said to be a "winning" one.

[10] Cf. here the classic paper by David Gale and F. M. Stewart, "Infinite Games with Perfect Information", in H. W. Kuhn and A. W. Tucker, editors, *Contributions to the Theory of Games*, vol. 2 (Annals of Mathematics Studies, vol. 28), Princeton University Press, Princeton, 1953, pp. 245-66, and cf. Morton David, "Infinite Games of Perfect Information", in M. Dresher, L. S. Shapley, and A. W. Tucker, editors, *Advances in Game Theory* (Annals of Mathematics Studies, vol. 52), Princeton University Press, Princeton, 1964, pp. 85-101.

[11] See here section II (viii) of the bibliography.

[12] For the distinction, see, e.g., John von Neumann and Oskar Morgenstern, *Theory of Games and Economic Behavior*, Princeton University Press, Princeton, 1953, pp. 76-84.

[13] See here chapter 3 below.

[14] See section II (v) of the bibliography.

[15] This observation was first made in the following papers: A. Mostowski, "On a System of Axioms Which Has No Recursively Enumerable Arithmetic Model", *Fundamenta Mathematicae* 40 (1953), 56-61; A. Mostowski, "A Formula with No Recursively Enumerable Model", *Fundamenta Mathematicae* 42 (1955), 125-40; G. Kreisel, "A Note on Arithmetic Models for Consistent Formulae of the Predicate Calculus", *Proceedings of the XIth International Congress of Philosophy*, vol. 14, Amsterdam & Louvain, 1953, pp. 39-49.

[16] See Leon Henkin, "Completeness in the Theory of Types", *Journal of Symbolic Logic* 15 (1950), 81-91 (but cf. Peter Andrews, "General Models and Extensionality",

Journal of Symbolic Logic 37 (1972), 395-97); Jaakko Hintikka, "Standard vs. Nonstandard Logic: Higher-Order, Modal, and First-Order Logics", in Evandro Agazzi, editor, *Modern Logic: A Survey*, D. Reidel, Dordrecht, 1980, pp. 283-96; Jaakko Hintikka, "Is Alethic Modal Logic Possible?" *Acta Philosophica Fennica* 35 (1982), 89-105; and the further literature referred to in the last two papers.

17 See section II (v) of the bibliography and chapter 3 below.

18 For their logical theory, and for applications to natural languages, see section II (i) of the bibliography.

19 See Jaakko Hintikka, "Quantifiers vs. Quantification Theory", *Linguistic Inquiry* 5 (1979), 153-77, and cf. M. Krynicki and A. H. Lachlan, "On the Semantics of the Henkin Quantifier", *Journal of Symbolic Logic* 44 (1979), 184-200.

20 See Jon Barwise, "On Branching Quantifiers in English", *Journal of Philosophical Logic* 8 (1979), 47-80.

21 For a discussion of such reduction problems, see W. J. Walkoe, Jr., "Finite Partially Ordered Quantification", *Journal of Symbolic Logic* 35 (1970), 535-55.

22 See section II (iii) of the bibliography.

23 See Jaakko Hintikka, "Leibniz on Plenitude, Relations, and the 'Reign of Law'", in Simo Knuuttila, editor, *Reforging the Great Chain of Being*, D. Reidel, Dordrecht, 1980, pp. 259-86, especially p. 272.

24 See section II (ix) of the bibliography.

25 See, respectively, Veikko Rantala, *Aspects of Definability* (Acta Philosophica Fennica, vol. 29, nos. 2-3), North-Holland, Amsterdam, 1977; and Jaakko Hintikka, "Impossible Possible Worlds Vindicated", *Journal of Philosophical Logic* 4 (1975), 475-84, reprinted (and expanded) in Saarinen, *Game-Theoretical Semantics*, pp. 367-79.

26 Cf. Lauri Carlson and Alice ter Meulen, "Informational Independence in Intensional Contexts", in Esa Saarinen et al, editors, *Essays in Honour of Jaakko Hintikka*, D. Reidel, Dordrecht, 1979, pp. 61-72.

27 See Jaakko Hintikka, "Questions with Outside Quantifiers", in Robinson Schneider et al., editors, *Papers from the Parasession on Nondeclaratives, CLS, April 17, 1982*, Chicago Linguistic Society, Chicago, 1982, pp. 83-92; "On Games, Questions, and Strange Quantifiers", in Tom Pauli, editor, *Philosophical Essays Dedicated to Lennart Aqvist on His Fiftieth Birthday*, Philosophical Society and Department of Philosophy, Uppsala University, Uppsala, 1982, pp.

159-69.

[28] Various further explanations are needed here. For instance, more has to be said about how anaphoric relations are determined in the output sentence of (G. some). Even more obviously, something ought to be said about what happens when the restrictions just mentioned are removed. A detailed discussion of these matters will not be attempted here, however.

[29] See chapter 9 below; and see sections 10, 12, and 13 of chapter 4.

[30] In other formal and natural languages negation can nevertheless be treated in a more informative way by giving explicit rules as to how the (semantical) negation (contradictory) of a given sentence can be formed syntactically. Such a treatment would be more informative, but is has not yet been attempted in print. See here chapter 4 below for problems with syntactical rules for negation-forming.

[31] See Jaakko Hintikka and Jack Kulas, "Towards a Semantical Theory of Pronominal Anaphora" (in preparation).

[32] See Richmond Thomason, editor, *Formal Philosophy: Selected Papers of Richard Montague*, Yale University Press, New Haven, 1974; Noam Chomsky, *Aspects of the Theory of Syntax*, The MIT Press, Cambridge, Mass., 1965 (see especially pp. 224-25, note 9).

[33] These ordering conventions clearly are closely related to various linguistic principles, such as the cyclic principle of transformational grammarians and George Lakoff's "derivational constraints" in his generative semantics. Unlike the claims made for these principles, however, my ordering conventions admit exceptions.

[34] See Tanya Reinhart, "Syntactic Domains for Semantic Rules", in F. Guenthner and S. J. Schmidt, editors, *Formal Semantics and Pragmatics for Natural Languages*, D. Reidel, Dordrecht, 1979, pp. 107-30. For a more extensive discussion of syntactic domains, see her dissertation, *The Syntactic Domain of Anaphora*, 1976, unpublished, M.I.T. Guy Carden has pointed out problems with her view, in his "Blocked Forward Coreference", presented at the 56th Annual Meeting of the Linguistic Society of America, New York, 1981. See also Susumu Kuno, "Reflexivization in English", *Communication and Cognition* 16 (1983), 65-80.

[35] This means that the "logical form" of (12) is $(x)F(x) \rightarrow$

G while that of (13) is (x)(F(x) → G), which can be re-written as (Ex)F(x) → G.

[36] See chapter 7 below.

[37] See chapter 8 below.

[38] This approach is represented in Joan Bresnan, editor, *The Mental Representation of Grammatical Relations*, The MIT Press, Cambridge, Mass., 1982.

[39] See here Jaakko Hintikka, "Quantifiers in Natural Languages: Some Logical Problems", in Saarinen, *Game-Theoretical Semantics*, and see chapter 10 below. See also Jaakko Hintikka, "On the Limitations of Generative Grammar", in (no editor given) *Proceedings of the Scandinavian Seminar on Philosophy of Language*, Vol. 1, (Filosofiska Studier, Vol. 26) Philosophical Society and Department of Philosophy, Uppsala University, Uppsala, Sweden, 1975, pp. 1–92.

[40] See Noam Chomsky, *Rules and Representations*, Columbia University Press, New York, 1980, pp. 122–28.

[41] See chapter 10 below.

[42] Cf. here Jaakko Hintikka, "A Counterexample to Tarski-Type Truth-Definitions As Applied to Natural Languages", *Philosophia* 5 (1975), 204–12.

[43] Cf. here chapter 8 below.

[44] John Stuart Mill, *A System of Logic*, London, 1843 (8th edition, New York, 1881), Book I, Chapter IV, §1.

[45] Augustus De Morgan, *Formal Logic*, Taylor and Walton, London, 1847 (reprinted by The Open Court Co., London, 1926), pp. 49–50.

[46] On this subject, see chapter 7 below, as well as Jaakko Hintikka and Simo Knuuttila, editors, *The Logic of Being: Historical Studies* (forthcoming).

[47] Cf. here chapter 8 below.

[48] Aristotle uses different question words (and phrases) in ancient Greek as names for his categories; he introduces categories as semantically determined classes of simple predicates; he treats categories as the widest genera of entities we can meaningfully consider together; and he frequently says that the several categories go together with different senses or uses of τὸ εἶναι, the Greek verb for being.

[49] See Jaakko Hintikka, *The Semantics of Questions and the Questions of Semantics* (Acta Philosophica Fennica, vol. 28, no. 4), North-Holland, Amsterdam, 1976; and cf. idem, "New Foundations for a Theory of Questions and Answers", forthcoming.

[50] See here chapter 5 below.
[51] See here chapter 3 below, and Jaakko Hintikka and Lauri Carlson, "Conditionals, Generic Quantifiers, and Other Applications of Subgames", in Saarinen, *Game-Theoretical Semantics*, pp. 179–214.
[52] See Jaakko Hintikka and Lauri Carlson, "Pronouns of Laziness in Game-Theoretical Semantics", *Theoretical Linguistics* 4 (1977), 1–29.
[53] See Jaakko Hintikka and Jack Kulas, "Towards a Semantical Theory of Pronominal Anaphora" (in preparation).
[54] Important work in this direction has been done by Lauri Carlson. See his book, *Dialogue Games: An Approach to Discourse Analysis*, D. Reidel, Dordrecht, 1983.
[55] See chapter 4 below.
[56] See Lauri Carlson, *Dialogue Games*.
[57] See Jaakko Hintikka, "Language-Games", in Jaakko Hintikka et al., editors, *Essays on Wittgenstein in Honour of G. H. von Wright* (Acta Philosophica Fennica, vol. 28, nos. 1–3), North-Holland, Amsterdam, 1976, pp. 105–25, (reprinted in Saarinen, *Game-Theoretical Semantics*, pp. 1–26); and cf. "Language-Games for Quantifiers", in Jaakko Hintikka, *Logic, Language-Games and Information*, Clarendon Press, Oxford, 1973, pp. 53–82.
[58] See Jaakko Hintikka, "Transcendental Arguments Revived", in A. Mercier and M. Svilar, editors, *Philosophers on Their Own Work*, vol. 9, Peter Lang, Bern, 1982, pp. 119–33.

Chapter 2

SEMANTICAL GAMES AND TRANSCENDENTAL ARGUMENTS

1. Kant on the Logic of Existence

Kant had the right idea in his theory of mathematics, but he was misled by an antiquated philosophical dogma.[1] Following his general transcendental point of view, he maintained that our ways of reasoning about existence (especially inferences from the existence or nonexistence of an individual to the existence or nonexistence of a different individual) must be grounded in the human activities through which we come to know the existence of individuals. This is a deep and intriguing idea, and Kant's identification of the types of reasoning in question as mathematical rather than logical marks only a difference in terminology between Kant and contemporary philosophers of logic. What Kant was dealing with is unmistakably such logical reasoning as is now codified in the modern logic of quantification theory – not anything we would any longer consider distinctively mathematical reasoning.

However, Kant went astray in identifying the activities through which we in fact come to know the existence and nonexistence of individuals. He located these "activities" in sense perception. In doing so, he was following a long tradition that goes back to Aristotle. This is, nevertheless, a *false* tradition. It is only in rare cases that we can wait until the relevant individuals kindly prove their existence by showing up in our passive sense perception. Normally, we have to get up and look for them. Hence, the true basis of the logic of existence and universality lies in the human activities of seeking and finding – we shall borrow a term from Wittgenstein and call them "language-games" – not in the structure of our faculty of sense perception, as Kant mistakenly claimed.

2. Seeking and Finding, and Game-Theoretical Semantics

Notwithstanding this mistake, Kant's interesting argument

allows for analogous conclusions when applied, mutatis mutandis, to modern logic. Even though logical and mathematical inferences do not reflect the structure of our outer
and inner senses, they reflect the structure of our language games of seeking and finding. The right approach
to the contemporary philosophy of logic and logical semantics is therefore through a study of the rule-governed
activities of seeking and finding. These activities, con-
ceived of as games against Nature, are precisely my semantical games.[2] Game-theoretical semantics thus admits of
a transcendental deduction in precisely the same sense as
Kant's transcendental arguments for his theory of space,
time, sense perception, and the mathematical method.
Game-theoretical semantics is the true Kantian approach to
language, I am thus led to say, even though I must qual-
ify it as a neo-Kantian or, more accurate still, meta-
Kantian approach in that it means adhering to Kant's basic
idea but correcting his crucial mistake.[3] This basic idea
is to focus on the activities through which we come to
know the relevant propositions, that is, the propositions
whose logical form is determined by the concepts of existence and nonexistence of individuals (plus propositional
connectives). These propositions are the ones that are
studied in modern first-order logic (quantification theory),
and the activities in question are our processes of verifying such propositions. In game-theoretical semantics,
these verification processes are conceptualized as games
against a recalcitrant Nature, who tries to frustrate my
attempts. These games are thus two-person games. (We
can call the players *Myself* and *Nature*.) Their usefulness
is largely due to the fact that they are games in the strict
sense of the mathematical theory of games.

3. A Transcendental Refutation of Certain Related Views

Thus we can see the close kinship of game-theoretical semantics and Kant's philosophy. We can also see that my
game-theoretical semantics is not without interesting philosophical antecedents, even apart from the connection with
Wittgenstein's concept of language game, which I have discussed elsewhere.[4] The same observation also suggests
further consequences. It helps to put into perspective
certain similar approaches to the philosophy of logic and
semantics. We can usefully discuss them by reference to

the question whether they allow for analogous "transcendental deductions".

Indeed, at first it might look as if several recent approaches to logical semantics are very much along the same
meta-Kantian lines as game-theoretical semantics.   Both
Michael Dummett and Dag Prawitz have proposed treating
the theory of meaning, not by means of static truth conditions, but in terms of the actual process through which
we come to know the propositions whose logic we are dealing with.[5]   For instance, Dummett characterizes his theory
of meaning as one that "takes verification and falsification
as its central notions in place of those of truth and falsity".[6]   Likewise, Prawitz emphasizes that "the meaning
of a sentence cannot be treated in isolation from the
question of how the truth of the sentence may be established".[7]   I could not agree more, nor, on my interpretation, could Kant.

However, both Dummett and Prawitz give their approach
what I cannot help but consider an unfortunate turn.
They both use mathematical language as their paradigm
case, and interpret the relevant methods of verification as
methods of proof.   This may be fine as a theory of mathematical truth (though even such a claim would be highly
controversial in its own right).   However, it seems to me
perfectly hopeless as a step towards a general theory of
meaning.   When we move outside of purely mathematical
languages, the truth of a proposition can seldom be established by means of formal proof procedures.   *Pace* Leibniz,
we cannot establish the truth or falsity of empirical propositions by calculation.   Hence the kind of theory Dummett
and Prawitz envisage cannot serve as a general theory of
meaning.

4. A Test Case: Branching Quantifiers

This general argument can be buttressed by more specific
ones.   It seems to me that there are several semantical
phenomena in both natural and formal languages that cannot be satisfactorily accounted for on the basis of the
Dummett-Prawitz approach.   Here I shall mention only one
of them.   It is the semantical behavior of branching (more
generally, partially ordered) quantifiers.[8]   The simplest
nontrivial example of a proposition containing branching
quantifiers is a sentence of the following form:

$$(1) \quad \begin{matrix} (x) \ (Ey) \\ \\ (z) \ (Eu) \end{matrix} \rangle \ M(x,y,z,u).$$

Here M(x,y,z,u) can be assumed to contain no quantifiers, though it may contain propositional connectives.

The meaning of (1) is immediately obvious in game-theoretical semantics. In this semantics, an existential quantifier represents my move (in a game against Nature): I select an individual from the given domain (universe of discourse) whose name is to be substituted for the quantified variable. Likewise a universal quantifier represents a similar choice of an individual by Nature. (Of course, not any random choice will do if a player wants to win. A player must try to find the right kind of individual; this is what makes semantical games games of seeking and finding.)

All that is needed in game-theoretical semantics to handle branching quantifiers is one of the most important general concepts of game theory, namely, the concept of information, with its associated notions of informational dependence and independence of different moves, codified in the notion of information set.[9] The information set of the move prompted by a quantifier Q_1 includes the moves prompted by only those quantifiers Q_2 that bear a certain partial-ordering relation to Q_1, i.e., which, intuitively speaking, are "to the left of" Q_1 in some one branch. For instance, in (1) the value of "y" is chosen independently of the choices of values of "z" and "u", but not independently of the choice of the value of "x".

In game-theoretical semantics, the truth of a proposition is defined as the existence of a winning strategy for Myself. The existence of such a strategy can be expressed by a second-order proposition, which in the case of (1) is clearly (2):

$$(2) \quad (Ef)(Eg)(x)(z) \ M((x,f(x),z,g(z)).$$

In comparison, we may note that for the following sentences, which contain only linear (totally ordered) quantifiers,

$$(3) \quad (x)(Ey)(z)(Eu) \ M(x,y,z,u)$$

and

$$(4) \quad (x)(z)(Ey)(Eu) \ M(x,y,z,u),$$

the analogous "translations" will be

$$(5) \quad (Ef)(Eg)(x)(z) \ M(x,f(x),z,g(z,x))$$

and

$$(6) \quad (Ef)(Eg)(x)(z) \ M(x,f(x,z),z,g(z,x)),$$

respectively.

Thus, game-theoretical semantics yields a translation of both first-order logic and the logic of partially ordered quantifiers into fragments of second-order logic. The enormous strength of second-order logic (with standard semantics in Henkin's sense)[10] prompts one to ask: How strong is the fragment that serves as the translation of the theory of partiallly ordered quantifiers? In other words, how strong is this theory? An interesting answer is in fact forthcoming. I have shown that the theory of partially ordered quantifiers is as strong as the whole of second-order logic, in the sense of having an equally difficult decision problem.[11] Hence it cannot be axiomatized, and the semantics of partially ordered quantifiers cannot be captured by any considerations that pertain to the actual means of proving (showing the logical truth of) sentences containing partially ordered quantifiers. Hence, the Dummett-Prawitz program is doomed to remain incapable of handling sentences that contain branching quantifiers.

Such sentences are not formal curiosities, either. I have shown[12] that branching quantifiers are indispensable for the semantical representation of a large number of natural-language sentences. I have even argued that all irreducible structures that contain partially ordered quantifiers are needed for the purpose. Hence one cannot dismiss this semantical phenomenon as being merely a marginal one.

One may of course try to get around this conclusion. However, I believe that all such attempts are ultimately going to be defeated by the naturalness of the game-theoretical treatment of such sentences containing partially ordered quantifiers.

For instance, why cannot one use the same idea of

informational independence in the formal "games" of theorem proving as is used in semantical games to give
branching-quantifier sentences their meaning? The answer
is that there cannot be incomplete information in games of
formal proof and disproof. A logician may forget or overlook earlier steps in his or her argument, but such
failures are mistakes, and cannot be subject to semantical
rules. Likewise, in the formal rule of existential instantiation it does not even make sense to ask what the substituting term depends on, for any singular constant not
previously used can serve as one. Hence the notion of
informational independence does not apply to the formal
games of theorem proving.

5. Material vs. Logical Truth, Formal Argumentation, and Semantics

I suspect that mistakes in this general direction have been
encouraged by a false analogy between ordinary material
truth (truth simpliciter) and philosophers' artificial notion
of "logical truth". The two are of course related to each
other, but they are not analogous. Logical truth is not
truth in some particular Platonic domain of logical entities
(or in some mind-created domain, either). It is much more
appropriately characterized as truth (plain truth) in each
possible world. It follows that the activities by which we
establish logical truths are not special cases of the
activities for establishing ordinary (material) truth. Yet
the false analogy between the two "kinds of truth" still
seems to mislead many philosophers. Activities that can
lead to our knowing certain logical truths are, because of
the false analogy, assumed to be representative also of
how material truths are established.

  Apart from such detailed criticisms, the analogy with
Kant enables us to locate the overall shortcoming of these
competing approaches. In a sense, they go wrong in ex-
actly the same place that Kant does, but in a different
direction. In the "transcendental argument" adumbrated
above, I located Kant's mistake in a wrong answer to the
question: What are the activities by means of which we
come to know the truth of a proposition we are dealing
with? Kant's answer - for propositions whose logic is
essentially that of quantification theory - was seen to be
perception, rather than the activities of seeking and find-

ing. In the approaches I am criticizing, a yet different answer is, in effect, given to the same question. It amounts to identifying formal argumentation as the relevant kind of knowledge-acquiring activity. In my opinion, this is quite as fatal a mistake as Kant's, and in some ways it is a much less plausible answer than the Kantian one.

Yet mistakes in this general direction are surprisingly persistent. It is almost a dogma among many philosophers of logic that the "language games" that constitute the "logical home" (to use Wittgenstein's metaphor) of our basic logical notions – for instance, quantifiers – are those of argumentation or consequence-drawing. For example, this view is unmistakably present in P. F. Strawson's *Introduction to Logical Theory*, and it occurs in a slightly different form in his later idea of communication as a semantically important activity.[13] Another version of the same general view is Lorenzen's idea[14] that the rules of certain competitive dialogues are constitutive of the rules of our logic. The ultimate hopelessness of the view that dialogues can provide the foundation of logic and semantics should nevertheless be obvious. Dialogues are intralinguistic activities. They cannot create or maintain the links between language and reality that lend our language its significance. On the contrary, they presuppose these links. Thus the theory of argumentation cannot serve as the foundation of logic and semantics. The real dependencies obtain in the opposite direction.

This helps us to understand the relation of game-theoretical semantics to other current approaches.[15] It is not, of course, the whole story. For instance, within the Lorenzen-Lorenz theory of dialogical logics there now are certain recently developed conceptualizations that can serve some of the same purposes as my semantical games.[16] It is nevertheless highly misleading philosophically to assimilate such games to dialogical games. "Hide-and-seek" is as little a variant of conversation as football is a variant of chess. One of the virtues of the Kantian analogy is that it serves to bring out the reasons why it is misleading to try to associate the semantical games of seeking and finding with dialogical games.

Thus it may look as if the Kantian analogy has given me a conclusive argument in favor of game-theoretical semantics and against its competitors as philosophical theories. Whatever merits Prawitz, Dummett, and Lorenzen may possess as mathematical logicians, their theories can-

not have the philosophical significance they ascribe to
them. Neither the theory of inference nor the theory of
argumentation can serve as the basis for semantics or the
philosophy of logic in the ways that have been claimed for
them.

6. From Semantical Games to Dialogical Games

My observations above do in fact show, it seems to me,
that the philosophical foundations of the competitors of
game-theoretical semantics are in need of much closer
scrutiny than they have been so far given in the literature. However, the matter is not quite as clear-cut as I
have made it out to be. As it so often happens in philosophy, there are further ways of looking at our problems. Once again the Kantian (transcendental) point of
view proves its mettle by suggesting a further line of
thought. It is true that the activities by which we come
to know the truth of quantificational propositions are
better taken to be activities of seeking and finding than to
be activities of formal argumentation. However, it does
not follow that there is not some more general description
of the relevant activities of verification and falsification
that would enable us to relate them to the language games
of argumentation. After all, it is clear that rules of proof
are not unrelated to the semantical games of seeking and
finding, even on my own account.[17] Instead of disparag-
ing the language activities of formal proof, I should instead show their connection with semantical games.

Dummett, Prawitz, and Lorenzen were seen to be wrong
in their unqualified philosophical claims. However, it does
not follow that the language games they have actually
studied are uninteresting or unimportant. The constructive task here is to put these language games into perspective by means of a closer analysis of their structure.
An important step in so doing is to spell out explicitly the
epistemic element that is implicit in the idea of verification,
and in the idea of defending a proposition in a dialogical
game. It seems to me that here is one of.the many cases
where the resources of epistemic logic have been neglected
by logicians, to the detriment of their arguments.

These tasks largely remain to be done. We can find
clues about how they can be accomplished, however. One
thing we can do is to try to conceptualize the activities of

verification and falsification as sequences of questions put to Nature.[18]   This is in keeping with the Kantian viewpoint.   As it happens, the idea of acquiring information by putting questions to Nature is even in literal agreement with what Kant says.[19]

By construing the process of coming to know the truth or falsity of relevant propositions as a series of questions put to Nature, we can subsume the study of the activities of verification and falsification – at least in some of its aspects – under the more general study of information-seeking dialogues that consist of questions and answers. These games can then be related – we may hope – to the dialogical games of Lorenzen and to the proof-theoretical methods of Dummett and Prawitz.

With respect to both tasks, most of the work remains to be carried out.   A beginning is being made, however. Dialogical games of the information-gathering sort are dealt with in my joint paper (with Merrill B. Hintikka) "Sherlock Holmes Confronts Modern Logic".[20]   They deserve a much more detailed study than they have so far received, both in their own right and in their relation to games of seeking and finding.   Furthermore, these interrogative games need to be related to Lorenzen's dialogical games and to the Dummett-Prawitz proof procedures, and it remains to be seen how many of the claims of these philosophers can be vindicated in this way.   There are indications, in any case, that not everything can be saved.   For instance, the three logicians just mentioned have claimed that the natural logic resulting from their respective approaches is an intuitionistic one.   I have put forward an argument that appears to show that their natural "logic" – in a sense that evolves from my dialogical games – is neither classical nor intuitionistic.[21]

Moreover, these questioning logics, whether intuitionistic or not, are not rock bottom logics in the way several philosophers have thought.   On the more fundamental level of the games of seeking and finding, game-theoretical semantics suggests that these logics are also nonclassical (incidentally also assigning to them ipso facto a viable pragmatics).   This logic is not an intuitionistic one, however, but of the nature of a functional interpretation in Gödel's sense.[22]   In general, as an important but so far neglected application of game-theoretical semantics, we could show how various functional interpretations of logic and arithmetic can be given an eminently natural "transcendental deduction" from my general point of view.²³

The most important task here is nevertheless a deeper analysis of the information-acquiring interrogative games themselves. It is here that our paper "Sherlock Holmes Confronts Modern Logic" is calculated to make a beginning. It has also become clear that certain dialogical games that generalize ours have extremely interesting applications to different problems (including linguistic problems) quite apart from their relation to competing approaches.²⁴ Lauri Carlson's recent work is an impressive demonstration of the promise of such applications.²⁵ It may be that such concrete applications are a better index of the merits of my approach than philosophical arguments are.

NOTES

¹ The interpretation summarized here of Kant's theories of mathematical reasoning, space, time, and perception is presented in my books, *Logic, Language-Games, and Information*, Clarendon Press, Oxford, 1973, chapters 5-9, and in *Knowledge and the Known*, D. Reidel, Dordrecht, 1974, chapters 6-8. (See especially the former, chapter 5, "Logic, Language-Games and Transcendental Arguments".)
² See *Logic, Language-Games, and Information* chapter 3, "Language-Games for Quantifiers". Many of my subsequent contributions to the development of game-theoretical semantics are collected in Esa Saarinen, editor, *Game-Theoretical Semantics*, D. Reidel, Dordrecht, 1979. See also chapter 1 above.
³ Several of the philosophical implications of game-theoretical semantics were spelled out in my *Logic, Language-Games, and Information* prior to its main applications to linguistic and logical semantics.
⁴ See my paper, "Language-Games" in Saarinen, *Game-Theoretical Semantics*, pp. 1-26, originally in Jaakko Hintikka et al., editors, *Essays on Wittgenstein in Honour of G. H. von Wright* (Acta Philosophica Fennica, vol. 28, nos. 1-3), North-Holland, Amsterdam, 1976, pp. 105-25.
⁵ For Michael Dummett, see "What Is a Theory of Meaning? I", in Samuel Guttenplan, editor, *Mind and Language*, Clarendon Press, Oxford, 1975, pp. 99-138; "What Is a Theory of Meaning? II", in Gareth Evans and John McDowell, editors, *Truth and Meaning*, Clarendon Press, Oxford, 1976, pp. 67-137; "The Justification of De-

duction", *Proceedings of the British Academy* 59 (1973), 1-34; *Elements of Intuitionism*, Clarendon Press, Oxford, 1977; "The Philosophical Basis of Intuitionistic Logic", in H. E. Rose et al., editors, *Logic Colloquium '73*, North-Holland, Amsterdam, 1975, pp. 5-40. For Dag Prawitz, see "Meaning and Proofs: On the Conflict between Classical and Intuitionistic Logic", *Theoria* 43 (1977), 2-40; "On the Idea of a General Proof Theory", *Synthese* 27 (1974), 63-77; "Intuitionistic Logic: A Philosophical Provocation", in the *Entretiens de Düsseldorf*, Institut International de Philosophie, 1978 (unpublished); "Proofs and the Meaning and Completeness of the Logical Constants", in Jaakko Hintikka et al., editors, *Essays on Mathematical and Philosophical Logic*, D. Reidel, Dordrecht, 1978, pp. 25-40; "Ideas and Results from Proof Theory", in J. E. Fenstad, editor, *Proceedings of the Second Scandinavian Logic Symposium*, North-Holland, Amsterdam, 1975, pp. 235-50.

[6] Dummett, "Theory of Meaning? II", p. 115.

[7] Dag Prawitz, "Meaning and Proofs", p. 3.

[8] See here my papers "Quantifiers vs. Quantification Theory" and "Quantifiers in Natural Languages: Some Logical Problems", in Saarinen, *Game-Theoretical Semantics*, pp. 49-79 and 81-117, respectively.

[9] The information set of a move M by a player P is the set of those moves whose outcome is known by P at M. See also R. Duncan Luce and Howard Raiffa, *Games and Decisions*, John Wiley, New York, 1957, p. 43.

[10] Leon Henkin, "Completeness in the Theory of Types", *Journal of Symbolic Logic* 15 (1950), 81-91. Cf. Jaakko Hintikka, "Standard vs. Nonstandard Logic: Higher-Order, Modal, and First-Order Logics", in E. Agazzi, editor, *Modern Logic: A Survey*, D. Reidel, Dordrecht, 1980, pp. 283-96.

[11] See "Quantifiers vs. Quantification Theory", in Saarinen, *Game-Theoretical Semantics*. (Originally published in *Linguistic Inquiry* 5 (1974), 153-77.)

[12] Ibid.

[13] P. F. Strawson, *Introduction to Logical Theory*, Methuen, London, 1952; "Meaning and Truth", in *Logico-Linguistic Papers*, Methuen, London, 1971.

[14] The basic writings of the Lorenzen school are conveniently available in Paul Lorenzen and Kuno Lorenz, editors, *Dialogische Logik*, Wissenschaftliche Buchgesellschaft, Darmstadt, 1978 (with ample further references to the

literature). See also Wolfgang Stegmüller, "Remarks on the Completeness of Logical Systems Relative to the Validity-Concepts of P. Lorenzen and K. Lorenz", *Notre Dame Journal of Formal Logic* 5 (1964), 81-112.

[15] Frequently game-theoretical semantics enables us to deepen the insights obtained in the competing approaches. For instance, the verificationists have pointed out repeatedly that in their view there is no valid general reason to believe in the law of bivalence, according to which each proposition S is either true or false. In game-theoretical semantics, the truth of S means that there is a winning strategy for Myself in the correlated semantical game G(S), and the falsity of S means that Nature has a winning strategy in G(S). Not only is it immediately clear on the basis of these definitions that there is in general no reason to expect S to be either true or false, but in the game-theoretical approach we see at once what the law of bivalence amounts to. It amounts to an assumption of determinateness for semantical games, that is, to an assumption that one of the two players always has a winning strategy. Now it is known from game theory and its applications to logic that determinateness postulates are often especially strong and especially interesting assumptions. Indeed, there exists a flourishing branch of foundational studies examining the consequences of different determinateness assumptions. For example, see J. Mycielski and H. Steinhaus, "A Mathematical Axiom Contradicting the Axiom of Choice", *Bulletin de l'Academie Polonaise des Sciences* (ser. II) 10 (1962), 1-3; J. Mycielski, "On the Axiom of Determinateness", *Fundamenta Mathematicae* 53 (1964), 205-24; Jens Erik Fenstad, "The Axiom of Determinateness", in Jens Erik Fenstad, editor, *Proceedings of the Second Scandinavian Logic Symposium*, North-Holland, Amsterdam, 1971, pp. 41-61 (with further references to the literature).

[16] I am referring to what Lorenzen and Lorenz call material games. The introduction of these games has not led the architects of this approach to change the label "dialogical", however.

[17] One way of looking at the activity of attempting to prove S is as an enterprise of trying to construct a counterexample to S, i.e., trying to construct a domain in which I don't have a winning strategy in G(S).

[18] See here especially my joint paper with Merrill B. Hintikka, "Sherlock Holmes Confronts Modern Logic:

Toward a Theory of Information-Seeking through Questioning", in E. M. Barth and J. L. Martens, editors, *Argumentation: Approaches to Theory Formation*, Benjamins, Amsterdam, 1982, pp. 55-76. Cf. also "Sherlock Holmes Formalized", in L. Geldsetzer, editor, *Festschrift* for A. Diemer, forthcoming, and "Towards an Interrogative Model of Scientific Inquiry", in W. Callebaut et al., editors, *Theory of Knowledge and Science Policy*, Communication & Cognition, Ghent, 1979, pp. 208-20.

[19] *Critique of Pure Reason*, B xiii.

[20] See note 18 above.

[21] Jaakko Hintikka and Esa Saarinen, "Information-Seeking Dialogues: Some of Their Logical Properties", *Studia Logica* 32 (1979), 355-63.

[22] See Kurt Gödel, "Über eine bisher noch nicht benutzte Erweiterung des finiten Standpunktes", in (no editor given) *Logica: Studia Paul Bernays dedicata*, Editions Griffon, Neuchatel, 1959, pp. 76-83. (See also section II (v) of the bibliography at the end of this volume for references to the literature on functional interpretations.) Note here how the translation into second-order logic exemplified by (2) and (5)-(6) above is of the nature of a functional interpretation. It can be varied further in different ways, e.g., by limiting the values of function variables (including those of a higher type) to recursive functions.

[23] As was first pointed out by Dana Scott ["A Game-Theoretic Interpretation of Logical Formulae", McCarthy Seminar, Stanford University, July 1968 (unpublished)], we can, for instance, in this way obtain an eminently natural motivation for Gödel's interpretation of elementary arithmetic (see the preceding note). For other uses of functional interpretations, cf. Jaakko Hintikka and Lauri Carlson, "Conditionals, Generic Quantifiers, and Other Applications of Subgames", in Saarinen, *Game-Theoretical Semantics*, pp. 179-214. See also the next chapter. Cf. also Jean-Yves Girard, "Functional Interpretation and Kripke Models", in Robert Butts and Jaakko Hintikka, editors, *Logic, Foundations of Mathematics, and Computability Theory* (Part One of the Proceedings of the Fifth International Congress of Logic, Methodology, and Philosophy of Science), D. Reidel, Dordrecht, 1977, pp. 33-57.

[24] Cf., e.g., the papers mentioned in notes 8, 18, and 23 above.

[25] Lauri Carlson, *Dialogue Games: An Approach to Discourse Analysis*, D. Reidel, Dordrecht, 1983.

Chapter 3

SEMANTICAL GAMES, SUBGAMES, AND
FUNCTIONAL INTERPRETATIONS

(Coauthored by Jaakko Hintikka and Jack Kulas)

1. Game-Theoretical Semantics Creates
a Higher-Order Translation

There is a way of looking at game-theoretical semantics
(GTS) that is not directly related either to its philosophical motivation or to some of its linguistic applications, but
that establishes potentially interesting links between it and
certain developments in logic and in the foundations of
mathematics.[1] These links have not been examined in detail in the literature, but they appear extremely promising.
In order to see these links, a certain idea introduced into
GTS by Hintikka and Carlson is needed: the idea of a
subgame.[2]
    The nature of this development of game-theoretical se-
mantics can be seen from the way formal first-order languages are treated in it. In this treatment, the truth of a
sentence S is equivalent to the existence of a winning
strategy for the player called *Myself* in a two-person game
(against *Nature*) G(S), which is correlated with S. Strategies are determined by the functions that tell the player
in question how to move, given the earlier history of the
game. Such functions are mathematical entities of a higher
type. Hence, the existence of a winning strategy for Myself in G(S) can be expressed in the language of higher-
order - in the first place, second-order - logic by an explicit sentence h(S). The force of the game-theoretical
treatment is thus reflected in and largely captured by the
translation h(S) of S, and, more generally, captured by a
certain translation from first-order languages into higher-order languages.
    This includes the interpretation of finite partially or-
dered quantifiers as an especially instructive special case.
Indeed, the translation thus accomplished is one of the
most direct ways of spelling out the interpretation of such
quantifiers. In fact, it has been used by all logicians who
have studied them. Let us consider some sentences that

47

contain linear quantifiers, as well as some sentences that contain branching quantifiers. We will assume that the interpretation of propositional connectives is not affected, and that M contains no quantifiers.

(1)   (x)(Ey) M(x,y)

translates as

(2)   (Ef)(x) M(x,f(x)).

Likewise,

(3)   (Ey)(x) M(x,y)

is unaffected by the translation, while

(4)   (x)(Ey)(z)(Eu) M(x,y,z,u)

translates as

(5)   (Ef)(Eg)(x)(z) M(x,f(x),z,g(x,z)).

This may be compared with

(6)   (x)(z)(Ey)(Eu) M(x,y,z,u),

which translates as

(7)   (Ef)(Eg)(x)(z) M(x,f(x,z),z,g(x,z)).

Furthermore,

(8) $\begin{matrix} (x) \\ (Ey) \end{matrix} \Bigg\rangle M(x,y)$

translates as

(9)   (Ey)(x) M(x,y),

while

(10) $(x)(Ey)$
$(z)(Eu)$ $\Big\} M(x,y,x,u)$

translates as

(11) $(Ef)(Eg)(x)(z)\ M(x,f(x),z,g(z))$.

The translation $h(S)$ immediately helps us to master the logical relations between different sentences that contain partially ordered quantifiers. For example, we can see that (8) reduces to a linear form (with the existential quantifier outside), while (10) does not, at least not equally obviously. It can easily be shown that it generally does not, as Henkin pointed out in his first paper on branching quantifiers.[3] (For special choices of M it can sometimes be reduced to an equivalent linear form, but this is not always possible.)

We can also see that the following ordering is an ordering of increasing logical strength: (6), (4), (10). Witness, for the purpose, the matrices of their respective translations:

(7) $M(x,f(x,z),z,g(x,z))$
(5) $M(x,f(x),z,g(x,z))$
(11) $M(x,f(x),z,g(z))$.

It can be at seen once that the fewer the arguments that a winning strategy depends on (i.e., the less information one needs to follow it), the stronger the statement is that such a winning strategy exists. This makes (4) stronger than (6), and (10) stronger than (4). It also makes the weakest of the three, (6), the candidate favored by the principle of charity to be the preferred interpretation of an utterance whose surface force could be any of them.

Moreover, any restrictions we might want to impose on Myself's strategies can be spelled out explicitly with the aid of the translation $h(S)$. For instance, one can argue that if those strategies are to be actually usable, they must be recursive. For how can one possibly play a game using a noncomputable strategy? For example, it has been argued in the literature that the existence of nonrecursive solutions to systems of differential equations does not make these systems deterministic. Similarly, following a non-recursive strategy is tantamount to having one's moves not

really determined at all. Hence, there seems ample motivation for allowing in our semantical games only strategies
codifiable by recursive functions (hereafter called *recursive strategies*). Such restrictions can be effected by
simply restricting the higher-order variables in h(S) to
recursive values.

By means of the higher-order translation we can even
show that the decision problem for the theory of partially
ordered quantifiers is as difficult as the decision problem
for the whole of second-order logic with standard interpretation. This can be seen by combining the reduction of
the decision problem (for satisfiability) for second-order
logic by Hintikka[4] with a result by Walkoe.[5] The former
reduces the decision problem for second-order logic to that
for formulas of the following form:

$$(12) \quad (X) \; M(X, \; Y_1, \; Y_2, \; ...),$$

i.e., to formulas that contain only one bound (universally
bound) second-order one-place predicate variable (over
and above free predicate variables and first-order quantifiers occurring in M). Walkoe's result shows how to express (12) in terms of partially ordered (but otherwise
first-order) quantifiers.

Even though the expressive power of second-order languages is, as one can easily see, stronger than that of
languages with finite partially ordered first-order quantifiers, the two languages have decision problems (for satisfiability) with the same degree of logical difficulty. This
is interesting because a great many unsolved logical and
mathematical problems are equivalent to questions concerning the satisfiability of certain second-order formulas - the
continuum hypothesis is only the most conspicuous of
them. Thus the theory of finite partially ordered quantifiers is an incredibly strong logical theory, even though it
is a first-order logic in the sense that all its quantifiers
range over individuals.

2. The Subgame Notion

This idea of higher-order translation can be extended further in two different but interrelated directions. One extension is to think of a game as consisting of a number of
separate units called *subgames*. Another is to change the

rules for propositional connectives in the same spirit that quantifiers were restricted to recursive strategies above.

Employing the subgame idea allows us to partition an overall semantical game into smaller constituent games (subgames), each of which is played out completely before the players move on to the next. Why does this make a difference? The answer must lie in the requirement that each subgame is played out completely in its own right. Now what does it mean, in game-theoretical terms, to play a game? The idea of a *normal form* gives us an answer.[6] To play a game is for each player to choose a strategy. Such strategy choices by all players conjointly uniquely determine the course and the outcome of the game. Hence, the upshot of the idea of completely playing out a subgame is that each player chooses a strategy and at least one of them reveals his or her strategy to his or her opponent. This makes an essential difference to the logical situation. Before the introduction of the concept of subgame, a player's strategy was a first-order function whose arguments were other players' earlier moves. After the change, a player's strategy in subsequent subgames may depend on certain earlier moves in earlier subgames, not just on an opponent's entire strategy. The former strategy has the logical type of a first-order function, while the latter strategy, involving as it does only certain moves in earlier subgames, is representable by a higher-order function (functional). Thus it is the subgame idea that forces us to go higher than second-order logic in the translation of first-order sentences. This is of course a significant difference.

3. Rules for Subgames

The subgame idea can be illustrated by means of the game-theoretical treatment of conditionals. How are they to be treated? One's first impulse is probably to treat them purely truth-functionally, i.e., to treat $(X \rightarrow Y)$ as if it were $(\sim X \vee Y)$. But the disadvantages of so doing are well known. One's second impulse is probably to strengthen the link between the antecedent and the consequent by introducing suitable modal or intensional notions, for instance, by treating $(X \rightarrow Y)$ as if it were $N(X \rightarrow Y)$, where "N" is the necessity operator or some other analogous intensional operator. Something obviously has to be done in this direction. But, however much we strengthen the link between antecedent and consequent, we come no closer to grasping the *conditional* character of conditionals. Now, what is this character? What is conditional about conditionals? Consider the game associated with (13):

(13) $(X \rightarrow Y)$.

The conditional element can be taken to mean that the game G(Y) for the consequent Y is played only if X turns out to be true; and then it should be played in a way that depends on how X was verified. Now the game G(X) is precisely a game in which Myself tries to verify X. So, the game rule can be formulated as follows: First, the game G(X) is played with the two players' roles interchanged. If Myself wins, i.e., manages to falsify X, Myself wins the overall game $G(X \rightarrow Y)$. If Nature wins, i.e., verifies X, G(Y) is played with Myself knowing the particular verifying strategy that Nature used in G(X). This corresponds to the idea that the way Y enters into the semantics of the conditional (13) depends on the way its antecedent X is verified. The resulting game rule can be summed up in flowchart (15) on the next page. That rule can also be expressed by a translation rule. In formulating it, we shall assume that X and Y have translations of the form $(E\zeta)(\xi) X'(\zeta,\xi)$ and $(E\phi)(\eta) Y'(\phi,\eta)$, respectively. Here ζ and ϕ are thought of as codifying the strategies of Myself, and ξ and η those of Nature. Hence, the two quantifiers $(E\zeta)$ and $(E\phi)$ may have to be replaced by strings of existential quantifiers of higher type (possibly also first-order quantifiers), and (ξ) and (η) by strings of function or functional quantifiers of different types, all universal, possibly including first-order universal quantifiers. Then the translation of (13) is (14):

(14) $(E\phi)(E\xi)(\zeta)(\eta)[X'(\zeta,\xi) \rightarrow Y'(\phi(\zeta),\eta)]$.

However, this is not the only game rule we have to consider. First, the idea that the antecedent of a conditional must be verified before the players consider the consequent can be given a different twist. If the antecedent is true, then Nature (playing the verifier's role in G(X)) must be able to win against any opposing strategy, even if Myself knows which strategy Nature is using. This means making Myself's strategy in G(X) a function

(15)   G(X → Y):

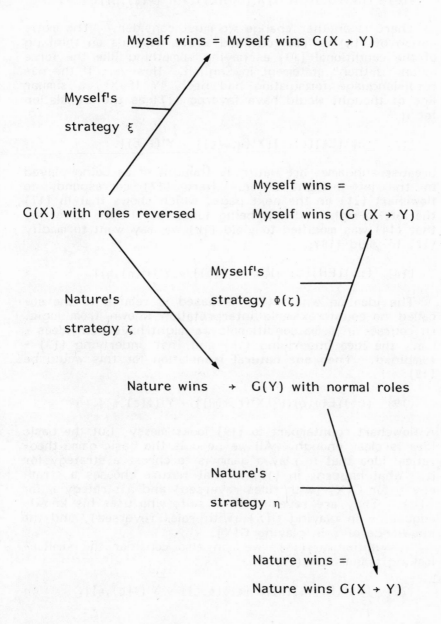

Myself wins = Myself wins G(X → Y)

Myself's

strategy ξ

G(X) with roles reversed

Myself wins =
Myself wins (G (X → Y)

Myself's

strategy Φ(ζ)

Nature's

strategy ζ

Nature wins   →   G(Y) with normal roles

Nature's

strategy η

Nature wins =

Nature wins G(X → Y)

of ζ, i.e., $\xi = \Xi(\zeta)$. Then (14) is replaced by the slightly different translation (16):

(16) $(E\Phi)(E\Xi)(\zeta)(\eta)[X'(\zeta,\Xi(\zeta)) \rightarrow Y'(\Phi(\zeta),\eta)]$.

There is another change we must consider.[7] The motivation of (14) or (16) outlined above depends on thinking of the conditional (13) as having something like the force of an "if-then" statement in English. However, if the natural-language formulation had been "Y if X", a similar line of thought would have favored (17) as the translation for it,

(17) $(E\psi)(E\xi)(\zeta)(\eta)[X'(\eta,\psi(\zeta)) \rightarrow Y'(\xi,\zeta)]$.

because subgames are naturally thought of as being played in the left-to-right order. Here (17) corresponds to flowchart (21) on the next page, which shows that in (17) the left-to-right order is being followed. In the same way that (14) was modified to yield (16) we may want to modify (17) to yield (18):

(18) $(E\Phi)(EH)(\zeta)(\eta)[X'(\zeta,\Phi(\eta)) \rightarrow Y'(H(\eta),\eta)]$.

The idea on which (17) is based is related to the so-called no-counterexample interpretation known from logic. Of course, in some conditionals we might have both ideas – i.e., the idea underlying (16) and that underlying (17) – combined. Then one natural translation for this would be (19):

(19) $(E\Phi)(E\Psi)(\zeta)(\eta)[X'(\zeta,\Psi(\eta)) \rightarrow Y'(\Phi(\zeta),\eta)]$.

A flowchart counterpart to (19) looks messy, but the basic idea is clear enough. All we need is the basic game-theoretical idea that to play a game is to choose a strategy for it. What happens in (19) is that Nature chooses a strategy ζ for G(X) (with roles reversed) and a strategy η for G(Y). They are revealed to Myself, who uses his knowledge of η in playing G(X) (with roles reversed), and the knowledge of ζ in playing G(Y).

In addition to (19), we can also consider the similar-looking translation (20):

(20) $(E\Phi)(E\psi)(\zeta)(\eta)[X'(\zeta,\psi(\eta,\zeta)) \rightarrow Y'(\Phi(\zeta),\eta)]$.

(21)   G(X → Y):

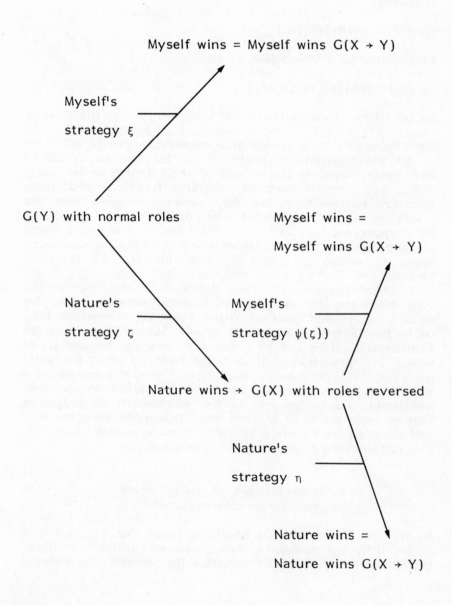

Myself wins = Myself wins G(X → Y)

Myself's
strategy ξ

G(Y) with normal roles

Myself wins =
Myself wins G(X → Y)

Nature's
strategy ζ

Myself's
strategy ψ(ζ))

Nature wins → G(X) with roles reversed

Nature's
strategy η

Nature wins =
Nature wins G(X → Y)

Along the same lines, we may want to formulate a game rule for negation that does not make $\sim X$ simply the truth-functional contradictory of X.   Rather, the idea is that any attempt to verify X will provide a way to verify $\sim X$.

If we assume again that the translation of X is the following:

$$(E\zeta)(\xi)[X'(\zeta,\xi)],$$

(22) would be a translation of $\sim X$:

$$(22) \quad (E\Phi)(\zeta)[\sim X'(\zeta,\Phi(\zeta))].$$

In all these formulations, we can intuitively think of a choice of ζ in $X'(\zeta,\xi)$ as a choice of an example of X, and the choice of ξ as a choice of a counterexample to X.

All the translations provided so far can be combined with restrictions on the values of their higher-order variables, e.g., restrictions to recursive functions and functionals.   Furthermore, we may want to require that the choice by Myself connected with disjunction be governed by a recursive function.   In other words, the requirement of recursiveness for strategies used by Myself should also apply to moves governed by the rule (G. v) for disjunction.

Each of these translations involves a step up in the type hierarchy for the functions and functionals used by Myself.   Repeated uses of these rules can therefore take us to functionals of any finite type.   Second-order quantification thus does not in general suffice for a game-theoretical interpretation of first-order formulas when the subgame idea is being employed.   For it is the subgame idea that leads immediately to the type-theoretical ascent just mentioned.   It is integral to the employment of subgames that in later parts of a game the strategy Φ used by Myself depends on Nature's strategy ζ in an earlier subgame, and is thus of a higher logical type than ζ.

4. Interrelations of the Different Functional Interpretations

So far, we have not said anything about the interrelations of the different competing functional interpretations, illustrated by the differences between the various translations given above, nor about whether they give us anything new. Let us consider, for instance, the higher-order translation (16) of the conditional $(X \rightarrow Y)$ (with the same translations of X and Y as above):

(16) $(E\Phi)(E\Xi)(\zeta)(\eta)[X'(\zeta,\Xi(\zeta)) \rightarrow Y'(\Phi(\zeta),\eta)]$.

Here the higher-order functions Φ, and Ξ mark choices by Myself that depend on ζ alone. Hence, the force of these choices is captured by using a lower-order existential quantifier that is within the scope of (ζ) but not of (η). In other words, (16) is equivalent to (23), which is trivially equivalent to (24):

(23) $(\zeta)(E\xi)(E\phi)(\eta)[X'(\zeta,\xi) \rightarrow Y'(\phi,\eta)]$.

(24) $(E\zeta)(\xi)[X'(\zeta,\xi)] \rightarrow (E\phi)(\eta)[Y'(\phi,\eta)]$.

But (24) is precisely what $(X \rightarrow Y)$ was defined to be. Thus, the translation (16) does not yield anything new. Moreover, from the argument just given it is seen that this observation is completely independent of whether the values of function and functional variables are restricted to recursive ones.

Analogously, (14) can be seen to be equivalent to (25), and hence reducible to (26):

(25) $(E\xi)(\zeta)(E\phi)(\eta)[X'(\zeta,\xi) \rightarrow Y'(\phi,\eta)]$.

(26) $(\xi)(E\zeta)[X'(\zeta,\xi)] \rightarrow (E\phi)(\eta)[Y'(\phi,\eta)]$.

But (26) is not the same as the original. However, if the semantical game associated with X is determinate, the antecedent of (26) is equivalent to (27):

(27) $(E\zeta)(\xi)[X'(\zeta,\xi)]$.

Then (26) is equivalent with (24), i.e., with $(X \rightarrow Y)$. The reason that the rule (14) yields something new is that in it we strengthen the conditional by waiving the requirement that the antecedent be true, allowing it merely not to be false.

Gödel's interpretation of conditionals – i.e., (20) – when treated analogously yields (28), which also reduces to (24):

(28) $(\zeta)(E\phi)(\eta)(E\xi)[X'(\zeta,\xi) \rightarrow Y'(\phi,\eta)]$.

Hence, we have reached the remarkable result that Gödel's rule for conditionals is redundant. He could have let conditionals be translated simply as conditionals. All the work in his translation is done by the other rules and by the restriction to recursive functions and functionals.

Likewise, (17) turns out to be equivalent to (29), and therefore to (26):

(29) $(E\xi)(\eta)(E\phi)(\zeta)[X'(\zeta,\phi) \rightarrow Y'(\xi,\eta)]$.

Thus the same things can be said of (17) as of (14).

Moreover, (18) reduces first to (30), and then to (31):

(30) $(\eta)(E\xi)(E\phi)(\zeta)[X'(\zeta,\xi) \rightarrow Y'(\phi,\eta)]$.

(31) $(\xi)(E\zeta)[X'(\zeta,\xi)] \rightarrow (\eta)(E\phi)[Y'(\phi,\eta)]$.

Here both the antecedent and the consequent are weakened in the same way as the antecedent of (13) was weakened in (26).

The most interesting translation rule for conditionals is (19). If we try to replace the term $\Psi(\eta)$ by a variable bound to an existential quantifier, we need a quantifier that is in the scope of (η) but not in the scope of (ζ). If we try to replace $\Phi(\zeta)$ by a variable bound to an existential quantifier, we need a quantifier that is in the scope of (ζ) but not in the scope of (η). It is clear that these two desiderata cannot be realized by means of any linearly ordered quantifier prefix. However, it is obvious that the desired equivalent can be obtained by means of a branching-quantifier prefix. Indeed, (19) is clearly equivalent to (32):

(32) $(\zeta)(E\phi)$
      $(\eta)(E\xi)$ $\Big\rangle [X'(\zeta,\xi) \rightarrow Y'(\phi,\eta)]$.

The branching-quantifier structure exemplified in (32), known as "the Henkin quantifier", is known to be irreducible in general. It is also easy to see that the same irreducibility is true of (32). Thus the translation rule (19) for conditionals is quite different from all the others we have considered. The other changes in our rule for conditionals either do not change our logic or change it only in relation to the law of excluded middle. The translation rule (19) amounts to a long step beyond the usual interpretations of first-order logic. For it is known that the extra logical power yielded by Henkin quantifiers is very great indeed. It is therefore a little surprising that it has not received the same attention as Gödel's rule (20).

These observations illustrate the power of game-theoretical ideas in dealing with different problems concerning subgames. It is also relevant to note here that restricting the values of higher-order variables to recursive functions and functionals makes a difference.[8] There are first-order formulas S such that S is satisfiable but h(S) is not, if the restriction is imposed on the values of the variables.

5. Semantical Games and Functional Interpretations

For many logicians, the translations we have formulated have a distinctly déjà vu aura. They all represent different kinds of functional interpretations of first-order logic.[9] The oldest of these interpretations was given by Gödel in 1959. It incorporates, in effect, the translation rules (20) and (22), the change in (G. v) mentioned above, and a restriction of the values of higher-order variables to recursive objects (recursive functions and functionals).

Indeed, the translation rules that are the gist of Gödel's interpretation can be formulated as follows, assuming that the translation t(X) of X and t(Y) of Y are $(E\xi)(\zeta)[X'(\xi,\zeta)]$ and $(E\phi)(\eta)[Y'(\phi,\eta)]$, respectively:

(T. &) $t(X \ \& \ Y) = (E\xi)(E\phi)(\zeta)(\eta)[X'(\xi,\zeta) \ \& \ Y'(\phi,\eta)]$.

(T. v) $t(X \ v \ Y) = (E\xi)(E\phi)(E\psi)(\zeta)(\eta)[(\psi=0 \ \& \ X'(\xi,\zeta)) \ v$
$(\psi=1 \ \& \ Y'(\phi,\eta))]$.

(T. U) $t((x)X) = (E\xi)(x)(\zeta)[X'(\xi(x),\zeta]$.

(T. E) $t((Ex)X) = (E\xi)(Ex)(\zeta)[X'(\xi,\zeta)]$.

(T. →) $t(X \rightarrow Y) = $ (20).

(T. ∿) $t(\sim X) \quad = $ (22).

The game-theoretical approach thus enables us to spell out the motivation – or at least *a* motivation – for Gödel's interpretation much more clearly than Gödel's own paper does. Indeed, we suspect that we are not the only readers who had trouble with Gödel's ideas – until, that is, we noticed their relationship to game-theoretical semantics. The possibility of giving a game-theoretical motivation to Gödel's proposal was first pointed out by Dana Scott.[10] In general, as far as traditional (of the Frege-Russell type) formal languages are concerned, functional interpretations *are* the logic of game-theoretical semantics when the latter is made completely explicit. (The sense of explicitness used here was indicated above. Let the h(S) be the higher-order translation that gives to us the functional interpretation of a first-order sentence S. This h(S) is precisely the sentence that asserts that there exists a winning strategy for Myself in the first-order game G(S) associated with S.) Hence the literature on functional interpretations is potentially highly relevant to the enterprise of game-theoretical semantics. Once again, it turns out that game-theoretical semantics has in fact played a much larger role in logic and foundational studies than one might have first thought. For, as Justus Diller puts it, "Functional interpretations have proved to be a useful tool in proof theory."[11] However, it does not follow that the perspectives in which functional interpretations have been considered are all philosophically satisfactory. Moreover, the situation turns out to be somewhat different in the semantics of natural languages, as we shall find below.

The relevance of functional interpretations to game-theoretical semantics in the past has been reduced somewhat by two factors. First, the literature on functional interpretations has been geared to foundational problems rather than general semantical ones. Second, beginning with Gödel's original paper, functional interpretations have often been discussed in reference to ideas of the intuitionists. This seems to us less than fortunate. Notwithstanding the impression one easily gets from papers dealing with Gödel's functional interpretation, it is in fact not a true interpretation of Heyting's intuitionistic predicate logic. Everything provable in Heyting's logic is valid on Gödel's functional interpretation, but the converse does not hold. It is not clear whether the upshot of the Gödel interpretation is an argument against intuitionistic logic as the most natural logic, or an argument for it. In any case, it

has been shown that Gödel's interpretation has to be modified if it is to be extended in a natural way to intuitionistic arithmetic of higher types.[12]

It is also not clear what the motivation for Gödel's interpretation of the conditional - represented as (20) above
- is, as distinguished from such rivals as (19). As we
saw in section 4, the two are not equivalent and (19) is in
some ways more interesting than (20).

Such technical discrepancies between Gödel's interpretation and intuitionistic logic and mathematics are connected with a philosophical difference between the two that
has not been sufficiently emphasized in the literature.
What game-theoretical semantics (and hence a functional
interpretation à la Gödel) brings about is a new *semantics*,
that is, a reinterpretation of what it is for a sentence to
be true in a model, in the sense of ordinary ("material")
truth. Game-theoretical semantics is geared to the ways in
which such truth is actually established. This may look
very much like the ideas of the intuitionists, but it is not.
For what they have in mind is not how the *de facto* truth
of a sentence is established by looking for and finding
suitable individuals, but how the logical (or mathematical)
truth of a sentence is established by finding a proof for
it. So it is not surprising at all to find that Gödel's functional interpretation does not capture Heyting's ideas.

For the same reason, it is misguided to try to use
game-theoretical semantics to argue for intuitionistic logic
and mathematics. Both game-theoretical semanticists and
intuitionists (more generally, constructionists) admittedly
focus on ways of establishing truth. But in intuitionism it
quickly turns out that what is intended is logical or mathematical truth and not truth *simpliciter*, as in game-theoretical semantics. The latter deals squarely with truth
conditions, not conditions of assertability or defensibility.

One particular way in which the confusion between material and logical truth can mislead philosophers is the following. Quite independently of how one thinks about the
processes (e.g., semantical games) through which the material truth of a given sentence S in some given model
(world) is established, it is eminently natural to think of a
logical proof of S as a frustrated attempt to *construct*,
step by step, a model in which S is not true. Now this
stepwise building process can be constructivistic and fini-
tistic even when the verification processes involved in the
establishment of material truth are not. If philosophers

overlook the distinction between these two "kinds of truth", they are thus easily led to think of the notion of truth-in-general in constructivistic terms. This involves a dangerous fallacy, however, and can be seriously misleading philosophically.

These remarks apply, mutatis mutandis, to Lorenzen's attempts to base intuitionistic logic on game-theoretical ideas.[13] However, Lorenzen has changed his mind so many times and has combined so many different ideas with each other, that his approach needs a much more extensive and detailed discussion than it can be given here.

There are, nevertheless, interesting general connections between the foundational studies based on functional interpretations and game-theoretical semantics. One particularly important line of foundational investigation is the classification of the functionals used in the interpretation of different formulas according to their complexity.[14] Typically, transfinite ordinals are used for the classification; then the degree of complexity goes together with the ordinal up to which one has to use such inferential principles as the descending-chain condition. Now the functionals needed in the interpretation codify precisely the strategies used by Myself in the corresponding semantical game. So, classifying these functionals by complexity is really classifying the correlated semantical games by their difficulty for Myself. This is one of the first ideas likely to occur to anyone studying semantical games. In this way, this part of foundational inquiries into functional interpretations has a strong game-theoretical motivation.

The relation of game-theoretical semantics to intuitionistic logic requires further comment. It is true that the logic that results from a functional interpretation is in some ways very close to intuitionistic logic. As Dana Scott has pointed out, the only thing that separates the logic of Gödel's functional interpretation from intuitionistic logic is that the law of excluded middle is valid in the former but not in the latter. In game-theoretical semantics, the law of excluded middle amounts to a determinateness assumption for the semantical games with which we are dealing. This determinateness is likely to fail when the games in question become more complicated. Therefore, the reason that the law of excluded middle holds in the logic of Gödel's functional interpretation is merely that it is a game-theoretical translation of a relatively simple part of logic, namely, first-order logic, which does not yet give rise to failures of determinateness. A general logic that encompassed more complicated formulas would give up determinateness, thus rejecting the law of excluded middle. Such a logic, presumably, would coincide with intuitionistic logic.

However, it remains questionable to what extent the above amounts to a vindication of intuitionists' ideas. Failures of the law of excluded middle can, on the contrary, result from blatantly nonintuitionistic procedures. For instance, if we are dealing with sentences that give rise to infinitely long semantical games, e.g., infinitely deep sentences, we have no reason to expect the law of excluded middle to hold. Such reasons are totally unrelated to intuitionism, though. Therefore, this attempt to vindicate the ideas of intuitionists strikes us as unconvincing.

6. Subgames in the Semantics of Formal and Natural Languages

So far, we have discussed only formal languages and the forms that the subgame idea takes in them.[15] What light does the subgame idea throw on natural-language phenomena? What differences, if any, are there between formal and natural languages with respect to the conceptualizations we have studied? At first sight, it might appear that the subgame idea is not likely to make much difference here. It is, of course, likely that natural-language conditionals are best treated by means of some form of the subgame idea. Indeed, it is intuitively plausible that such a treatment can capture what is conditional about conditionals. But it also appears unlikely that natural-language semantics should rely on such complicated two-way dependencies as are captured, e.g., by (20). What we can reasonably expect are relatively simple rules that can be captured by such flowcharts as, e.g., (15), and codified in (14) or (17). But from the viewpoint of conventional formal logic this makes little difference yet. It was shown in the preceding section that, with or without restricting higher-order variables to recursive entities, the change from the usual truth-functional rule for conditionals to (16) or (20) *makes no difference*. Moreover, the changes codified in (14), (17) or (18) are relatively small. The only odd man out is the change formulated in (19), but

this particular interpretation apparently has not been discussed earlier in the literature.

Hence, it might seem that little new light can be thrown
on natural-language phenomena by subgames or by the
closely related functional interpretations. However, this
impression is mistaken. There are features in natural-
language semantics that have no counterparts in the semantics of conventional formal languages. Because of
them, even the modest step to such game rules as are
codified in (14), (16)-(18), or (20) will affect the semantics of natural languages. This is one of the reasons for
the importance of the subgame idea in the semantics of
natural languages.

7. Towards a Treatment of Anaphora

The most important phenomenon with no simple counterpart
in conventional formal languages is anaphora. This is not
the place, however, to develop a full-fledged theory of it.
But we have made a start in another work that is still in
progress.[16] There we expect to show that the semi-formal
idea that suffices for the purposes of the present chapter
can be used in the formulation of an explicit game rule for
the semantical behavior of certain types of anaphora.

This idea in its basic form is simplicity itself. An
anaphoric pronoun is "interpreted" by means of a game
rule applied to it. This game rule involves a selection by
Myself of an individual from a set of individuals available
to the two players of a semantical game at the time when
they come to "process" the pronoun. There are several
different ways in which an individual can become available
in the sense intended here:

(i)   It is one of the individuals chosen by the players
        earlier in the same game or subgame.

This clause requires a couple of explanations, however.
First, individuals whose choice involves the whole strategy
of one of the players in an earlier subgame are available
only on the condition that these strategies are "remembered", in a sense to be spelled out. Second, individuals
whose choice depends on some player's earlier strategy are
normally not "remembered" by, or available to, the players
in subsequent subgames.

(ii)   It is referred to by a proper name or a compar-
           able expression occurring in the initial sentence
           of the game.

(iii)   It can be obtained from (i) or (ii) by means of
           strategies that are codified in certain functions
           and functionals and "remembered" from earlier
           subgames.

Several further remarks are needed to define fully the set
of individuals available, but it would take us too far from
our present topic to make them here.

This construal of the way anaphoric pronouns work has
no counterpart in conventional logical languages. It marks
an important difference between the usual Frege-Russell
type of formal logic and the logic of ordinary language,
and a complete break with the widespread idea of assimilating the mode of functioning of anaphoric pronouns to the
mode of functioning of bound variables of quantification
theory.

Before this rule for anaphoric pronouns (which will not
be completely defined here) can be used in all cases, we -
or, rather, the players - must know what principles govern the order of its application vis-à-vis other game rules.
A full account of these ordering principles is an important
part of a satisfactory treatment of anaphora in game-theoretical semantics.   Though such an exhaustive account
won't be undertaken here, a few observations are in order. It has been in effect pointed out by Hintikka and
Carlson, though within a slightly different theory, that
the rule for anaphoric pronouns has priority over several
other rules, including rules for propositional connectives
that don't involve subgames.[17] And also it appears that
the rule for pronominal anaphora does not have an auto-
matic priority over quantifier rules.

8. Anaphora and Subgames in Natural
Languages: Simple Cases

A few concrete examples will show how these ideas, in
combination with our earlier results, illuminate actual natural-language phenomena. Consider, for example, (33):

(33)   If Tom owns a cat, he spoils it.

Here the subgame G(Tom owns a cat) connected with the
antecedent is played first, with the roles of the two
parties reversed. The only rule (so far formulated) that
applies here is (G.a(n)). Since the players' roles are reversed, the choice prescribed in (G.a(n)) is made by Nature playing the role of Myself. Nature's strategy in this
first subgame is completely specified by the individual chosen. For the sake of argument, let's assume that the individual chosen by Nature is Morris. Then Nature wins
the subgame G(Tom owns a cat) if and only if both "Tom
owns Morris" and "Morris is a cat" are true. In this case,
and in this case only, the players go on to play G(he
spoils it), assuming that (15) (or (14)) is being used. As
can be seen from flowchart (15), Myself "remembers" the
strategy Nature used in the first subgame. As was indicated above, the rationale for remembering *Nature's* strategy here is that Nature's role in that subgame, which is
the role of Myself (due to the role reversal), is to verify
the sentence. The subgame played on the consequent is
played only after the antecedent has been shown to be
true. This dependence is how GTS captures the conditionality of conditionals: only the verifier's strategy is remembered. As was seen earlier, this means remembering
Nature's choice of an individual in G(Tom owns a cat),
i.e., remembering Morris. The only rule that can be applied in the game G(he spoils it) connected with the consequent is the rule for anaphoric pronouns. Then, by (i)
and a remembered strategy, Morris serves as the obvious
value for "it", and Tom, by (ii), as the obvious value for
"he". So, the second subgame reduces to G(Tom spoils
Morris), i.e., reduces to a win for Myself if "Tom spoils
Morris" is true, and a win for Nature if it is false.

   The truth of (33) means that there exists a winning
strategy for Myself in the correlated game, i.e., a strategy that wins against any strategy of Nature's. Now Nature's strategies are, in effect, so many choices of cats
owned by Tom, since other choices of individuals would
lead to a win for Myself already on the basis of the subgame connected with the antecedent. Putting all these observations together, it can be seen that the force of (33)
can be represented by (34):

(34) (x)[(Tom owns x & x is a cat) → (Tom
      spoils x)].

This is obviously the intended meaning of (33), confirming the correctness of our analysis. However, this "output" sentence (34) tells us nothing about the mechanism of the translation.

One interesting feature of this treatment of (33) is that it not only allows, but it *requires* us to treat the indefinite article "a" in the antecedent as an existential quantifier, even though in the resultant representation (34) it corresponds to a universal quantifier. This and other representations like it in conventional logical notation have led some theorists to postulate two different readings for the indefinite article: one giving it the force of a universal quantifier, the other that of an existential quantifier. Apart from the arbitrariness of such a postulation, it has the more serious drawback of failing to account for the mechanism through which the actual force (34) of (33) comes about.

In contrast to (33), consider the following sentence:

(35)   *If Tom owns every cat, he spoils it.

Here the choice of an individual in the first subgame G(Tom owns every cat) is made by Myself in a falsifier's role. The chosen individual is Myself's complete strategy. From (15) it can be seen that this strategy is not carried over to, or remembered in, the second subgame. For Myself's aim in the first subgame is to falsify "Tom owns every cat", and falsifying strategies don't carry over. Hence, there is nothing available to the players in the subgame G(he spoiled it) that could serve as a value for "it". The prediction from our theory, then, would be that (35) is anomalous (unacceptable), which is obviously the case. However, we don't want to prejudge the question whether such anomaly should be classified as ungrammaticality rather than some other kind of deviance.

9. Anaphora and Subgames:
More Complicated Cases

The following somewhat more complex example also illustrates what has been said:

(36) Even if you send a personalized invitation to each
      of your friends, some friend will throw it away
      unread.

Let us consider the meaning of this sentence. There
are in principle at least four ways of trying to interpret it
that are neither natural in this particular case nor of interest to us here:

(i)   One might try to interpret the pronoun "it" as
          referring to some contextually given individual.

(ii)   One might try to interpret the pronoun "it" as
          referring to no individual at all, but rather to
          the fact mentioned in the antecedent, in analogy
          with one reading of (37):

   (37)   Even if you send a letter of protest to everyone,
          it will be ignored.

          This is the reading on which "it" does not refer
          to any particular letter, but instead to the
          "archetype", as it were, of the letter sent to all
          of the recipients.

(iii)   In the first subgame G(you send...your friends),
          one might try to apply a game rule first to "a
          personalized invitation" before one is applied to
          "each friend".

(iv)   One might try to interpret "it" as a pronoun of
          laziness, i.e., to understand it as if it meant
          (38):

   (38)   Even if you send a personalized invitation to each
          of your friends, some friend will throw a person-
          alized invitation away unread.

We are not going to discuss fully why all these readings
are filtered out here, though some remarks on this subject
will be made below.
    The remaining reading - the only *natural* one here - is
obtained as follows. First, a subgame G(you send...your
friends) is played on the antecedent of (36), with the two
players' roles reversed. The strategy of Nature, whose

aim is to verify the antecedent, consists of a function f. If Nature is going to win this subgame, this function has to correlate with each friend whom Myself might choose a personalized invitation sent to that friend.   Then, in the second subgame G(some friend will throw it away unread), the first rule to be applied is undoubtedly (G. some). For one thing, this rule is favored by the left-to-right ordering.   Furthermore, by the second qualification made to (i) in section 7 above, no individual would be available as a value for "it" anyway, even if the players tried to apply the rule for anaphoric pronouns first.

This is worth spelling out.   The needed invitation (the one sent to the "some friend"), which was chosen by Nature in the first subgame, is not now available, because its choice depended on an earlier choice by Myself playing Nature's role.   And it's no help that the function f is remembered, because the only possible argument would be the corresponding friend chosen by Myself in the first subgame.   But that choice embodies Myself's winning (falsifying) strategy in that subgame.   Since that strategy is not remembered, the needed argument for the function f is not available to the players.

An application of (G. some) yields a sentence like (39):

(39)   Harry will throw it away unread, and Harry is a friend.

Now let us assume (this assumption can be shown not to be a critical one) that the next rule to be applied is the rule for anaphoric pronouns. It applies to "it". The only individual (of the right sort) available to the players at this point is f(Harry), i.e., the invitation to be sent to Harry. So, the force of (39) is to say that Harry will throw away unread the particular personalized invitation that was sent to him. This yields just the right reading of (36), the one on which it has roughly the same force as (40):[18]

(40)   Even if you send a personalized invitation to each of your friends, some friend will throw his or her invitation away unread.

Our success in treating (36) provides further evidence for our theory.

James Higginbotham has claimed that our game-theo-

retical treatment allows, and even prefers, a nonexistent
reading for the following sentence: [19]

(41)   If everyone else consults two doctors, I'll con-
       sult them too.

It is nevertheless clear why (41) cannot be treated in
analogy with (36), as Higginbotham claims our theory must
treat it. The function correlated with the first subgame of
(41), and remembered in the second, associates two doctors with everyone other than the speaker (the "I") - so,
not automatically with Myself. In order for Nature to win
that first subgame, so the second will be played, Nature
will have to use for a strategy a function g that correlates
with each person *except the speaker (Myself)* two doctors
consulted by that person. However, the sentence (41) itself gives us no reason to expect that this function should
be defined for Myself as an argument, let alone yield some
specified kind of value. Hence there is no context-
independent reading of (41) that would assign to it a
reading analogous with the preferred reading of (36).

Since existential quantifiers resemble disjunctions in
that each marks a move by Myself, and since universal
quantifiers are like conjunctions in that each marks Nature's move, our theory predicts that there should be examples with propositional connectives that are analogous to
(33) and (35). This expectation is fulfilled by examples
like (42) and (43): [20]

(42)   If Tom owns a cat or a dog, he spoils it.
(43)   *If Tom owns a cat and a dog, he spoils it.

10. Relation of Informal and Formal Analyses

At this point, it may be of interest to see how our informal treatment of natural-language examples is related to
the formal treatment explained above that uses a translation to higher-order notation as its main tool. We have
seen that, other things being equal, (16) reduces to (13).
(See section 4 above.) Why are things not equal when
there is an anaphoric cross-reference between the antecedent and the consequent, as, e.g., in (33)?

What happens when there is an anaphoric back reference from the consequent to the antecedent is, in effect,

that the "logical form" (higher-order translation) of a conditional like (33) is, not (16), but something like (44):

(44) $(E\Phi)(E\Psi)(y)(z)[A(y,\Psi(y)) \rightarrow B(\Phi(y),z,y)]$.

In other words, the presence of anaphora means that "y",
in effect, also occurs in B otherwise than as the argument
of Φ.

In the same way as (16) reduces to (23), (44) reduces
to (45):

(45) $(y)[(x)A(y,x) \rightarrow (Eu)(z)B(u,z,y)]$.

But here the scope of "(y)" cannot be reduced to the
antecedent only, for "y" occurs also in the consequent.
Now (45) is obviously the logical form of the simplest natural-language sentences in question (viz., those with
anaphoric cross-reference), provided that there are no
other quantifiers present than those represented in (44).
Here we can see what the precise formal counterpart is to
the informal line of thought presented above in section 8
concerning sentences like (33).

It is worth emphasizing that, even though we can thus
represent the "deduction" of the logical form of such sentences as (33) in familiar logical notation, the motivation
and the formulation of some of the most interesting regularities is possible only in the framework of game-theoretical semantics. For instance, the sense in which the
indefinite pronoun in examples like (33) is an *existential*
quantifier – thus preserving an important semantical regularity – can only be seen from the game-theoretical reasoning that leads to our game rule for conditionals. Formal-
istically speaking, we need to know, among other things,
when it is justifiable to stick this extra variable "y" into
the consequent, as in (44). Such questions can only be
answered adequately by means of game-theoretical semantics.

The examples given in this section and its predecessors
show that a game-theoretical treatment of natural-language
sentences normally yields, as a by-product, a translation
into some kind of logical notation. Typically, the translation is a higher-order sentence, not a first-order one.
Nevertheless, let us first consider a case in which we obtain a first-order translation, in order to gain some feeling
for the nature of the translation process:

(46)   If you give a Christmas gift to each boy today,
        some boy will open it right away.

(It would be more natural here to say "his" instead of
"it", but this makes no essential difference to our argument, while avoiding the extra complication of the genitive
case mentioned above.)   Let us use the following abbrevi-
ations:

   A(x,y) = you give to x the Christmas gift y today
   B(z,u) = z will open u right away.

Then the game-theoretical interpretation (higher-order
translation) according to (16) or (20) will be (47):

   (47) $(E\Phi)(E\Psi)(f)[A(\Psi(f),f(\Psi(f))) \rightarrow B(\Phi(f),f(\Phi(f)))]$.

Here Φ and Ψ are functionals whose arguments are one-
place functions of individuals and whose values are individuals.   In usual fashion (47) reduces to (48), which is
equivalent to (49):

   (48) $(f)(Ex)(Ey)[A(x,f(x)) \rightarrow B(y,f(y))]$.
   (49) $(f)[(x)A(x,f(x)) \rightarrow (Ey)B(y,f(y))]$.

Assuming the principle of choice, this reduces to (50):

   (50) $(x)(Ey)A(x,y) \rightarrow (Ey)(Ez)B(y,z)$.

   The crucial step in the argument is the use of the term
$f(\Phi(f))$ as the second argument of the predicate B in (47).
Once again, this step can only be motivated by a game-
theoretical analysis of the situation.
   For the following sentence (51), no translation into
first-order notation is possible:

   (51)   Everybody has a different hobby.

(This example was given to us by Lauri Carlson.)   The
game-theoretical formulation of (51) is clearly (52),

   (52) $(Ef)(x)(y)(u)[H(x,f(x))$ & $[(y \neq u$ &
          $H(y,f(y))$ & $H(u,f(u))] \rightarrow (f(y) \neq f(u))]$.

where: $H(x,y) = y$ is a hobby of x.

In order to translate (52) into first-order notation, we would have to replace the $f(x)$, $f(y)$, and $f(u)$ there by variables bound to existential quantifiers that are at the same time within the scope of only (x), only (y), and only (u), respectively. But this is impossible, so the earlier translation strategy does not work. We do get, however, a translation of (51) into *branching-quantifier* notation without higher-order quantifiers,[21] viz., (53),

(53)　(y)(Ev)
　　　　　　　＼
　　　　　　　　＞M
　　　　　　　／
　　　(u)(Ez)

where $M = (54)$:

(54)　$[H(y,v)$ & $H(u,z)$ & $((y \neq u) \equiv (v \neq z))]$.

It is known that branching-quantifier prefixes of the form (53) don't always reduce to linear form. It can be argued that (53) in particular is one such that doesn't.[22]

It is not known, however, whether every higher-order translation like (52) can be reduced to a branching-quantifier notation.

In general, we can see that the subgame idea does yield something new in natural-language semantics, even when it is implemented by rules like (16) or (20) that in formal languages don't give us anything new. One reason why these rules enrich our natural-language semantics is that they uncover mechanisms of anaphora that are actually used in natural languages but that simpler rules not involving subgames cannot cope with. Such simpler rules are likely to effect a translation into first-order notation. But we have seen that such a translation is impossible in some cases.

In particular, we can by means of the subgame idea obtain a beginning of a treatment of anaphoric pronouns with quantifier phrases, conjunctions, or disjunctions as their antecedents. Even though our treatment is restricted so far to singular quantifier phrases, it helps us to understand an especially subtle part of natural-language semantics.

11. Subgames in Discourse Semantics

Much of what has been said earlier in this chapter applies immediately to segments of discourse larger than individual sentences. The reason is that the subgame idea applies in a most natural way to discourse. Each sentence S uttered in a discourse gives rise to a semantical game $G(S)$ that can be considered a subgame in a larger "supergame" determined by the entire discourse.

In the simplest case, consecutive sentences S_1, S_2 are assertions by the same speaker. The subgames $G(S_1)$ and $G(S_2)$ are combined conjunctively, and Myself together with Nature, assuming their normal roles, play $G(S_1)$ first. If Myself wins, they go on to play $G(S_2)$ in the usual way, letting its outcome be the outcome of the combined game. If Nature wins $G(S_1)$, Nature wins the combined game.

When successive utterances bear more complicated discourse relations to each other, for instance, the relation of a question to its answer(s), the correlated subgames are combined in more complicated ways. Studying the interrelations of successive subgames is an important part of discourse semantics, though far too large a subject to be investigated here.

It can already be seen, however, that many of the ideas expounded in this chapter can be extended to more complicated cases. One reason is that the mechanism of discourse anaphora, which involves more than one sentence, is very similar to the mechanism of sentence anaphora, which involves more than one subsentence constituent. The following examples (55)-(57) illustrate this:

(55)   Which cat does Tom own? Whichever it is, he spoils it.
(56)   Has everybody written a book? If so, someone will not be able to get his published.
(57)   Every professor has been assigned two advisees. You better start working with yours soon!

Note that (57) carries an implication that you are a professor. Thus most of our discussion in this chapter can be extended immediately to the discourse level.

NOTES

[1] For game-theoretical semantics, see Esa Saarinen, editor, *Game-Theoretical Semantics*, D. Reidel, Dordrecht, 1979, the rest of the present volume, and its bibliography below.

[2] Jaakko Hintikka and Lauri Carlson, "Conditionals, Generic Quantifiers, and Other Applications of Subgames", in F. Guenthner and S. J. Schmidt, editors, *Formal Semantics and Pragmatics of Natural Languages*, D. Reidel, Dordrecht, 1979; reprinted in Saarinen, *Game-Theoretical Semantics*, pp. 179-214.

[3] Leon Henkin, "Some Remarks on Infinitely Long Formulas", in (no editor given), *Infinitistic Methods*, Pergamon Press, Oxford, 1961, pp. 167-83.

[4] Jaakko Hintikka, "Reductions in the Theory of Types", *Acta Philosophica Fennica* 8 (1955), 61-114.

[5] W. J. Walkoe, Jr., "Finite Partially Ordered Quantification", *Journal of Symbolic Logic* 35 (1970), 535-55.

[6] The concept of a normal form for a game goes back at least to John von Neumann and Oskar Morgenstern, *Theory of Games and Economic Behavior*, Princeton University Press, Princeton, N.J., 1953, especially pp. 76-84.

[7] For the logical relations between the different game rules mentioned in this section, see section 4 below.

[8] This insight goes back to A. Mostowski, "On a System of Axioms Which Has No Recursively Enumerable Model", *Fundamenta Mathematicae* 40 (1953), 56-61; and "A Formula with No Recursively Enumerable Model", ibid. 42 (1955), 125-40; see also G. Kreisel, "A Note on Arithmetic Models for Consistent Formulae of the Predicate Calculus", in (no editor given), *Proceedings of the XIth International Congress of Philosophy*, vol. 14, Amsterdam & Louvain, 1953, pp. 39-49.

[9] See Kurt Gödel, "On a Hitherto Unexploited Extension of the Finitary Standpoint", *Journal of Philosophical Logic* 9 (1980), 133-42, and the bibliography at the end of the present volume, section II (v).

[10] Dana Scott, "A Game-Theoretic Interpretation of Logical Formulae", McCarthy Seminar, Stanford University, July 1968, (unpublished).

[11] Justus Diller, "Functional Interpretations of Heyting's Arithmetic in All Finite Types", *Nieuw Archief voor Wiskunde* 3 (1979), 70-97, especially p. 70 (with further references to the literature).

[12] See, e.g., Justus Diller, "Functional Interpretation of Heyting's Arithmetic in All Finite Types".

[13] See P. Lorenzen and K. Lorenz, editors, *Dialogische Logik*, Wissenschaftliche Buchgesellschaft, Darmstadt, 1978, and the bibliography at the end of the present volume, section IV (i).

[14] See, e.g., C. Spector, "Provably Recursive Functionals of Analysis", in (no editor given), *Recursive Function Theory: Proceedings of Symposia in Pure Mathematics*, vol. 5, American Mathematical Society, Providence, R.I., 1962, pp. 1-27.

[15] For differences between formal and natural languages from a game-theoretical point of view, see chapter 1 of this book.

[16] Jaakko Hintikka and Jack Kulas, "Towards a Semantical Theory of Pronominal Anaphora" (in preparation).

[17] See Jaakko Hintikka and Lauri Carlson, "Pronouns of Laziness in Game-Theoretical Semantics", *Theoretical Linguistics* 4 (1977), 1-29.

[18] Frequently, (40) and similarly constructed examples are more natural candidates for the intended interpretation than (36) and its analogues. However, this makes no crucial difference to our discussion, for it turns out that the semantical mechanism operative in the anaphora in (40) is effectively the same as is operative in (36). The only difference is an additional complication due to the genitive case. In some of the examples in the sequel, it would be "more natural" to use a genitive pronoun to get the intended reading.

[19] James Higginbotham, "Comments on Hintikka's paper", *Notre Dame Journal of Formal Logic* 23 (1982), 263-71.

[20] These examples seem to be due to Lauri Karttunen.

[21] For branching quantifiers, see Jaakko Hintikka, "Quantifiers vs. Quantification Theory", *Linguistic Inquiry* 5 (1974), 153-77; and "Quantifiers in Natural Languages: Some Logical Problems", in Saarinen, *Game-Theoretical Semantics*, pp. 81-117; and see the bibliography at the end of the present volume, section II (i).

[22] General results concerning such reducibility and nonreducibility have been established by Walkoe, "Finite Partially Ordered Quantification".

Chapter 4

ANY PROBLEMS - *NO* PROBLEMS

(Coauthored by Jaakko Hintikka and Jack Kulas)

I. The Problem of Negation in Game-Theoretical Semantics

This paper is a development and extension of the semantical theory for natural languages proposed and developed by the senior author under the name of game-theoretical semantics (GTS).[1] The topics discussed include the general explanatory strategies for natural-language semantics employed by GTS, the treatment of negation in GTS, and the thesis that the English quantifier-word "any" is always to be considered a universal quantifier. We shall start with *no*-problems and then consider *any*-problems, all the while keeping an eye on methodological considerations.

In several game rules for the semantics of English that have been used in GTS, mention is made of an operation, called *neg*, that is supposed to take us from a given sentence S to its negation or contradictory. For example, the following version of the rule for conditionals in English makes essential use of this operation:[2]

(G. if) If a game has reached a sentence of the form

If X, Y,

Myself may choose either neg[X] or Y. The game is then continued with respect to Myself's choice.

Three more examples of the essential role of neg in game rules follow:

(G. knows whether) If a game has reached a sentence of the form

b knows whether X

(where b is a proper name) the game is continued with respect to

77

b knows that X or b knows that neg[X].

(G. only)   If a game has reached a sentence of the form

X - only Y - Z

an individual, say d, may be chosen by Nature, whereupon the game is continued with respect to

X - Y - Z, but neg[X - d - Z] if d is not Y.

Qualifications are needed here, but they do not affect the role of the neg operation in this rule.

(G. neg + believes)   If a game has reached a sentence of the form

b doesn't believe that X

(where b is a proper name) and a world w_1, then Myself may select a doxastic b-alternative w_2 to w_1. The game is then continued with respect to w_2 and the sentence neg[X].

There are other rules that involve neg essentially, e.g., (G. no). Furthermore, all of the rules for universal-quantifier words, e.g., "all", "every", "each", and "any", make essential use of conditionals, which in turn make essential use of neg. Since the neg operation has such an extensive use in the game-theoretical account of English semantics, an adequate account of it is essential for the viability of this approach.

It is thus important to understand the operation neg as fully as possible. However, there are difficulties here. In each of the above formulated rules, neg is an operation that is supposed to take us from a sentence S to its contradictory. But what happens if S is not a grammatical sentence? Consider the result (ii) of applying (G. neg + believes) to (i):

(i)   Bill doesn't believe that anyone came.
(ii)   neg[anyone came].

"Anyone came" is not a bona fide English sentence. So can we even suppose that it has a contradictory? In this paper we propose to extend neg to handle such cases by suggesting a general explanatory principle that is meant to reveal a special affinity between syntax and semantics.

2. A Set of Rules for Negation and Quantifiers

The natural first idea in dealing with an operation like neg is to try to formulate explicit syntactical rules for it. We shall do so, albeit only as an experiment. Ultimately, however, we want to show the eliminability of neg as a purely syntactical operation.

The interaction of negation and quantifiers has been of particular interest to semanticists. We shall begin our account of neg by proposing a set of rules for its application when it is juxtaposed with various quantifier words. The following rules for the operator neg, which we shall call *N-Rules*, are reasonably obvious. In them, we assume that the displayed quantifier word is the first expression to which any game rule applies in the sentence in question. Also, we assume that "b" is a placeholder for an arbitrary proper name (different from all those occurring in the sentences under discussion and thus operating as a variable) of the appropriate category, and that "Z(W/T)" is the result of replacing T by W in Z.

(N. every)   neg[X - every Y - Z] =
                   neg[X - b - Z](some Y/b).

(N. some)   neg[X - some Y - Z] =
                   neg[X - b - Z](every Y/b).

(N. no)   neg[X - no Y - Z] = X - some Y - Z.

For "each" and "any" there is an N-rule that is the same as the N-rule for "every", and for "a(n)" an N-rule that is the same as the N-rule for "some".

(N. and)   neg[X and Y] = neg[X] or neg[Y].

(N. or)   neg[X or Y] = neg[X] and neg[Y].

(N. if)   neg[If X, Y] = X, but neg[Y].

(N. atomic)   For simple sentences with the structure

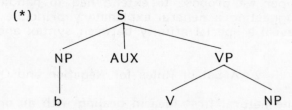

(*)

(where b is a proper name) the negation
can be obtained by turning it into

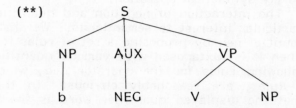

(**)

Conversely, the negation of (**) (or of any sentence
formed from it by further grammatical transformations) is
(*).

These rules give the right account of many cases.
Consider, for example, the negation of the tricky conditional (1) containing "any".

(1)   If anyone comes, I'll be surprised.

By the N-rules formulated above, and given that (G. any)
has priority over (G. if), we have the following derivation:

(2a)   neg[If anyone comes, I'll be surprised]
(2b)   neg[If b comes, I'll be surprised](someone/b)
(2c)   (b comes but neg[I'll be surprised])(someone/b)
(2d)   (b comes but I won't be surprised)(someone/b)
(2e)   Someone comes but I won't be surprised
(2f)   Someone will come but I won't be surprised.

(2f) is obviously the right negation (contradictory) of (1). Again, consider the negation of (3), which is very similar to (1):

(3)   If everyone comes, I'll be surprised.

Using the N-rules, and given that (G. every) does not have priority over (G. if), we get:

(4a)   neg[if everyone comes, I'll be surprised]
(4b)   Everyone comes, but neg [I'll be surprised]
(4c)   Everyone comes, but I won't be surprised
(4d)   Everyone will come, but I won't be surprised.

(4d) is obviously the right negation of (3).
   Our N-rules can handle even more complicated cases, such as (5):

(5)   If Johnnie can beat anyone, he can beat anyone.

Application of the N-rules gives us:

(6a)   neg[If Johnnie can beat anyone, he can beat anyone]
(6b)   neg[If Johnnie can beat x, he can beat anyone] (someone/x)
(6c)   (neg[If Johnnie can beat x, he can beat y] (someone/x))(someone/y)
(6d)   ([Johnie can beat x, but neg[he can beat y]] (someone/x))(someone/y).
(6e)   ([Johnnie can beat x but he can't beat y] (someone/x))(someone/y)
(6f)   (Johnnie can beat someone, but he can't beat y) (someone/y).
(6g)   Johnnie can beat someone, but he can't beat someone(else).

(The addition of "else" in (6g) can be motivated, but it is not important for our present purposes to do so here.) Once again, we obtain what is obviously the right negation or contradictory by means of the N-rules.

3. The Insufficiency of the N-Rules

Though the N-rules give the right result in many cases,
they fail to do so in all. First, the effect of an application of an N-rule to a complex sentence involves the
replacement of one logical word by another, as follows:

$$
\left.\begin{array}{l} \text{every} \\ \text{each} \\ \text{none} \\ \text{no} \end{array}\right\} \;\rightarrow\; \text{some}
$$

$$
\left.\begin{array}{l} \text{some} \\ \text{a(n)} \end{array}\right\} \;\rightarrow\; \text{every}
$$

$$
\text{and} \;\;\rightarrow\;\; \text{or}
$$

$$
\text{or} \;\;\rightarrow\;\; \text{and}
$$

Clearly, we obtain the true semantical negation (contradictory) of X only if the scope of the new logical word
in neg[X] corresponds to the scope of the old logical word
in X. (Strictly speaking, we should speak of the order of
application of the relevant rules, but no harm is done in
this chapter if we indulge in the more common parlance by
speaking of "scopes".)   But, as it turns out, there seems
to be no general guarantee that their scopes always match
up, and there seems to be no other way of formulating the
N-rules to assure coincidence of scopes.

But then can't we find better rules?   Is the apparent
semantical character of negation formation an inevitable
feature of the semantics of natural languages? We strongly
believe that effective, purely syntactical rules for forming
the semantical negation of English sentences cannot be
complete.   An argument for this position will be given below in section 5 (see also section 11).   That argument applies only to a fragment of English that includes certain
specifiable complex structures.   Whether purely syntactical
rules, like the N-rules, can be given for the part of English that doesn't contain those complex structures is an
issue that can only be decided "in the lab".[3]

What does all this mean?   It suggests an interesting
way of looking at what happens when we as competent

speakers of English try to form the semantical negation of a given sentence. Our observations strongly suggest that this procedure is not governed by purely syntactical rules, but that it essentially relies on semantical clues. For any given sentence, the first thing we do is give it a semantical interpretation. Then we construct a new sentence from the contradictory of that semantical interpretation. In a formal treatment such as ours here, this can be approximated by thinking of negation formation as involving, first, a translation of a given sentence X into some logical formalism, for example, first-order notation. Then the translation tr(X) is negated, and the result is translated back into English. (It is not clear that such a back translation is always possible, nor is it clear that such a back translation can be made in accordance with recursive rules.) The negation-forming rules given above should be construed as attempts to find regularity where ultimately, we believe, there isn't any.

4. Examples and Discussion

Even though a conclusive general argument can't be given at this time, the difficulties just mentioned can be illustrated by examples. These examples, and others like them, will also prompt comments on the behavior of negation in English.

First, the rule-ordering problem is illustrated by what happens when one tries to form the negation of (11):

(11)   Someone will solve every problem.

The preferred reading of (11) gives "someone" wide scope, so its logical representation is (12):

(12) $(Ex)(y)[(y$ is a problem) $\rightarrow (x$ will solve $y)]$.

If we form the negation of (11) using the N-rules, we obtain the following:

(13a)   neg[(11)]
(13b)   neg[x will solve every problem](everyone/x)
(13c)   (neg[x will solve y](everyone/x)) (some problem/y)
(13d)   ((x will not solve y)(everyone/x)) (some

problem/y)
(13e)   (everyone will not solve y)(some problem/y)
(13f)   Everyone will not solve some problem.

On what appears to us to be the preferred reading of (13f), it has the logical form (14),

(14)   (Ey)(y is a problem) & $\sim$(x)(x will solve y)).

which is not the contradictory of (12), the logical form of (11). Likewise, the other fairly plausible reading of (13f) yields (15) as its logical force:

(15)   (Ey)(x)(y is a problem & $\sim$(x will solve y)).

But this is not the contradictory of (12), either.

In diagnosing this problem, we note that in (11) (G. some) has priority over (G. every). In an application of the N-rules, "some" changes into "every" and "every" into "some". Consequently, we will get the right negation only if, for the purported negation (13f), (G. every) has priority over (G. some). But it doesn't for the preferred reading of (13f).

Another problem is illustrated by an attempt to form the negation of (16), whose logical form is clearly (17):

(16)   Everyone admires somebody.
(17)   (x)(Ey)(x admires y).

The N-rules yield the following derivation of the negation of (16):

(18a)   neg[16]
(18b)   neg[x admires somebody](someone/x)
(18c)   (neg[x admires y](someone/x))(everybody/y)
(18d)   ([x   doesn't   admire   y](someone/x))
          (everybody/y)
(18e)   (someone doesn't admire y)(everybody/y)
(18f)   Someone doesn't admire everybody.

The logical representation of (18f) is obviously (19):

(19)   (Ex)$\sim$(y)(x admires y).

This is not the right contradictory of (16). The right

contradictory is (20):

(20) (Ex)(y)∿(x admires y).

This problem is easy to diagnose. What happens is that
in the negation-forming process a new operator, viz., negation, enters the picture. We get the right result only if
all the new replacement operators have wider scope than
negation. Otherwise, the new operators are, logically
speaking, within the scope of negation. This is what happened with the derived negation of (16). In (19), "everybody" has narrow scope with respect to negation, though
in the right negation of (16) - viz., (20) - the universal
quantifier that replaced "somebody" should have wide
scope.

This particular problem case can be eliminated by
modifying the N-rules rules so that (i) "some" and "a(n)"
replace "any", and (ii) "every", "any", and "each" replace
"some". This guarantees that both newly introduced
quantifiers will have wider scope than negation, which is
the last operator to be introduced into the output sentence. Furthermore, this provides insight into the English
quantifier system by providing a raison d'etre for certain
words that always have wide scope vis-à-vis negation.
Without them, negation formation would be a much clumsier
operation. It also shows why "any" and "some", of all the
English quantifier words, have played a special role in the
theory of English negation.

However, the proposed cure is no panacea. First, it
does not eliminate problems due to relative priorities among
quantifier rules themselves, illustrated by (11)-(15) above.
Second, the proposed change is viable only as applied to
post-Aux occurrences of quantifiers. For instance, if applied to (21),

(21) Someone has won every match.

the modified N-rules would yield the following derivation:

(22a)   neg[(21)]
(22b)   neg[x has won every match](anyone/x)
(22c)   (neg[x has won y](anyone/x))(some match/y)
(22d)   ([x has not won y](anyone/x))(some match/y)
(22e)   (anyone has not won y)(some match/y)
(22f)   *Anyone has not won some match.

But (22f) is ungrammatical. So the problem illustrated by (16)-(19) not only forces us to make changes in the N-rules; it forces us to make them context-sensitive. Moreover, the influence of context has so far been analyzed only for those very simple sentence-structures that contain one S-node, i.e., that contain no subordinate or coordinate clauses. For more complicated cases, the dependence will be very tricky, and it will be exceedingly hard to capture with a simple formulation.

Further anomalies can be seen by trying to form the negation of even apparently simpler sentences. Consider (23), where "someone" occurs in a pre-Aux position:

    (23)   Someone loves somebody.

The modified N-rules give us the following derivation of the negation of (23):

    (24a)   neg[23]
    (24b)   neg[x loves somebody](everyone/x)
    (24c)   (neg[x loves y](everyone/x))(anybody/y)
    (24d)   ((x doesn't love y)(everyone/x))(anybody/y)
    (24e)   (everyone doesn't love y)(anybody/y)
    (24f)   Everyone doesn't love anybody.

But this is not the right negation of (23). The logical form of (23) is (25), while the logical form of (24f) is (26), which is not equivalent to the right negation (27):

    (25) $(Ex)(Ey)(x \text{ loves } y)$.
    (26) $\sim(x)(Ey)(x \text{ loves } y)$.
    (27) $(x)(y)\sim(x \text{ loves } y)$.

The underlying reason for this problem is that "every" tends to take smaller scope than negation. For this reason, the negation-sign is before "(x)" in (26). A further examination would show that the third universal quantifier in English, "each", cannot be used to get us out of our problem here, either. (We met this problem earlier in connection with (15).)

It is tempting to try to solve this problem by changing the N-rule for "some" into a mirror image of (N. no), as follows:

(N. some)*   neg[X - some Y - Z] = X - no Y - Z.

However, when applied to the first constituent of (23) to which a game rule is applicable, this new rule yields (28):

(28)   No one loves somebody.

But the most natural reading of (28) gives "somebody" wide scope.   Indeed, this reading is in keeping with our ordering principles.   The right negation of (23), however, is (29):

(29)   No one loves anybody.

This example strongly suggests that a satisfactory set of rules for forming the idiomatic negation of sentences like (23) can't be constructed if they are to operate on quantifier phrases one by one independently of context. But if in negation-forming rules we have to take into account the interplay between different quantifiers (and perhaps other constituent expressions), it should not come as much of a surprise if a complete set of satisfactory rules turns out to be unconstructible in recursive terms.   In sections 5 and 11 below we offer further support for this position.

Notice that we can pinpoint the reason for the "anybody" in (29).   We need either a universal quantifier that has wider scope than negation,   or else an existential quantifier that has narrower scope.   "Everybody" and "somebody" fill neither bill, while "anybody" satisfies the former.   The latter is filled by the indefinite article, wherefore the desired negation is also (30):

(30)   No one loves a (single) person.

However, in other cases, this procedure will not work.

The very inconclusiveness of the considerations presented in this section supports our suggestion of the impossibility of mechanical rules for negation-formation in English.   We have not proven that effective rules for negation formation are impossible, but we have shown, by way of examples, that such rules must accommodate the effects of several complicating factors, such as the relative order of different quantifier rules, their relative order with respect to the game rule for negation, the position of a quantifier phrase in a sentence relative to Aux, etc.   A set of rules that accommodates the effects of all these factors must clearly be quite complicated.

5. Negation and Branching Quantifiers

In this section, we offer an argument that a set of complete rules for English negation can't be fabricated. Elsewhere Hintikka has shown that there exist informationally indepedent ("branching") quantifiers in natural languages like English.[4] Moreover, there are irreducible (nonlinearizable) partially ordered quantifier structures present in English. Barwise has shown that a sentence with a partially ordered quantifier prefix is linearizable if its negation can also be expressed in a branching-quantifier form with first-order quantifiers.[5] Now it is known that not all branching-quantifier structures are linearizable, not even all those that are exemplified in natural languages like English. Therefore, there are English sentences whose negation cannot be expressed even in the branching-quantifier extension of first-order languages.

In so far as the total expressive power of the English quantifier system is that of a first-order language amplified by partially ordered quantifier prefixes, there is no reasonable hope that negations for all English sentences can be expressed in idiomatic English. The presence of irreducibly branching (nonlinearizable) quantifier structures suggests that there are no exceptionless rules for the formation of the semantical negation of each English sentence. There cannot be exceptionless negation-forming rules for all English sentences that contain linear or nonlinear first-order quantifiers, if it is required that the negation (contradictory) also contains only first-order quantifiers (linear or partially ordered). The N-rules formulated above are of this kind - the output contains only singular quantifier words (no plural ones) if the input sentence does. Thus, we have found a sense in which the approximate N-rules formulated above can't be transformed into strict ones.

But can we assume that the negation of a partially ordered quantifier sentence S must be a sentence similar to S in specifiable ways? Unfortunately, we cannot give any knockdown argument on behalf of this assumption. However, a look at the N-rules formulated above shows that alternative rules not subject to the limitation just mentioned would have to be entirely different. There does not even seem to be any way of anticipating what such alternative rules might look like. Admittedly, plural quantifier phrases of English are essentially second-order quantifiers, and thus have more expressive power. However, it is very hard to see how this expressive power can be put to the service of natural negation-forming rules.

6. Comparisons with Other Treatments

In spite of the inevitable incompleteness of the N-rules formulated above (and, we might add, other possible rules like them), they can serve as an object of comparison and as a reference point for further remarks. Prima facie, the existence of explicit rules for negation formation is one of the most important topics in the semantics of natural languages. For instance, how can we compare natural and formal languages to each other if we don't have anything that corresponds to the easy negation-forming operation of formal languages? In spite of their apparent importance, there are fewer rules in the literature to which our N-rules can be compared than might be expected.

Purely syntactically, negation used to be introduced by a single sentence-initial constituent in the deep structure, as was done by Klima in his classic early paper on negation.[6] In so far as linguists also believed that transformations were meaning preserving, the transformations that turned negated deep structures into surface structures are roughly comparable with the steps involved in the negation formations using the N-rules above, e.g., (2a-f), (4a-d), (6a-g), (13a-f), etc.

Much that was said by such authors as Klima, Fillmore, Stockwell, Schachter and Partee can be compared with what can be brought out by examining our N-rules.[7] In so far as we can better understand, and put in wider perspective, our predecessors' rules by means of our own, we can enhance the credibility of our own approach. It turns out that certain features of their treatments enjoy a much more limited validity than they themselves spell out.

Several examples of these observations can be given. Later in this chapter, it will turn out that the central feature of the Klima-type approach, the sentence-initial deep-structure constituent for negation, is appropriate only in virtue of a general principle of language understanding that, roughly speaking, enjoins us to maximize the agreement between semantics and syntax. (See section 11 below.)

Another feature of Klima's treatment of negation was discussed in section 4 above. It was seen that in many cases "some" has to be replaced by "any" as part of the negation-forming process. This is raised by Klima to the level of a general rule that he codifies in terms of the addition of a feature "INDEF(inite)" into a constituent already marked "INDET(erminate)". We have seen, however, where the need for replacing "some" by "any", rather than by "every" or "each", comes from. The intro-duction of a negative constituent into a sentence does not limit the logical scope of the quantifier in question (initially "some", later "any") in the way it would do if "some" were replaced by "every". (Cf. (16)-(20) above.) This is the real motivation for the so-called some-any suppletion rule. However, it justifies only some cases of this suppletion rule.

This is seen from the fact that this motivation is not operative if the replacement of "some" had sufficiently wide scope for other reasons. This will be the case if instead of (16) we tried to form the negation of (31):

(31)   Someone admires everybody.

The N-rules will then yield the following derivation of the negation of (31):

(32a)   neg[31]
(32b)   neg[x admires everybody](everyone/x)
(32c)   (neg[x admires y](everyone/x))(somebody/y)
(32d)   ([x   doesn't   admire   y](everyone/x))
           (somebody/y)
(32e)   (everyone doesn't admire y)(somebody/y)
(32f)   Everyone doesn't admire somebody.

If we used the modified N-rule, we would obtain the un-grammatical negation (33):

(33)   *Anyone doesn't admire somebody.

Hence, the applicability of the some-any suppletion rule is conditional on the particular way the ordering principles affect the readings of one's sentences.

The same general point is illustrated by the derivation (32) where we need a different kind of suppletion. For (32f) has a reading on which it is not the contradictory of (31), viz., the reading on which its logical form is (34):

(34) $\sim(x)(Ey)(x \text{ admires } y)$.

This reading is caused by the tendency of the rules for "every" and "everyone" to come in the rule ordering after the rule for negation. To counteract this, we can in our negation-forming process replace "some", not by "every" or "any", but by "each". This would yield (35),

(35)   Each person does not admire somebody,

which clearly is the right negation (contradictory) of (31), even though it is a bit clumsy idiomatically. This shows, incidentally, that it is not enough to make the some-any suppletion rule optional as Klima does. Some other changes are also needed.

Admittedly, we have seen that in some related cases, such as (16)-(20), we are pushed back to a some-any suppletion. However, this is an accidental feature of the situation, even though it probably has encouraged linguists to believe in the generality of some-any suppletion.

All this illustrates further the way in which ordering principles are the real basis of any satisfactory treatment of negation. By means of our approach, other features of earlier treatments of negation can be shown to have their limited justification and also their deeper reasons, which do not emerge from those earlier discussions. For instance, in incorporating the negative constituent into indefinites, a linguist using a Klima-type treatment has to make several stipulations without any deeper theoretical motivation. First, he has to stipulate that this transformation is obligatory if any indefinite is in a pre-Aux position. Second, its optional applicability to post-Aux *any*-words is limited by Klima to the leftmost one. Both of these restrictions can be explained in terms of our rule-ordering principles, which also show how to find exceptions to Klima's rules.

For instance, our ordering principles show immediately that (36) and (37) are synonymous:

(36)   I didn't show anyone anything.

(37) I showed no one anything.

In contrast, (38) is not even well formed:

(38) *I showed anyone nothing.

This shows why the position of the the first (outmost) post-Aux "any" is a crucial position.

Of course, in other contexts we don't get the right negation in this way. For instance, (39) and (40) are not synonymous:

(39) I did not tell anything to everybody.
(40) I told nothing to everybody.

For, on one of its readings - apparently the most natural one - (39) has as its logical form (41) (as is indeed predicted by our ordering principles), whereas the logical form of (40) is clearly (42):

(41) $(x)\sim(y)(I$ told x to $y)$.
(42) $(y)\sim(Ex)(I$ told x to $y)$.

Thus our approach helps put earlier treatments of negation into wider perspective.

7. Negation and Conditionals

What follows from our view for the game rules in which negation-formation is involved? One thing is that there may be an unavoidable "yield" in these rules: their application has an interpretive element that does not reduce completely to hard-and-fast syntactical rules. In any case, we have to have a closer look at these rules, one by one.

First, the rule for conditionals (G. if) as it is formulated above is only an approximate one. More adequate rules are discussed in a paper by Hintikka and Carlson,[8] and in chapter 3 above. The rules they formulate are in terms of subgames, and are closely related to the functional interpretations first suggested by Gödel in 1959.[9] The details are not important here. The relevant results include the following:

(i) A conditional sentence S is interpreted by a high-

er-order sentence h(S) that says that there exists a winning strategy for Myself in the game G(S) associated with
S. h(S) has the form (43):

(43) $(E\Phi_1)(E\Phi_2)\ldots\ (\Psi_1)(\Psi_2)\ldots\ M(\Phi_1,\Phi_2,\ldots,\Psi_1,\Psi_2,\ldots)$

The game-theoretical negation of S is interpreted by means
of a sentence of almost the same form, represented by
(44):

(44) $(E\Psi_1)(E\Psi_2)\ldots\ (\Phi_1)(\Phi_2)\ldots\ \sim M(\Phi_1,\Phi_2,\ldots,\Psi_1,\Psi_2,\ldots)$

(44) says that Nature has a winning strategy in G(S), and
is equivalent to the ordinary negation (contradictory) of
(43) only if conditional (45) is true:

(45) $(\Phi_1)(\Phi_2)\ldots\ (E\Psi_1)(E\Psi_2)\ldots\ \sim M(\Phi_1,\Phi_2,\ldots,\Psi_1,\Psi_2,\ldots)$

$\rightarrow (E\Psi_1)(E\Psi_2)\ldots\ (\Phi_1)(\Phi_2)\ldots\ \sim M(\Phi_1,\Phi_2,\ldots,\Psi_1,\Psi_2,\ldots)$

In the jargon of game theorists, (45) says that G(S) is
determinate, that is, that one of the two players has a
winning strategy. From game theory we also know that
assumptions of determinateness are far from trivial: sometimes they are tantamount to extremely powerful set-theoretical assumptions. Hence determinateness may in some
cases fail, and thereby invalidate the law of excluded
middle.

What all this means for negation-formation is the following. First, in the reformulated game rule for conditionals,
we don't need the neg operation any longer. This syntactical operation is replaced by the semantical device of role
switching by the two players in a certain subgame. This
seems to be characteristic of the best treatments of many
of those game rules that, prima facie, involve the syntactic
operation neg.

Second, what we want here is an operation for forming
the contradictory (semantical negation) of a given S. The
game-theoretical negation (44) of (43) will not always yield
it, since the law of excluded middle sometimes fails. The
obvious alternative for forming the contradictory of S
seems to be to prefix a negation-sign to the higher-order
representation (43) of the given sentence. The problem of
forming the contradictory of a given sentence whose higher-order representation is (44) will then amount to the

problem of finding a natural-language expression whose higher-order translation is the contradictory of the higher-order translation of S, i.e., is logically equivalent to (46):

(46) $(\Phi_1)(\Phi_2) \ldots (E\Psi_1)(E\Psi_2) \ldots \sim M(\Phi_1, \Phi_2, \ldots, \Psi_1, \Psi_2, \ldots)$

We may expect that such a natural-language sentence does not always exist. The reason for this is that (46) is not always a translation of a sentence with first-order quantifiers. In so far as it is reasonable to expect the contradictory of a natural-language sentence with first-order quantifiers to be expressible as another sentence with similar quantifiers, it appears hopeless to try to form exceptionless syntactical rules for forming the contradictory of every English sentence.

8. Principles vs. Rules

In the case of other rules that involve negation, other observations are in order. Before discussing any particular rule, however, certain general considerations should be presented. There is an important difference between GTS and many other recent approaches to language study. Whatever their differences, most of the alternative approaches operate with just one set of rules, all on a par. In GTS, there is a two-level explanatory system, naturally motivated by the game framework. Besides the *rules* for making individual moves, we inevitably also need *principles* to govern their order and perhaps also to govern other things about their formulation and application as well.

Indeed, many of the subtler features of the semantical behavior of natural languages are governed indirectly by such principles rather than directly by game rules. The behavior of "any" is a case in point. Our discussion in section 4 above offers additional illustrations. What was found there was that, even though the ordering principles governing different game rules are reasonably clear-cut, it is extremely hard to capture all the different consequences of the principles in one generalization. But this is nothing new for well-informed methodologists. Newton's gravitational law is extremely simple, but the analysis of the behavior of configurations of three or more bodies on the basis of the law is enormously complicated. Further examples are given in section 13 below.

Here we meet a principle that is less clear-cut than those governing the order of application of the different game rules. It says in its roughest and most general form that semantics and syntax go together, or that semantics parallels syntax. We shall thus call it the *SPS principle*. It may be considered a heuristic rather than a strict principle, though it yields quite definite predictions. Indeed, the force of the SPS principle is seen better from its consequences than from attempted general formulations of it.

9. Negating Quantifier Phrases

One consequence of the SPS principle is directly relevant to the theory of negation. When a quantifier phrase occurs in subject position of a sentence S, there are two different ways of trying to form the negation (contradictory) of S. One is to negate the quantifier phrase by prefixing a "not" to it; the other is to negate the verb of the main clause of S. We shall call the latter *regular negation*, and the former *term negation*.

The basic fact about term negation is that it is not always acceptable. (47) contains a sample of grammatically permissible term negations, while (48) a sample of impermissible ones:

(47)   not every
       not a
       not many
       not all
       not both

(48)   *not some
       *not any
       *not few
       *not several
       *not either

The regularity these lists exemplify is predicted by the SPS principle. The syntactical operation of term negation can yield the contradictory of a given sentence only if the quantifier to which it is prefaced does not have priority over – i.e., wide scope with respect to – negation. If it does, the syntactical operation of term negation does not

go together with its semantical result in that it does not
yield the contradictory of the original. This violates the
SPS principle, which predicts that term negation is acceptable only for quantifier words whose game rules do not
have priority over the negation rule in semantical games.
In heuristic terms, we can thus say that competent speakers reject such phrases as (48) because the negative particle "not" in them, which is a syntactic item, does not do
its obviously intended semantical job, viz., form the contradictory of the sentence.

    This prediction is confirmed by the evidence summed up
by the two lists (47) and (48) above. All the quantifiers
in the second list have a wider scope than "not", while
none in the first list does. This is illustrated by examples
(49)-(58):

    (49)   John did not win every match.
    (50)   John did not win a match.
    (51)   John did not win many matches.
    (52)   John did not win all matches.
    (53)   John did not win both matches.

    (54)   John failed to win some matches.
    (55)   John failed to win any matches.
    (56)   John failed to win few matches.
    (57)   John failed to win several matches.
    (58)   John failed to win either match.

    As a generalization of our remarks on term negation, it
can be said that there is a strong tendency in natural language to interpret the semantical operation neg as a fairly
simple syntactical operation. Cases where such an interpretation is not possible are easily considered deviant.

                   10. Negative Belief-Sentences

There are other applications of the SPS principle beyond
the issue of the acceptability of term negations. One is
the following. It may happen that in some applications of
our game rules, we end up considering a neg[X] where X
itself is not acceptable. A case in point arises in connection with the rule (G. neg + believes). This rule has
a double interest to us, for in it we are dealing with the
formation of a neg[X] where X is a "believes that" sen-

tence, in addition to this rule's involving the operation neg[Y] for a certain component clause Y of X.

Suppose we apply (G. neg + believes) to sentence (59):

(59) Tom doesn't believe that Dick has dated any girl.

Here a choice by Myself of a doxastic alternative with respect to Tom leads the players to consider (60) with respect to the chosen alternative:

(60) neg[Dick has dated any girl].

But the bracketed sentence in (60) is unacceptable. So the intended interpretation of neg as forming the contradictory of a given sentence fails for (60). To preserve the rule (G. neg + believes), we have to extend the operation neg to apply also to certain unacceptable strings. In such cases, the original semantical interpretation of neg cannot guide us, for speakers are not likely to associate any interpretation to an unacceptable string. Rather, we must rely on principles that speakers of English are likely to depend on. It is our position that the SPS principle is one such principle.

From a purely technical point of view, we are in the same position as a mathematician who is extending a function beyond the argument values for which it was originally defined. The mathematician in such a position is not constrained by hard-and-fast rules, but rather is guided by a desire to preserve the important laws that have been found to govern the function in the realm of values for which it was originally defined. In our case, these regularities can be thought of as the game rule (G. neg + believes) on the one hand, and the SPS principle on the other.

In light of these considerations then, what sense can we – or the players – make of (60)? Here a suggestion ensues from the SPS principle. If the semantical operator neg were expressed by a syntactical constituent that preceded "any", (60) would be acceptable. The parallelism between syntax and semantics asserted by the SPS principle suggests how (60) is to be interpreted: "neg" should be expressed by a clause-initial syntactical constituent. In other words, a consequence of the SPS principle is that (60) should be taken as (61):

(61)   Dick hasn't dated any girl.

This obviously gives the right reading to (59).

The same idea works in other cases. But notice that neg[X] cannot uniformly be taken to amount to regular negation, i.e., the operation of negating the main verb. A counterexample to such uniformity is offered by (62):

(62)   Tom doesn't believe that any girl has dated Dick.

If here we take (63) to amount to (64), we get an unacceptable string:

(63)   neg[any girl has dated Dick].
(64)   *Any girl hasn't dated Dick.

The reason is that in (64) "any" could have wide scope even if (O. any) were not in force. (63) has to be taken to have the force of (65):

(65)   Dick hasn't been dated by any girl.

This supports the consequence of the SPS principle that neg be dealt with in (63) as if it were a sentence-initial constituent.

This diagnosis of the situation is confirmed by observing that the interpretation of neg[X] is different when X is acceptable on its own. For instance, consider (66):

(66)   Jim doesn't believe that John can beat any opponent.

The preferred reading for this is obtained along the same lines as our treatment of (60). That this reading of neg[X] is obtained, even though X itself is acceptable, is an indication of the tendency registered above to interpret neg as a clause-initial syntactical constituent. This reading has (67) as the logical representation of (66):

(67)   ∿ Jim believes that (Ex)(x is an opponent & John can beat x).

In this representation, the quantifier "any" of (66) corresponds to an existential quantifier. For this reason, examples like (59) and (66) have sometimes been put forward

as alleged counterexamples to the thesis put forward by
Hintikka that "any" is always a universal quantifier. We
can now see that they are not genuine counterexamples.
Starting from the assumption that "any" is a universal
quantifier, we have been led to the right reading of (59)
and to one of the two possible readings of (66). This
shows vividly that the temptation to use (59) and (66) as
counterexamples to the universal-*any* thesis stems from an
oversimplified view of semantical explanation and semantical
representation. If it is mistakenly assumed that the logical
representation (67) has to be obtained somehow fairly directly from the surface form (66), the only apparent possibility is to consider "any" as an existential quantifier.
This strategy is not only unnecessary, but it also hides
the real mechanism that yields the differences between (59)
and (66), as well as the different readings of (66). This
is witnessed by the failure of the competing accounts to
explain these differences.

The other reading of (66) can be represented by (68):

(68) $\sim$ Jim believes that $(x)[(x$ is an opponent) $\rightarrow$
(John can beat x)].

This reading arises by an application of (G.neg +
believes). A choice of an alternative world by Myself
leads the players to consider (69) in the world chosen:

(69)   neg[John can beat any opponent].

Now the bracketed expression in (69) is acceptable on
its own. Hence (69) should amount to its contradictory.
This yields (68).

Another, more general way of describing the situation
is the following. In such sentences as (66) we have a
conflict between two different partial definitions of neg.
There is, first, the original interpretation of this operation
as forming the contradictory of a given sentence, and,
second, the extension of this operation to unacceptable
strings. When the regularities governing the latter are
applied in cases of acceptable strings, we get results different from those obtained from simply going by the original semantical import of neg. In such cases, we have two
different readings of the overall sentence. This shows
that the SPS principle can be operative in interpreting
neg[S] also when S is an acceptable sentence in its own

right. In such cases, speakers sometimes are willing, in effect, to deal with neg as if it were a sentence-initial syntactical constituent. This is what yields the reading (67) of (66). The SPS principle accounts for this.

11. The Nonrecursivity of Negation in English

Our treatment of a sample problem in the preceding section suggests two remarkable general conclusions. First, one of the implications of the SPS principle in that example can be expressed by saying that our semantical operator neg is to be dealt with as if it were a sentence-initial syntactical constituent. As was anticipated earlier, this can be thought of as the basic reason why Klima and others were able to treat negation - up to a point at least - by means of a sentence-initial deep-structure constituent.

A second observation is even more important. A comparison between the readings of (59) and (66) illustrates a general point. When our game rules lead us to consider neg[X], it may happen that X is unacceptable as predicted by the *any*-thesis of Hintikka.[10] In other cases, X is acceptable. The comparison between (59) and (66) shows that these two cases behave differently.

This fact has an important consequence. Suppose one is trying to formulate explicit rules for neg[X]. The observation just made implies that, when X has the form (70),

(70) b doesn't believe that Y.

the negation-forming operation neg[X] works differently when Y is acceptable by itself and when it is unacceptable. It has been argued by Hintikka that the two cases cannot be distinguished from each other recursively: neither the set of acceptable Xs nor the set of unacceptable Xs is recursively enumerable.[10] If so, the negation-forming operation that takes us from X to neg[X], when considered as a syntactical operation, cannot be recursive. The way it applies in certain cases will depend on whether a certain constituent Y of X is acceptable or not. And Hintikka's argument purports to show that this cannot be ascertained by recursive means.

Hintikka's thesis has stood up well against criticisms.[11] If it is right, we obtain the result that the operation of forming the semantical negation (contradictory) of a given sentence in English is not an effective (recursive) one. This result prompts several comments.

First, it shows vividly how differently negation is handled in formal and natural languages. In most formal languages, the semantical negation (contradictory) of a sentence X is formed by means of a simple syntactical operation, viz., by prefixing "$\sim$" to X. (The best-known exception to this case is probably the language of finite partially ordered quantifier prefixes, where there may not be any negation to a given X in the same language.) However, such simplicity is only an ideal for natural languages. Admittedly, the SPS principle implies that in natural languages syntax and semantics should go together as closely as possible. We have found, however, indications to the effect that in some areas, e.g., in the case of the negation-forming operation, no effective syntactical operation can do the whole semantical job. "Together as closely as possible" does not mean "together all the way".

Second, our result vindicates what we did earlier in this chapter when we did not continue trying to patch up the N-rules to cover all cases. What we have found implies that no explicit set of recursive rules like the N-rules can be complete.

Third, it is worth emphasizing that there exists a handy test case for the impossibility claim made in this section. If a reader is not happy with the claim, he has a most straightforward way of arguing for his position, viz., by producing an explicit set of rules for forming the semantical negation of a given English sentence, even only within the relatively meager fragment of English that contains the usual quantifier phrases, propositional connectives, and a few other fairly simple notions, including epistemic and doxastic ones.

Fourth, a supplementary remark is in order here. We are assuming, of course, that the fragment of English we are dealing with does not include such artificial operators as "it is not the case that". However, it can be argued that this does not make any essential difference to our argument.[12]   For consider a sentence with a nonrestrictive subordinate clause, like (71):

(71)   John came, which surprised me.

By prefixing "It is not the case that" mechanically to (71)

we obtain (72):

    (72) It is not the case that John came, which sur-
           prised me.

Of course, (72) is not the contradictory of (71).

It will not do, either, to try to somehow prefix "It is
not the case that" to the whole (71). For something like
(73) is certainly not an acceptable sentence of English, if
it is supposed to differ from (72):

    (73) It is not the case that: John came, which sur-
           prised me.

For one thing one cannot utter (73) without falling back
to (72). Thus, there is no reason to assume that one can
escape the impossibility here surmised by using the prefix
"It is not the case that".

Our thesis of the nonrecursivity of negation (in the
sense explained above) was prompted by an examination of
negated belief-constructions. It turns out that similar remarks can be made in relation to some other constructions
in English.

12. "Knowing Whether" and Negation

Indeed, closely related observations can be made concerning "knows whether" constructions. Consider, for instance, (74), which has the form (75).

    (74)   Jim knows whether John has beaten anyone.
    (75)   b knows whether X.

An application of (G. knows whether) gives Myself a
choice between (76) and (77).

    (76)   b knows that X.
    (77)   b knows that neg[X].

For (74), these are (78) and (79), respectively.

    (78)   Jim knows that John has beaten anyone.
    (79)   Jim knows that neg[John has beaten anyone].

Here X (= "John has beaten anyone") is not acceptable alone.   Hence (78) and (79) have to be interpreted by means of a general principle like the SPS principle.

Indeed, this principle applies here in two different ways.   First, it is obviously integral to the semantics of "whether"-constructions that in the two horns of the "whether"-constructions, (76) and (77), the propositions known are contradictories of each other. Since syntax and semantics go together, no matter what neg[X] is syntactically, it will here be the contradictory of X. This implies that, as soon as we can interpret either of the two expressions X or neg[X] in (76) or (77), we can interpret the other one, too, for it will be the contradictory of that first one. For instance, we can interpret both (78) and (79) as soon as we can interpret one of them.

Second, the same things can be said of (79) on the basis of the SPS principle as were said above for (60) using that principle. In other words, (79) is to be understood as if the semantical operation neg were a syntactical operation. This yields (80) as the force of (79):

(80)   Jim knows that John has not beaten anyone.

In other words, neg[X] is to be taken in (79) to have the force of (81):

(81)   John has not beaten anyone.

But now our first observation tells us that the that-clause in (78) can be interpreted, and has to be interpreted, as the contradictory of (81). Here (G. any) applies, yielding (82):

(82)   John has beaten someone.

Consequently, (78) must be taken to have the force of (83):

(83)   Jim knows that John has beaten someone.

This yields precisely the right semantical interpretation of (74).

Besides yielding the right interpretation of (74), our line of thought enables us to make several observations analogous to those made on the basis of our examination of negated belief-sentences.

First, sentences like (74) have been put forward as alleged counterexamples to the thesis that "any" is always a universal quantifier. We can now see that these alleged counterexamples are not conclusive. We have given an explanation of the force of (74) without giving up the assumption that "any" is always a universal quantifier. Admittedly, this explanation is in terms of principles rather than generalizations from particular cases. However, we believe that the significance of such general principles as the SPS principle has been underestimated in the literature.

Second, the line of thought outlined above is predicated on the assumption that the X in (77) is not acceptable in its own right. If it is, the situation is different. A case in point is (84):

(84)   Jim knows whether John can beat anyone.

The same line of thought as was applied to (74) results in taking the logical form of (84) to be (85):

(85)   Jim   knows   that   (Ex)(John   can   beat   x)   v
       Jim knows that (x)$\sim$(John can beat x).

However, in this case the instantiation of (76), viz., (86), is acceptable even without its relation to the instantiation of (77):

(86)   Jim knows that John can beat anyone.

In virtue of the requirement that the that-clause of (77) be the semantical negation of the that-clause of (76), we obtain (87) as the force of (77) in this case:

(87)   Jim knows that John cannot beat everyone.

From (86) and (87) we obtain another reading of (84) whose logical form is (88):[13]

(88)   Jim   knows   that   (x)(John   can   beat   x)   v
       Jim knows that (Ex)$\sim$(John can beat x).

Clearly (84) has precisely the two readings (85) and (88). Thus we see that it makes a difference for the interpretation of sentences of the form (75) whether X is acceptable by itself or not. Since this is, we believe, recursively undecidable, it is impossible to set up a complete, fully explicit set of rules for interpreting "knows whether" sentences. This nonrecursivity result does not concern only or even primarily the negation-forming process neg needed in the rule (G. knows whether). It concerns the process of interpreting sentences of the form (75). What we have found shows that this process, which we can for present purposes think of as a translation from English to the notation of epistemic logic, is not a mechanical one. This calls into question a dogma of contemporary semantics that says that the semantical interpretation of a given natural-language sentence S is a matter of applying fixed rules to a finite number of syntactical clues in S.

In spite of the difference in application, this new nonrecursivity result and the one registered in section 11 concerning the neg operation are due to the same underlying phenomena, and hence reinforce each other. That the SPS principle enables us to deal with negated belief-sentences and with the "knows whether" construction constitutes good evidence for it. Further evidence is obtained by showing that a similar treatment applies to a class of sentences containing the word "only".

13. "Only" and Negation

Most of the same things can be said, mutatis mutandis, of "only"-constructions as were said earlier about negated belief-constructions and "knows whether" sentences. Once again, "only"-sentences have been used as alleged counterexamples to the thesis that "any" is always a universal quantifier. (89) is a case in point:

(89) Only Tom has bought any books.

The logical form of (89) is, of course, (90):

(90) (Ex)[(x is a book) & (Tom has bought x)] & (y)[(y ≠ Tom) → ~(Ex)[(x is a book) & (y has bought x)]].

The problem here is to see how (90) comes about.

In the semantical game played on (89), (G. only) is applied first. If we suppose that Nature chooses Dick, and that (89) is parsed so that

$$X = \phi$$
$$Y = \text{Tom}$$
$$Z = \text{has bought any books},$$

the result is essentially (91):

(91) Tom has bought any books but neg[Dick has bought any books].

One problem with (91) is that neither the first conjunct (92) nor the bracketed expression (93) in the second conjunct is grammatical.

(92) *Tom has bought any books.
(93) *Dick has bought any books.

Thus, an indirect, but principle-governed way of interpreting (91) is needed.

The interpretational clue yielded by the operative word "only" here is that the two halves of (91) are contradictories, except that they speak of different individuals. In other words, (92) and neg[93] would be contradictories if their subject terms were the same. This fact alone does not yet help us, but other clues are available. In the same way as in earlier cases, the SPS principle implies that in (94),

(94) neg[Dick has bought any books].

the semantical operator neg should be treated as if it were a syntactical operator for negation, which means that (94) is to have the force of (95):

(95) Dick has not bought any books.

Notice that this step presupposes that "any" is interpreted as a universal quantifier having wide scope with respect to negation.

By the clue yielded by the word "only", (95) and (92) must be contradictories, except for the interchange of "Tom" and "Dick". This means that (92) must be taken to have the force of (96):

(96)   Tom has bought some books.

As in the case with negated belief-sentences and "knows whether" sentences, the situation is different when the expression "X – Y – Z" in the output of (G. only) is acceptable in its own right. A case in point is (97):

(97)   Only John can beat any opponent.

This has the two readings (98) and (99), the former being parallel to (90):

(98)   (Ex)[(x is an opponent) & (John can beat x)] &
       (y)[(y ≠ John) → ∿(Ex)[(x is an opponent) & (y
       can beat x)]].

(99)   (x)[(x is an opponent) → (John can beat x)] &
       (y)[(y ≠ John) → ∿(x)[(x is an opponent) → (y
       can beat x)]].

The way in which the reading (99) comes about is obvious. An application of (G. only) to (97) yields an output whose first conjunct is (100), which is grammatical on its own:

(100)   John can beat any opponent.

From this, the clue offered by the operative world "only" induces an interpretation on the second conjunct of the output of (G. only) having the form (101), which can be taken to have the force of (102):

(101)   neg[b can beat any opponent].
(102)   b cannot beat some opponent.

In this way, we obtain the other reading (99) of (97).

Once again, the same generalizations as were mentioned in sections (10)-(11) and (12) above can be seen to apply to yet another construction. For one thing, the same non-recursivity argument is applicable here. Likewise, a prima facie counterexample to the universal-quantifier character of "any" turns out to be wrong in light of a deeper analysis of the semantical principles on which it is based.

14. Ordering Principles and Negation

The importance of principles rather than rules in semantical theory is further illustrated by the role of ordering
principles in understanding the semantical behavior of
negation.   More specifically, the relative order of application of the negation rule and other rules is important in
the semantics of English.   (103) is a list of some rules
that have priority over the negation rule (G. neg), while
(104) is a list of some rules that don't:

(103)	(G. any)	for "any"
	(G. past)	for the simple past tense
	(G. the)	for "the"
	(G. some)	for "some"
	(G. several)	for "several"
	(G. either)	for "either"

(104)	(G. every)	for "every"
	(G. past perf)	for the past-perfect tense
	(G. only)	for "only" (or "the" only)
	(G. a(n))	for the indefinite article
	(G. many)	for "many"
	(G. both)	for "both"

These lists, which can easily be turned into rule-ordering principles, explain a great many features of the behavior of negation.   The following pairs of contrastive examples illustrate this:

(105)	Tom did not solve any problem.
(106)	Tom did not solve every problem.

(107)	Dick did not turn off the light.
(108)	Dick has not turned off the light.

(109)	Harry is not the man who loves Harriet.
(110)	Harry is not the only man who loves Harriet.

(111)	Thomas did not solve some problem (or other).
(112)	Thomas did not solve a (single) problem.

(113)	Richard failed to solve several problems.
(114)	Richard failed to solve many problems.

(115)   Harold didn't forget either message.
(116)   Harold didn't forget both messages.

Thus ordering principles do have a great deal of explannatory force when dealing with the behavior of negation.

15. Logic vs. Natural Language

It is often asserted that natural language is not logical.[14] Often, maybe typically, such assertions are taken to refer to the degree of exactness and unambiguity of natural languages, compared with the formal languages of a logician. This strikes us as a very superficial view. Attempts to develop a "fuzzy logic" have not yielded any major new insights into the interrelations of formal and natural languages. It seems to us that the difference between formal and natural languages is not so much a matter of the rules that govern the two kinds of languages. Rather, one important difference is that in natural languages the application of the semantical rules (game rules) is governed by second-order principles. Their applicability, unlike that of primary rules, depends on factors that are not purely syntactical, e.g., the acceptability of the strings involved *and* the general parallelism of syntax and semantics. These factors may even create nonrecursivities (unaxiomatizabilities). Such phenomena, rather than any simple-minded difference in the degree of precision, seem to us to be the true core in the claims of the "nonlogical" character of natural languages. If we are right, this character of natural languages is vividly illustrated by the nonrecursive character of semantical negation in English.

The new support that we have found for the thesis that "any" is always a universal quantifier offers indirect evidence for earlier nonrecursivity results based on the behavior of "any".[15] Concerning its universal-quantifier character, the opposite of what is stated by Davison is true:[16] if all we care about is a translation, by hook or crook, into a logical notation, it is not only prima facie possible but tempting to interpret "any" as sometimes being an existential quantifier. It is only when we take seriously the mechanism that yields the actual force of various English sentences that we can see the importance of always treating "any" as a universal quantifier.

NOTES

[1] See chapter 1 above for a general discussion, where further references to the literature are provided.

[2] This particular rule is oversimplified, as is shown in Jaakko Hintikka and Lauri Carlson, "Conditionals, Generic Quantifiers, and Other Applications of Subgames", in F. Guenthner and S. J. Schmidt, editors, *Formal Semantics and Pragmatics for Natural Languages*, D. Reidel, Dordrecht, 1979, pp. 1-36; and in chapter 3 above.

[3] One suggestion for such rules would be to formulate a rule for each pair and triple of interacting logical operators (quantifiers and connectives) in all their syntactically relevant positions. Sentences in which there is interaction among more than three operators are sentences to which our argument in section 5 applies. So, supposing our argument to be valid, there can be no rules like the N-rules for quadruples, etc., of interacting logical operators. Though probably comparatively rare in discourse, these latter sentences point up a fundamental limitation to purely "syntactical" negation rules.

[4] Jaakko Hintikka, "Quantifiers vs. Quantification Theory", *Linguistic Inquiry* 5 (1974), 153-77; also in *Dialectica* 27 (1973), 329-58. For a technical discussion of branching quantifiers, see J. Walkoe, Jr., "Finite Partially Ordered Quantification", *Journal of Symbolic Logic* 35 (1970), 535-55.

[5] Jon Barwise, "On Branching Quantifiers in English", *Journal of Philosophical Logic* 8 (1979), 56. Proposition 1 is the relevant claim, for which a proof is given on pp. 73-74.

[6] Edward Klima, "Negation in English", in Jerry A. Fodor and Jerrold J. Katz, editors., *The Structure of Language*, Prentice-Hall, Englewood Cliffs, N.J., 1964, pp. 246-323.

[7] Klima, "Negation in English"; Charles J. Fillmore, "On the Syntax of Preverbs", unpublished paper, Ohio State University, 1966; Robert P. Stockwell, Paul Schachter, and Barbara Hall Partee, *The Major Syntactic Structures of English*, Holt, Rinehart and Winston, New York, 1973, especially chapter 5.

[8] Hintikka and Carlson, "Conditionals, Generic Quantifiers, and Other Applications of Subgames".

[9] Gödel's 1959 article is translated into English as "On a Hitherto Unexploited Extension of the Finitary Standpoint", *Journal of Philosophical Logic* 9 (1980), 133-42.

[10] See, e.g., Jaakko Hintikka, "Quantifiers in Natural Languages: Some Logical Problems", in Esa Saarinen, editor, *Game-Theoretical Semantics*, D. Reidel, Dordrecht, 1979, pp. 81-117; and Hintikka, "Rejoinder to Peacocke", also in Saarinen, pp. 135-51.
[11] See Noam Chomsky, *Rules and Representations*, Columbia University Press, New York, 1980, pp. 123-27; and see chapter 9 below.
[12] This was first pointed out to us by Ernest LePore in discussion.
[13] This reading of (84) is the natural reading that results if "anyone" is emphatically stressed, as in (i):

(i) Jim knows whether John can beat *anyone*.

(85) is the natural reading if (84) is given its normal, unmarked intonation.
[14] Geach, for example, in a similar vein, talks about the "popular view that modern formal logic has applications only to rigorous disciplines like algebra, geometry, and mechanics; not to arguments in a vernacular about more homely concerns....The reason offered would be the complex and irregular logical syntax of vernacular languages." *Reference and Generality*, Cornell University Press, Ithaca, N.Y., 1962, p. vii.
[15] See Hintikka, "Quantifiers in Natural Language".
[16] Alice Davison, "Any as Universal or Existential?" in Johan Van der Auwera, editor, *The Semantics of Determiners*, Croom Helm, London, 1980, pp. 11-40.

Chapter 5

TEMPORAL DISCOURSE AND SEMANTICAL GAMES

1. Game-Theoretical Semantics

It has proven surprisingly difficult to construct explicit
formal semantics for English tenses and temporal adverbs.
If evidence is needed, the recent proliferation of attempted
formal treatments of English temporal discourse should be
testimony enough to the dissatisfaction of linguists and
logicians with existing theories.

This chapter is an attempt to bring game-theoretical semantics to bear on the problem. It represents a tentative
exploration of some of the most important problems and
prospects in this area rather than a fully worked-out
theory. It reflects my belief that a mark of a good theory
is to raise interesting problems and not merely to solve old
ones. Indeed, in spite of the tentative character of my
discussion, it leads to several conjectures of considerable
general interest.

I shall take the main ideas of game-theoretical semantics
for granted.[1] Basically, these games are two-person zero-
sum games. In the simplest cases, which correspond to
extensional logic, they are played on a given model or
"world" M in which all the concepts used in a given sentence S are defined. The game G(S) starts with S, and
the first player, who we will call *Myself*, can be thought
of as trying to verify S in M, while the other player, to
be called *Nature*, tries to falsify S. On the basis of this
idea, several specific game rules are easily found. For instance, in order to verify a sentence of the form

X - some Y who Z - W,

where "who" occupies the subject position in "who Z", Myself has to find an individual from the domain of M, say b,
so that the following sentence can be verified:

X - b - W, b is a Y and b Z.

113

This is a special case of the game rule (G. some) for the English quantifier word "some".

At each stage of the game, some sentence S' is considered by the players. The game ends with an atomic sentence. Since the concepts used in it are all defined on M, it is either true or false. In the former case, the winner is Myself, in the latter, Nature. The sentence S is true iff there is a winning strategy for Myself, and false iff there is one for Nature.

The way this approach can be extended to temporal discourse should also be obvious in its main features. The main difference is that the models on which the game is now conducted have to be somewhat richer in structure. Indeed, the model presupposed in a game will now be a branching time structure T – a tree, in the mathematical sense of the term. A sentence is at each move considered not only with respect to this structure, but also with respect to a moment of time t within the structure T. Tenses come in, roughly, as instructions to take a step from one time point to another, chosen by one of the players.

For instance, the game rule for the past tense can be tentatively formulated as follows:

(G. past)   When the game has reached a sentence S and the moment of time t_1, one of the players may choose an earlier moment of time t_2, $t_2 < t_1$. The game is then continued with respect to S' and t_2, where S' is like S except that the main verb in some clause in S has been changed from the past to the present tense. (It will be said that the rule (G. past) is applied to that verb.)

This rule will be modified later. An explicit formulation of most of the other rules discussed will not be attempted in this chapter. Instead, I will try to explain informally, or semi-informally, some of the advantages of a game-theoretical treatment.

What are these advantages? It seems to me that the following features of game-theoretical semantics are relevant here: the choice of the player who is making a move; the order in which different game rules are applied (roughly, but not quite accurately, the relative scopes of the words and phrases to which they are applied); the possibility of coordinating several applications of one and the same rule to ingredients of the sentence; and the relation of the game rules to the principle of compositionality. All these topics, plus others, will be discussed later in this chapter.

2. Underdetermination of the Next Move

One of the most interesting features of game-theoretical semantics, in general, is that many game rules leave open the question of which player (Myself or Nature) is to make the next move. This is neither an imperfection of the language (e.g., an ambiguity) nor a flaw in the game rules. Rather, it is an important part of how our language actually works.[2]

This phenomenon is naturally captured by game-theoretical semantics, as is illustrated by (G. past) above. It comes into play in temporal discourse in an important way. Consider, e.g., the following examples:

(1)   Joan was at MIT last year.
(2)   When Franklin came in, Eleanor left.

These sentences are, as linguists sometimes misleadingly[3] put it, ambiguous between an existential- and a universal-quantifier reading. This duality is readily captured by our game rules. If a play of a game has reached (1) or (2) and a moment of time t_0, the next move, in accordance with (G. past), may take the players to an earlier moment of time $t_1(< t_0)$, and to (3) or (4), respectively:

(3)   Joan is at MIT.
(4)   Franklin comes in, and Eleanor leaves.

In (3), the choice of t_1 is restricted by the temporal adverb "last year". In both, we get the "at one time" reading if the move (choice of t_1) is made by Myself, and the "all the time" reading if it is made by Nature.

3. Scope Ambiguities

By construing tenses as something rather like quantifiers, as we are doing in our game rules for them, we are in effect allowing them to interact with quantifiers and other quantifier-like operators. This interaction manifests itself mostly in the form of competition between the scopes of tenses and "other quantifiers". This in turn explains why many sentences that contain both admit of a multiplicity of readings. The following are cases in point:

(5)   Two hunters shot three tigers.
(6)   John will find every book he has lost.
(7)   Every senator has been re-elected.
(8)   The President of the United States and the Prime Minister of Canada will meet next year.

The different readings of these sample sentences can be captured by the different orderings that our game rules allow when applied to (5)-(8). For instance, in (5) the first application can be to the numerical quantifier "two", to the verb "shot" (by G. past), or to the other numerical quantifier "three". Correspondingly, we get the following obviously different readings:

(5a)   Each of two hunters shot three tigers.
(5b)   A pair of hunters shot a group of three tigers.
(5c)   Three tigers were each shot by two hunters.

The different readings of (6)-(8) can be accounted for similarly.

4. Scope Ambiguities and Quantification over Events

These observations pose an important large-scale question. Often, a distinction between two uses of the verb - the distributive and the collective - is postulated in order to account for multiple readings of sentences such as (9):

(9)   All the men lifted a boat.

If such a distinction is needed, we have indirect evidence for a Davidsonian ontology of events.[4] For the most natural explanation of the distinction is undoubtedly obtained by means of Davidson's idea that a verb like "lift" introduces (as if by a tacit, initial existential quantifier) an entity, viz., the event referred to.   In some cases there is just one individual bearing the agent relation to this event, in others there are several.   It is easy to see how this idea can be used to account for the different readings of (9).   An even simpler example is offered by a sentence like (10):

(10)   Tom, Dick, and Harry lifted Sue.

Here the different readings are, for a Davidsonian, presumably due to the different scope orderings of conjunction ("and") and the event quantifier tacit in "lifted".

It seems to me that we do not need the collective-distributive contrast in any size, shape, or form, and hence we do not need Davidson's ontology, either.   The tense-operator, which is present on any account in "lifted" in (10), suffices to explain the duality of readings of (10). For we can apply either (G. and) or (G. past) to (10). They yield (11),

(11)   Tom lifted Sue; Dick lifted Sue; and Harry lifted Sue (considered at the original time t_0).

of whose conjuncts Nature next chooses one, or (12), respectively:

(12)   Tom, Dick, and Harry are lifting Sue (considered at an earlier moment of time $t_1 < t_0$, chosen by Myself).

Some support for my view is obtained by noting that the ambiguity in (10) is no longer present in the present-progressive sentence (12).

But doesn't it still make a difference whether Tom, Dick, and Harry are each doing it separately, or whether they are doing it conjointly?

Yes, it can make a difference.   But what we then have is a further ambiguity, different from our original ambiguity.   The latter, hence, cannot be used as evidence for the presence of the collective-distributive contrast.   Moreover, the so-called collective reading sometimes seems to be merely a result of conversational expectations.   For instance, one of the readings of (13) has Jack and Jill getting married at the same moment:

(13)   Jack and Jill were married last week.

The unlikelihood of this for two separate weddings results in the assimilation of the "at the same time" reading to the "each other" interpretation. This link is detachable, however. There is no inconsistency or semantical abnormality in saying (14):

(14)   Jack and Jill were married last week, but not to each other, even though they tied the knot at the same time as part of a double ceremony.

Thus my theory tells against the reification of events.

5. Restraints on Rule Ordering

The interplay of tenses and quantifiers, however, seems to be more restricted than my theory allows. In other words, my theory seems to predict too much freedom and, hence, too many readings. But this appearance is not reality. There are different ways in which the multiplicity of readings is often reduced in particular cases.

The stipulation that a rule like (G. past) is to be considered as being applied to certain verbs (the verbs that are changed from the past tense to the present) is not a mere nominal definition. It makes it possible for our ordering principles to rely on the location of the verbs in question in a sentence. This comes into play both via the left-to-right order of rule application and via the subordination of the clauses where the expressions to which the game rules are applied are located. This enables us to explain how sundry multiplicities of readings are eliminated in ordinary discourse.

For instance, consider the following sentences:

(15)   Every senator will be re-elected.
(16)   In some election year, every senator will be re-elected.

Here "every" has a wide scope in (15) but a narrower one than "some" in (16). This is in keeping with the left-to-right preference in the ordering of game-rule application. This preference can be codified in an ordering principle (O. LR), which says that in applying rules to phrases in the same clause the players should work their way from left to right.

Likewise we can consider the contrast between the following sentences:

(17) Seven presidents died in office.

and

(18) Last week, seven miners died in an explosion.

In (17), the numerical quantifier "seven" can be expected to have wide scope, by (O. LR). In (18), it can be expected to have narrow scope, since the phrase "last week", which regulates the choice of an earlier moment of time, occurs to the left of "seven". This assigns precisely the correct preferred readings to (17) and (18).

Further problem cases can be dealt with similarly. For instance, the reason that the last reading of (5), namely, (5c), is less natural than the others is that it violates the (weak) ordering principle (O. LR). The same principle explains why the first two (numerical) quantifiers in the following sentence have to be treated alike:

Two senators and two congressmen introduced four interrelated items of legislation.

In this way, the precise preferred meaning of a large number of sentences containing both tenses and quantifiers can be predicted.

6. Quantifier Analogies

Various expressions that in effect quantify over time can be treated in game-theoretical semantics in a way that is analogous to the treatment of their nontemporal relatives. For instance, we have the following parallels, among which are a few so-called nonstandard quantifiers:[5]

always – all
never – no
sometimes – some
repeatedly – several
often – many
rarely – few
ever – any

7. Simple Past vs. Present Perfect

The game-theoretical apparatus enables us to capture interesting regularities in the semantics of tenses in English.
Consider, for instance, the following examples:

(19)   I turned off the stove.
(20)   I have turned off the stove.
(21)   I didn't turn off the stove.
(22)   I have not turned off the stove.

Here the truth conditions of (19)–(20) are essentially the
same.   Yet their respective negations, (21)–(22), differ
sharply in meaning.
    An explanation is easily forthcoming in game-theoretical
terms.   First, note that the game rule (G. pres perf) for
the present-perfect tense can be formulated, mutatis
mutandis, in the same way as (G. past).   Hence, what has
to be explained is not why (19)–(20) agree in meaning,
but why (21)–(22) differ in meaning.   For this purpose,
observe first that in (19)–(22) "turning off the stove"
refers to a momentary event.   In a game-theoretical
framework, this means that an application of the game rule
dealing with its tense must be made by Myself.   In the
technical formulation of (G. past) and (G. pres perf), this
means that the question of which player is to make the
next move is to be made dependent on the subcategorization of the verb to which it is applied, as expressing
either a momentary event or an ongoing state or activity.
    The difference between (21)–(22) occurs because the
negation rule (G. not) is supposed to be applied in (21)
after the choice of an earlier moment of time, whereas in
(22) it is applied after the game rule (G. pres perf) for
the present-perfect tense.   In other words, the explanation of the difference in meaning between (21) and (22)
lies – as it does in many other cases – in an ordering

principle regulating the sequence in which the different game rules are to be applied. There is plenty of collateral evidence for an ordering principle that tells us this. It is easily seen how it applies to (21)-(22). The ingredient in a sentence to which a rule is applied first has wide scope typically. Hence, our ordering principle says that in (21) the past-tense operator has wide scope, while in (22) negation has wide scope. This is precisely the difference between (21)-(22).

This phenomenon has led Tichy to the unusual view that the English simple past tense "is incomplete in isolation" semantically.[6] The cash value of this strange doctrine is captured by our ordering principle.

As was noted, in (19)-(22) we have an activity that does not take any interval of time. Hence, only the existential reading of the past tense comes into play. When this is not the case, we can also have Nature making the move sanctioned by (G. past), as is possible in the following examples:

(23) Susan stayed in Virginia this semester.
(24) Susan has stayed in Virginia this semester.
(25) Susan didn't stay in Virginia this semester.
(26) Susan hasn't stayed in Virginia this semester.

Here the ordering principle does not make any difference, because the tense can be, in effect, either an existential or a universal quantifier over time. This is confirmed by examples like (25)-(26).

It seems to me that both the alleged semantical incompleteness of the simple past and the differences between the simple past and the present perfect can be accounted for game theoretically. In semantical analysis, we do not need the mythical "reference time" that Reichenbach introduced, if we use the game-theoretical approach.

8. The Outside-In Direction of Semantical Games

Perhaps the most important difference between game-theoretical semantics and its closest rivals is that game-theoretical rules work their way from outside in, whereas the semantical rules of its closest rivals all operate from the inside out. This implies, e.g., that game-theoretical semantics is not constrained by the principle of compositionality, which I have argued elsewhere is wrong any-way.[7]

Part of the cash value of the failure of compositionality is that we can optionally allow certain game rules to be applied to several different expressions in the same sentence in one fell swoop. For instance, we have to modify the game rule (G. past) to allow it to be applied to the main verb of more than one clause in S at the same time.

In the modified rule (G. past), there will be no explicit indication whether it should be applied to one verb or to several. Hence it allows for a variety of readings for sentences that contain more than one main verb in the past tense. (27) and (28) are cases in point:

(27)   The woman who stole the book saw John.
(28)   The woman who stole the book saw the man who robbed the bank.

The readings thus obtained seem to be precisely the ones that they actually have.

Moreover, giving up the compositionality principle will enable a game-theoretical semanticist to allow the different choices of time-moments that are involved in the applications of (G. past) to different verbs to be interdependent in other ways. One familiar weak principle governing the order of choices is that the left-right order of verbs involved in a sentence should match the temporal order of the moments chosen, as in (29):

(29)   Jack and Jill were married and had a baby.

The weakness of this principle, which seems to be merely a conversational principle, is shown by the ease with which it can be overridden as in (30):

(30)   Jack and Jill were married and had a baby, but not in that order.

9. An Economy Principle for Rule Applications

Now these considerations might still seem to predict, in many cases, a greater variety of viable readings for sentences containing several verbs in the past tense than they actually possess. However, all that this objection shows is that there are further factors that in certain particular cases filter out some of the otherwise possible readings.

There is indeed a pragmatic principle that tells us to minimize the number of independent choices governed by one and the same game rule to phrases in one and the same sentence. This principle, together with the one that invites us to match the order of verbs with the order of time-moments, yields the most natural reading for the following sentence:

(31)   After he checked into his hotel, John went to the bar, where he had a drink, paid the bartender, and left a tip.

We know that we're dealing with a conversational principle because its effect is readily cancellable. For instance, (31) might be continued: "Well, to be precise, John left the tip before he actually paid for his drink."

The same pragmatic character of the principle is shown by its dependence on the availability of alternative formulations that would make the sentence in question unambiguous. For instance, consider again - this time a little bit more closely - our sample sentence (32)(=(28)):

(32)   The woman who stole the book saw the man who robbed the bank.

Not all the possible readings are equally plausible. On what clearly is the preferred reading, the choice associated with "robbed" is independent of the other choices governed by applications of (G. past) to the sentence. The reason seems to be that a simultaneity could have been imposed by reformulating (32) as follows:

(33)   The woman who stole the book saw the man who was robbing the bank.

These different principles tend to reduce the multiplicity of readings that sentences with several past-tense verbs have and that result from the freedom that is allowed by (G. past) with respect to coordinated or noncoordinated application. Of them, the principle that tells us to minimize the number of independent choices is especially interesting. It can be considered a special case of a much wider economy principle that operates in the semantical processing of a sentence by means of our game rules. I don't know how to state it in its most general form, but its import can be stated in rough-and-ready fashion as follows: Don't multiply the entities you need in a semantical game beyond necessity! Here we seem to be dealing with a general principle of language understanding that is operative in various other parts of semantics, e.g., in the interpretation of certain modal sentences. To see this, consider, the following:

(34)   Joan believes that a burglar might have broken into her apartment yesterday, and she believes that he might have stolen her pearls.

Here, "believes that...might have" represents a doxastic possibility. Appearances notwithstanding, the two halves of (34) describe one and the same possibility, not two independent ones. An explanation is forthcoming by modifying the game rule for doxastic possibility in the same way that (G. past) was modified, and then applying the general economy principle.

The generality of the principle is also suggested by the simultaneous application of game rules, since it may include several applications of (G. past) and also, at the same time, applications of the rule (G. past perf) for the past perfect. This rule can be formulated roughly as follows:

(G. past perf) When the game has reached a sentence S and a moment t_0, one of the players may choose an earlier moment of time $t_1 < t_0$. The game is then continued with respect to S' and t_1, where S' is like S except that the main verb in one or more of its clauses has been changed from the past-perfect tense to either (i) the past or (ii) the present-perfect tense.

Here the choice between (i) and (ii) is limited by general conditions on the acceptability of the two tenses in the resulting sentence. The terminology used in connection with (G. past perf) is the same as that used in connection with other rules.

One interesting thing about the general economy principle is that its proper formulation presupposes something like game-theoretical semantics. For what we are minimizing is not the number of entities in the *models* of our sentences. Hence no purely model-theoretical approach can allow for a formulation of the principle in question. What we are minimizing is the number of entities introduced in the course of the *semantical interpretation* of a sentence. This interpretation is here conceptualized by means of semantical games.

We must not overestimate the generality of the economy principle, however. It characterizes to some extent the applications of certain particular rules as distinguished from others. For instance, the economy principle applies very strongly to the uses of (G. past perf) and almost as strongly to those of (G. past). In contrast, it applies somewhat more weakly to the rule (G. fut) for the future tense, and only very weakly to (G. pres perf).

To illustrate these points by means of a simple example, let us go back to the rule (G. past perf). The choice between (i) and (ii) in (G. past perf) creates differences between different readings that are actually present in English. Consider, for instance, the following example:

(35) I had locked the door, but I had not turned off the stove.

A coordinated application of (G. past perf) to (35) implies that either (36) or (37) is to be defended by Myself at some earlier moment of time:

(36) I locked the door, but I did not turn off the stove.
(37) I have locked the door, but I have not turned off the stove.

I have assumed, as we obviously have to assume here, that, in simultaneous applications of (G. past perf) to several different verbs, they are all handled in the same way: either all according to (i) or all according to (ii).

Now the difference between (36) and (37) is clearly the difference between two possible readings of (35). Notice that if I add the words "the day before" to the first clause in (35) the second reading vanishes; in the output sentence (37) the corresponding addition would result in an ungrammatical sentence.

10. Generalizations to Discourse Semantics

One of the most useful features of my game-theoretical approach is that many semantical concepts and generalizations used in it can be extended from sentences to discourse. What was said in sections 8-9 above is a case in point. For instance, consider the following fragment of a narrative (I am borrowing the example from Dowty, with modifications):

> (38) John came to visit me yesterday. He was depressed when he arrived. He told me about his problems. He had not discussed them with anybody. He had hoped to have a chance of doing so. Gradually he became happier. He left in a good mood.

This illustrates the discourse-semantical applicability of several observations made in sections 8-9. They include:

(a) The simultaneous applicability of each one of such rules as (G. past) and (G. past perf) to the main verbs of several different sentences.
(b) The joint (coordinated) applicability of such rules as (G. past) and (G. past perf).
(c) The possibility of coordinated applications of rules like (G. past), with the left-right order in the discourse mirroring the temporal order.
(d) The strong tendency of (G. past perf) to be applied simultaneously with (G. past) (and with other occurrences of (G. past perf)).

The problem here is therefore not to extend some particular observations from sentences to discourse, but to show how the game-theoretical approach applies to discourse, and not only to individual sentences, in the first place.

Without trying to give a full treatment of the matter, I can perhaps refer the reader to the ideas put forward in an earlier paper by Jaakko Hintikka and Lauri Carlson.[8] Briefly, we can think of the semantical games associated with the successive sentences (S_1, S_2, ...) of a discourse as subgames within a larger "supergame". The idea of a subgame here includes not just the assumption that the game in question is played through, but primarily the idea that on its completion one of the players (sometimes both) reveals the strategies he or she used in the game. Knowledge of these strategies can therefore be used by the other player in later subgames.

The subgames involved in an ordinary narrative can be thought of as conjunctively connected. That is, the next subgame is played only if the present one is won by Myself, playing his (her) usual role. In more complicated types of discourse, for instance in question-answer dialogues, the overall game is more involved, and has to be specified separately. The recent work of Lauri Carlson can be thought of as an important step in this general direction.[9] In spite of being quite recent, this work has been carried out far enough to demonstrate not only its feasibility but its fruitfulness. Hence there is no obstacle to extending the discussion of the preceding two sections directly to discourse.

This amounts to an essential advantage of the game-theoretical approach: no competing account has brought all the relevant sentence phenomena and discourse phenomena together. For instance, some recent linguists have been forced to assume a special rule, restricted to narrative discourse, to be able to deal with different occurrences of the past tense referring to the same moment of time or to the same occasion. The phenomenon in question is nevertheless not restricted to discourse, but can occur within one and the same sentence, as we saw. It exemplifies a general economy principle that applies both to sentences taken one by one and to discourse.

11. Treating Temporal Adverbs

Likewise, because we have given up compositionality, we can, without any awkwardness, process several temporal adverbs simultaneously, and at the same time as the tense of a verb. Moreover, the adverbs may be plain time-indicators, or they may have the nature of temporal quantifiers.

An example of the former is a sentence like the following:

(39)   I first met John Smith at two o'clock in the afternoon noon on Thursday in the first week of June in 1962.

An example of the latter might be:

(40) Yesterday John sneezed rarely.

The rule for "rarely" (say, applied to the sentence "rarely X") calls for Myself to choose a number of moments of time, say t_1, t_2, ..., t_n, where n is smaller than some constant $n_0 > n$, whereupon Nature chooses a different moment of time t_N. These times are chosen in accordance with the tense of the main verb of X. Then the following will have to be defended by Myself:

(*)   X' (at t_i) (i = 1,2,...,n)
(**)   neg[X'] (at t_N),

where neg[Z] is the semantical negation of Z in English, and X' is like X except that its main verb is in the present tense. In other words, the game is then continued with respect to the conjunction of (*) and (**), and with respect to the times indicated. The temporal adverb "yesterday" in (40) ensures that the moments of time t_1, t_2, ..., t_n, t_N must all be chosen from yesterday.

It is extremely important to realize that, although I have spoken of the simultaneous application of several game rules, this characterization is inaccurate in one important respect. It would be less misleading to speak of *coordinated* applications. For even though the applications of different rules are coordinated, the order of these rules still matters. Witness, for instance, the following example:

(41) When Mary came to the party, John repeatedly went to the bar.

Allowing "when" to stand elliptically for "on the occasion(s) when", (41) is seen to be ambiguous in several ways. First, "when" can have either a universal-quantifier reading ("whenever"), or else an existential-quantifier reading. (For this point, see section 2 above.) The former reading allows "repeatedly" to govern either the whole sentence or else only the consequent. What makes the difference is the relative order of application of the rules (G. when) and (G. repeatedly).

The latter reading is possible only if the scope of "repeatedly" covers only the consequent. Precisely what the mechanism is that rules out the other larger scope is not discussed here.

The interplay of temporal adverbs and tenses is important, and can be different for different tenses (and also different in different languages for the same tense). For instance, it is a requirement in English that, in whatever way the choice of an earlier moment of time is restricted in (G. pres perf), the interval from which the choice is made must have as its upper bound the "present moment", i.e., the moment of time t_0 mentioned in the rule.

This restraint partly characterizes the present-perfect tense in English. However, the corresponding restraint is not present in the parallel rules for some other languages, e.g., German and Finnish. This observation shows, incidentally, that it would be a mistake to try to somehow derive this property of the English present-perfect tense from some deeper analysis of the English tense system.

12. Tenses and Temporal Connectives

By the same token, in game-theoretical semantics there is no awkwardness about the idea of evaluating tenses and temporal operators (e.g., temporal adverbs) at the same time. What many temporal adverbs do is to limit the range of moments of time from which the players make their respective choices. As such, their semantical force can only come into play in conjunction with the choice associated with a tensed verb.

The same applies to what might be called temporal connectives, such as "when", "before", "while", "after", "until", "since", and "as long as". The rules for them must be formulated to apply in cooperation with the tense rules. For instance, an approximation to the game rule for "before" might run as follows:

(G. before)   When the game has reached t_0 and a sentence of the form

(*) X before Y,

where X and Y are clauses, one of the players may choose a moment of time t_1 in accordance with the tense of the main verbs of X and Y. The game is then continued with respect to t_1 and

(**)   X' but neg[Y'],

where neg[Z] is the semantical negation of
Z, X' is like X except that the main verb is
in the present tense, and Y' is like Y except that the main verb is in the present-
perfect tense.[10]

(One thing we must heed here is the possibility that X or
Y has several main verbs. How the rule is to be extended
to cover this case is obvious.)

13. The *Any*-Thesis Generalized

One advantage offered by the game-theoretical approach is
that it enables us to extend to temporal discourse several
generalizations that have independently been found to obtain in other fragments of English. For instance, we can
obtain in this way an explanation of why we can say (42)
but not (43):

(42)   John left before anybody came.
(43)   *John left after anybody came.

An explanation is given by the *any*-thesis that I have formulated and defended elsewhere.[11] Briefly, (G. before)
yields, when applied to (42),

(44)   John leaves, but neg[anybody has come],

which reduces to

(45)   John leaves, but nobody has come.

This shows that on my analysis (42) differs in meaning
from (46):

(46)   John left before everybody came.

For, applied to (46), (G. before) yields

(47)   John leaves, but not everybody has come,

which is different in meaning from (45). According to the
any-thesis, this nonsynonymy makes the occurrence of
"any" in (42) grammatical.

In comparison, the game rule for "after" is

(G. after) When the game has reached t_0 and a sentence
            of the form

            (*)   X after Y,

            where X and Y are clauses, one of the players
            may choose a moment of time t_1 in accordance
            with the tense of the main verb of X and Y.
            The game is then continued with respect to t_1
            and

            (**) X' and Y',

            where X' is like X except that the main verb
            is in the present tense, and Y' is like Y ex-
            cept that the main verb is in the present-per-
            fect tense.

As the reader can readily ascertain, (G. after) does
not create the kind of asymmetry between "any" and
"every" that according to the *any*-thesis would authorize
the occurrence of "any". Hence the asterisk in (43).

More generally, the interplay between quantifiers and
temporal notions is, by and large, subject to the same
regularities that govern the interplay of quantifiers and
other operators elsewhere. For instance, observe a difference between the following:

(48) Frequently John denounced all his enemies.
(49) Frequently John denounced each one of his
      enemies.

The latter admits of a reading on which each of John's
enemies was a frequent subject of his denunciation, but
not necessarily jointly with other enemies. This is in
agreement with the fact that "each" elsewhere tends to
have the widest scope (i.e., the rule (G. each) tends to
have priority over other rules).

14. Indexical Time Reference

Some especially interesting temporal adverbs are those that
can be used to refer indexically to the moment of utterance
of their containing sentence. They include "now", "yesterday", "tomorrow", "X ago" (e.g., "two days ago"),
etc. They can be handled by means of rules that do not
look entirely different from the others. The following are
cases in point:

(G. now)   When a game has reached a sentence of the
            form

            $X - now - Y$,

            and a moment of time t_0, the players may con-
            tinue with respect to

            $X - at\ t_0 - Y$.

(G. ago)   When a game has reached a sentence of the
            form

            $X - Y\ ago - Z$,

            and a moment of time t_0, the players may con-
            tinue with respect to

            $X' - now - Z'$,

            and the time $t_0 - \delta$, where $X' - Z'$ is like $X - Z$
            except that the main verb in one or more of
            its clauses has been changed from the past
            tense to the present, and where δ is the time
            difference determined by Y.

One remarkable feature of these rules is that they have
priority over most others. Indeed, (G. now) seems to
have priority over practically all the other rules we have
formulated, and the rules for "yesterday", "tomorrow",
"ago", etc., likewise seem to have a relatively high
priority.

It is interesting to see that the possibility of dealing
with words like "now" in this relatively simple way is a di-

rect consequence of my giving up the principle of compositionality. As was noted above, in terms of game-theoretical semantics, compositionality means that the inside-out structure of a sentence determines the order of application of our rules: they are never applied to an ingredient in a lower clause if they can be applied to one in a higher clause. There is plenty of evidence to indicate that this assumption has to be given up anyway.[12] Here we have just seen another advantage of giving it up.

How great this advantage is is shown by the fact that it is expressions like "now" that are supposed to supply the best evidence for such complications in our semantics as the two-dimensionality of the tense logics of Kamp and others, the backwards-looking operators of Saarinen, etc.[13] We can turn the tables on both of the competitors here. We have just seen that a much simpler treatment is possible within the game-theoretical framework by means of rule ordering.

These comparative considerations can be deepened. If we believe in compositionality, we must consider the semantical evaluation of a sentence as proceeding step by step from inside out. In the model, some steps mean moving from one moment of time to another. This gives us a slightly different way of looking at the indexical notions like "now", "tomorrow", etc., that we have considered. They may be taken to be (in a temporal context) the notions that lead the players to consider moments of time that are no longer considered in the evaluation process, but which they did consider at earlier stages of the game (i.e., the evaluation). Typically, but not exclusively, the previously considered time is the starting time of the whole game. The work of David Kaplan, Hans Kamp, Esa Saarinen, et al., offers many examples of how they require for their semantics a "memory" of time moments considered earlier in the evaluation process.

Analysts who have tried to uphold compositionality have tried to cope with such expressions by making the semantical evaluation of a sentence relative to two time indices. From our game-theoretical viewpoint, they correspond to the time that is reached in the game and the original starting time of the game. Saarinen has argued, however, that this is not enough, since there can also be back references to moments of time considered in between, at intermediate stages of the game. This makes the use of the two-parameter approach very dubious.

15. The Rejection of the "Reference Point" Idea

From the sketch of a game-theoretical treatment of tenses
outlined above we can obtain a more general perspective on
the idea of a "reference point" (or "reference interval")
employed in many recent approaches to temporal discourse,
especially tenses. A "reference point" is essentially an
interim moment of time to which the players move and by
reference to which (here's the idea!) the further moments
of time considered in the game are chosen.

But, if so, we can see one reason why such attempted
reference-point accounts are bound to fail. The reference-point idea means essentially assuming only *one* reference point. It can work only if under any course of a
play of our game at most two moments of time are succes-
sively selected. It is likely to fail if a longer sequence of
choices of time-points is required. Now it is true that for
the semantical interpretation of any one tense *as such* two
choices are enough. However, the interplay of tenses with
other temporal notions may force us to consider more than
two interdependent choices. Then the reference-point account is in serious trouble.

However, the situation is not quite as simple as this.
The multiplicity of time-points does not matter in itself,
and hence does not give rise to insurmountable problems
as long as we don't have to consider them together, e.g.,
in the sense of "remembering" time-points we have considered earlier so as to be able to refer back to them.
Hence the inadequacy of reference-point accounts will become obvious only in contexts where we have anaphoric
back reference of some sort to several time-points considered earlier in a semantical game. In other words, it
may be expected that Esa Saarinen's counterexamples to
two-dimensional (and more generally many-dimensional)
model-theoretic semantics for tense-logics will serve also as
counterexamples to reference-point treatments of temporal
discourse. Whether this is the case depends on the particular form of the reference-point account. I will not try
to examine different accounts of this kind but will instead
merely announce my belief that serious difficulties face all
reference-point accounts in this direction.

16. Are There Backwards-Looking Operators?

Thus there are good reasons for suspecting that multiple-parameter and reference-point approaches to temporal discourse are not entirely satisfactory. It is not clear, however, that one of their partial competitors, the backwards-looking-operator idea, works much better. What we have seen earlier in this paper shows that a number of phenomena for the explanation of which backwards-looking operators have been evoked can be explained in other ways, partly through game-rule ordering and partly through the idea of simultaneous application of a game rule (or several game rules) to more than one phrase in a sentence. In fact, there does not seem to be any data among those for the explanation of which backwards-looking operators have been evoked that cannot be explained in one of these ways. Combined with the absence of all explicit, syntactically marked backwards-looking operators in natural languages, what we have found suggests that natural languages like English handle those logico-semantical phenomena that were supposed to be modelled by backwards-looking operators, in ways that differ both from these operators and also from the extra metatheoretical parameters of other theorists. Even though more discussion and more examples are needed here, the insights we have reached suffice to illustrate the fruitfulness of game-theoretical methods in this area.[14]

NOTES

[1] Much of the early work in game-theoretical semantics is collected in Esa Saarinen, editor, *Game-Theoretical Semantics*, D. Reidel, Dordrecht, 1979. For a fuller explanation of how this approach works see chapter 1 above.
[2] This phenomenon is illustrated by the two-barrelled character of English wh-words in their interrogative use. For it, see my monograph *The Semantics of Questions and the Questions of Semantics* (Acta Philosophica Fennica, vol. 28, no. 4), North-Holland, Amsterdam, 1976. As I emphasize there, such a multiplicity of readings must not be identified with ambiguity.
[3] Ibid.
[4] Cf. Donald Davidson, "The Logical Form of Action Sentences", in Nicholas Rescher, editor, *The Logic of Decision*

and Action, University of Pittsburgh Press, Pittsburgh, 1967, pp. 81-95.

[5] For a sketch of the treatment of such "nonstandard" quantifiers see my "Rejoinder to Peacocke", in Saarinen, *Game-Theoretical Semantics*, and Lauri Carlson's forthcoming paper on the subject; cf. section 11 below.

[6] Pavel Tichý, "The Logic of Temporal Discourse", *Linguistics and Philosophy* 3 (1980), 343-69.

[7] See chapter 10 below.

[8] Jaakko Hintikka and Lauri Carlson, "Conditionals, Generic Quantifiers, and Other Applications of Subgames", in Saarinen, *Game-Theoretical Semantics*, pp. 179-214.

[9] Lauri Carlson, "Focus and Dialogue Games", in Lucia Vaina and Jaakko Hintikka, editors, *Cognitive Constraints on Communication*, D. Reidel, Dordrecht, 1983, pp. 295-333; *Dialogue Games*, D. Reidel, Dordrecht, 1983.

[10] For semantical negation, see chapter 4 above.

[11] See "Quantifiers in Natural Languages", in Saarinen, *Game-Theoretical Semantics*, pp. 81-117.

[12] See chapter 10 below.

[13] See Esa Saarinen's own papers in *Game-Theoretical Semantics*.

[14] In working on this paper, I have greatly profited from discussions with Merrill B. Hintikka, Barry Richards, and Jack Kulas. They are not responsible for my excesses, however. I profited likewise from the papers and comments by many of the other participants in the 1980 Groningen Round Table.

Chapter 6

DEFINITE DESCRIPTIONS IN GAME-THEORETICAL SEMANTICS

(Coauthored by Jaakko Hintikka and Jack Kulas)

1. Can We Localize Russell's Theory?

The many attractive features of Russell's treatment of definite descriptions, or as we shall also call them, *the*-phrases, make its failure as an overall theory ever so poignant.[1] This failure needs few comments. Even if, *pace* Strawson, Russell's theory works perfectly when applied to definite descriptions like "the present King of France", it fail to account for the uses of *the*-phrases that pick up earlier reference. We shall call these the *anaphoric* uses of *the*-phrases. (1) is an example of such a use:

(1)   Joan was accosted by a stranger. Wisely, she didn't talk to the man.

Likewise, Russell's theory does not enable us to deal with the so-called generic uses of the definite article, as in the following example:

(2)   The tiger is striped.

But is it perhaps possible to modify Russell's treatment to overcome its limitations and failures? This is what we shall be striving to do in this chapter. David Hilbert once described his metamathematics as an attempt to regain Cantor's set-theoretical paradise from which paradoxes had banished us. In an analogous spirit, we may be said to be trying to regain the paradise that Russell's theory of descriptions represents to a logician, while trying to avoid its failures.

For reasons that we have spelled out elsewhere, we shall consider the anaphoric use of *the*-phrases as their semantically basic use.[2] By so doing we hope to be able to account for the other uses as being somehow derived from it, and explicable by reference to it.[3] Hence our

137

task here is to modify Russell's treatment of definite descriptions to enable us to handle anaphoric uses, while keeping its attractive features intact.   How can we do this?

One's first idea here is likely to be to try to "localize" Russell's theory in the sense of letting the quantifiers that he relied on range, not over the whole universe of discourse (or some category of entities in the universe), but rather over some contextually determined part of it.   This plausible idea works in some cases.   However, in spite of its plausibility, the idea of simply contextually restricting the ranges of Russell's quantifiers does not work.   Sometimes the existence requirement that is integral to Russell's treatment cannot be satisfied by any restriction; sometimes Russell's uniqueness requirement cannot be satisfied.   Examples of the former are the following:

> (3)   Nobody stole your missing diamonds, for a thief would have had to scale a slippery 50-foot wall. Moreover, the thief would have had to elude detection by an extemely sophisticated security system.

> (4)   Don't wait for the change, vote for it.

Here (4) is adapted from a political commercial.   For the sake of the argument, we may assume that no change of the intended kind will ever take place.

> (5)   "Yeah, I'll be there.   But how'll I know if you've been there?"
> "Well, if I get there first, I'll make a blue chalk mark, and if you get there first, you rub the mark out."
> (From an old vaudeville act of Mack and Moran.)

Examples of the second kind of failure are the following:

> (6)   Some man is capable of falling in love with any woman, at least if the woman is a blonde.
> (7)   Every year I send a birthday card and a check to my son, but last year he barely looked at the card.

If the relevant range of individuals is narrowed so as to include only one woman (as in (6)) or one birthday card (as in (7)) to obtain uniqueness, the whole force of the universal quantifier is lost; for the whole point of using a universal quantifier is to speak of several different individuals.

Furthermore, the attempted restriction cannot always stay constant throughout a discourse or even throughout a single (complex) sentence. Intuitively speaking, the individual picked out by one and the same *the*-phrase can change from one part of a discourse to another, and even from one part of one and the same sentence to another. The following are cases in point:

(8)   In the first inning the first batter struck out, but in the fourth inning the first batter hit a home run.

(9)   In the United States the president now has far greater powers than were enjoyed by the president in the nineteenth century.

2. Game-Theoretical Solution to the Localization Problem

Therefore, a simple restriction of the ranges of Russellian quantifiers does not vindicate his theory. This might suggest that nothing like Russell's treatment of *the*-phrases will work for their anaphoric uses. The suggestion is wrong, however. Indeed, it is here that game-theoretical semantics (GTS) comes to our assistance. One way of putting the main point is to say that GTS gives us a different and more dynamic way of restricting the ranges of quantifiers involved in Russell's treatment of definite descriptions. We have seen that it will not do to try to restrict the ranges of Russellian quantifiers to some contextually given (but otherwise fixed) part of the universe of discourse. GTS enables us to restrict those ranges relative to the stage a semantical game has reached at the time when a given *the*-phrase is treated in the game. This restriction is different in kind from the one envisaged earlier, and more dynamic.

The simplest restriction of the new kind confines the quantifiers that we rely on in a Russell-style treatment to the set of individuals chosen by either player in the game up to the move in which a definite description is assigned a reference. We can implement this idea by means of explicit game rules by starting from the game rule that codifies the generally accepted Russellian treatment. This game rule can be formulated as follows:

(G. Russellian *the*)   When a semantical game has reached a sentence of the form

(*)   X – the Y who Z – W,

an individual, say b, may be chosen by Myself, whereupon Nature chooses a different individual, say d. The game is then continued with respect to

(**)   X – b – W, b is a(n) Y, b Z, but d is not a(n) Y who Z.

Here the choices are thought of as being made from some fixed, comprehensive universe, as Russell thought, or from an appropriate category, as is more natural to do in dealing with natural language. This rule yields a game-theoretical treatment that is equivalent to Russell's theory of descriptions. To see this, note that a choice by Myself means an existential instantiation. Hence (**) amounts to

$$(Ex)[(X - x - W) \quad \& \quad (x \text{ is a(n) } Y) \quad \& \quad (x \text{ } Z) \quad \& \quad (y)[(y \neq x) \rightarrow \sim((y \text{ is a(n) } Y) \quad \& \quad (y \text{ } Z))]],$$

which is logically equivalent to Russell's contextual analysis of definite descriptions.

Furthermore, Russell's distinction between primary and secondary occurrences of definite descriptions[4] becomes a distinction between the relative order of the game rule (G. Russellian *the*) and some other game rule. But since there can be more than one such other rule, Russell's dichotomy is insufficient to cope with the full logical behavior of definite descriptions.

What can we do to adapt this treatment to the behavior of anaphoric *the*-phrases? We can restrict the two players' choices that are connected with the different Russellian quantifiers to a set (that we shall call *I*) of all those individuals chosen by the two players up to that point.

In brief, our tentative game rule for *the*-phrases in their anaphoric use is the following:

(G. anaphoric *the*) When a semantical game has reached a sentence of the form

(*)   X - the Y who Z - W,

then an individual, say b, may be chosen from a set *I* of individuals by Myself, whereupon Nature chooses a different individual, say d, from the same set *I*. The game is then continued with respect to

(**) X - b - W, b is a(n) Y, and b Z, but d is not a(n) Y who Z.

Here *I* is the set of all individuals chosen by either player earlier in the game. If *I* is a unit set, i.e., if *I* = {b}, then the game is continued with respect to

(***) X - b - W, b is a(n) Y, and b Z.

The motivation of the rule is clear. The only individuals that can considered by the two players (at the time they are supposed to apply the rule (G. anaphoric *the*) to (*)) are the members of *I*. If you believe in the spirit of Russell's theory of descriptions, you therefore keep his theory but let the Russellian quantifiers range over *I*. This is precisely what (G. anaphoric *the*) says.

The rule is subject to the same comments and qualifications as the usual quantifier rules used in GTS. They were discussed briefly in chapter 1 above. The main points are worth repeating here:

(i) Y and Z are assumed to be in the singular. A different rule is required to cover the case in which they are plural. However, we shall not try to formulate it here.

(ii) Instead of "who", in (*) we might of course have "that", "which", "where", "when", etc. They are treated analogously, except for small variations that will not be taken up here. Likewise in (*) we could have a prepositional phrase containing one of the words just listed. There are no major theoretical problems in extending (G. anaphoric *the*) to these cases.

(iii) The next question is how the realm of the choice of b in (**) is affected by the difference between the different words and phrases mentioned in (ii). This problem is discussed in chapter 8 below, so it won't be taken up here.

(iv) Game rules such as (G. anaphoric *the*) will have to be supplemented by provisions for making sure that anaphoric relations that obtain in (*) are preserved in (**). Once again, this problem is not discussed here. It pertains to all game rules for quantifiers and most rules for quantifier-like expressions, not just to (G. anaphoric *the*).

3. Anaphoric *The* in Formal Languages

In spite of these qualifications, the basic idea on which our rule (G. anaphoric *the*) is based is clear. This clarity is illustrated by the existence of a similar rule that can be set up for formal first-order languages containing a symbol analogous to Russell's (ιx) for anaphorically used "the". We shall use "(νx)" as such a symbol. The rule that corresponds to (G. anaphoric *the*) can then be formulated as follows:

(G. anaphoric νx)   When a semantical game has reached a sentence of the form

(*)   S [(νx)A[x]],

an individual, say b, from the set *I* of individuals chosen by the two players up to that time in the game, may be selected by Myself, whereupon Nature selects a different individual, say d, from the same set *I*. The game is then continued with respect to

(**)   (S[b]   &   A[b]   & $\sim$A[d]).

Here S is the relevant context of "νx" in (*). S[b] is like (*) except that some occurrences of "(νx)A[x]" have been replaced by occurrences of "b" and A[b] (and A[d]) are like A[x] except that all the free occurrences of "x" have been replaced by "b" (and "d", respectively). If *I* =

{b}, the game is continued with respect to

$$(***) \quad (S[b] \ \& \ A[b]).$$

This game rule gives rise to a semantics in which sentences can be shown to be valid, invalid, or neither. Examples of valid sentences include the following:

(10) $(x)(A[x] \rightarrow (B[x] \equiv B[(\nu x)A[x]]))$.
(11) $(x)(y)[A[x] \rightarrow (B[(\nu x)A[x]] \rightarrow$
         $(B[x] \ \& \ \sim A[y]))]$.
(12) $(y)(u)[(Ex)(x = (\nu z)A[z]) \rightarrow$
         $((A[y] \ \& \ \sim A[u]) \ v \ (\sim A[y] \ \& \ A[u]))]$.

4. Applications

It turns out that our game rule (G. anaphoric *the*) needs several further refinements. Before discussing them, however, we have to see how the rule just formulated works. Also, the problems into which the first simple-minded-restriction suggestion ran present challenges to our treatment. We have to show that our treatment succeeds where the other suggestion failed.

First, let us consider an example to see how (G. anaphoric *the*) works. In selecting such an example, it is useful to remember that (as was mentioned above in chapter 1) GTS is calculated to apply to discourse and not only to sentences one by one. In the treatment, successive declarative sentences by the same speaker or writer are treated as if they were conjuncts. Hence, consider the following example:

(13) A stockbroker and his mother live in a village close to Sturbridge castle. Every morning the stockbroker takes a train to London from the village, while the mother goes for a walk.

This is easily treated by means of GTS. The subgame associated with the first sentence has to be dealt with first by the players. Two applications of (G. a(n)) and one application of (G. genitive)[5] yield something like (14):

(14) Kenneth Widmerpool and Ethel Widmerpool live in Sturbridge Greens close to Sturbridge castle.

> Kenneth Widmerpool is a stockbroker. Sturbridge Greens is a village. Ethel Widmerpool is the mother of Kenneth Widmerpool.

The players move on to deal with later sentences only if all the clauses of (14) are true. Then the set *I* open for the next application of (G. anaphoric *the*) is {Kenneth Widmerpool, Ethel Widmerpool}. Hence the second sentence of (13) is true, i.e., there is a winning strategy for Myself, if and only if a choice of two individuals x, y by Myself from *I* is possible such that x is the only stockbroker in *I*, y the only mother in *I*, and it is true that (15):

> (15)   Every morning x takes a train to London from the village while y goes for a walk.

Clearly the only viable candidates are x = Kenneth Widmerpool and y = Ethel Widmerpool. In other words, the force of the second half of (13) is, given players' choices displayed in (14), to assert that Kenneth Widmerpool takes a train to London every morning while Ethel Widmerpool goes for a walk. This is of course precisely the intuitive force of (13).

   Our theory also enables us to deal with the problem cases that the "restricted range" idea was unable to handle. For instance, an application of the game rule (G. no) for "nobody" to (3) yields a sentence of the form (16):

> (16)   Bill did not steal your missing diamonds, for a thief would have had to scale a slippery 50-foot wall. Moreover, the thief would have had to elude detection by an extemely sophisticated security system.

Here Bill was chosen by Nature. Then an application of (G. a(n)) to (16), followed by an application of (G. anaphoric *the*) yields (in part) (17):

> (17)   Bill did not steal your missing diamonds, for Bill would have had to scale a slippery 50-foot wall, if Bill is a thief. Moreover, Bill would have had to elude detection by an extremely sophisticated detection system.

This shows how our game rules yield the right semantics for sentences of the first problem kind.

Likewise, our rule enables us to handle the second group of problem cases. For instance, (7) is handled clause by clause, in accordance with the subgame principle.[6] To handle this example, the set I has to be enhanced to include not only individuals chosen by either player, but also strategies used and "remembered". (See section 9 below.) For example, for the players to pick the particular birthday card sent to the son last year, the function used by Nature to verify the antecedent – i.e., the function from years to brithday cards – has to be available to the player who must choose "the birthday card". If such a function were not available, uniqueness would fail. This obviously assigns the right semantics to (7).

Likewise, the third class of problem cases is amenable to our approach. An explicit treatment would require rules for tenses, which we will not try to formulate here. (See chapter 5 above for explicit game rules for tenses.) Even without such rules, we can see that different individuals are picked out by different tokens of *the*-phrase of a certain type. If these occurrences are handled at different stages of the game, the set I mentioned in (G. anaphoric *the*) may be different on the two different occasions, which in turn can lead to the selection of different individuals for the role of b (see (G. anaphoric *the*)) for the two different occurrences.

5. Epithetic and Counterepithetic *The*-Phrases

Beyond the problem cases so far treated, our treatment handles several other problems. They include prominently the treatment of epithetic *the*-phrases, which are illustrated by (18) and (19):

(18)   Harry borrowed ten dollars from me, but the bastard never paid me back.
(19)   I challenged a kibitzer to a chess game, but the disguised grand master mated me in ten moves.

For instance, in the game associated with (19) an application of (G. a(n)) yields a sentence of the form

(20) I challenged Boris to a chess game, but the
      disguised grand master mated me in ten moves,
      and Boris is a kibitzer.

An application of (G. anaphoric *the*) to (20) yields (21):

(21) I challenged Boris to a chess game, but Boris
      mated me in ten moves, Boris is a kibitzer, and
      Boris is a disguised grand master....

Hence (20) is true only if Boris is a grand master. Thus
part of the force of the use of an epithetic *the*-phrase in
(19), on our theory, is to let it be known that the kibitzer in question is a disguised grand master. Of course
this is precisely the point of using the epithetic *the*-
phrase.

The other example, (18), can be dealt with after we
have made a small change in the rule (G. anaphoric *the*).
(See sections 8 and 9 below.) All the other epithetic uses
of *the*-phrases are likewise easily accounted for.

The success of our theory in dealing with epithetic uses
of *the*-phrases encourages us to continue further the exploration of the semantical behavior of these phrases. In
its epithetic use a definite description is employed to attribute properties to the entity described that are not attributed to it by the head of the anaphoric definite description. Conversely, an anaphoric *the*-phrase need not
mention all the properties specified by its head, as
illustrated by the following examples:

(22) An old fisherman walked toward the beach. The
      fisherman was thinking of the day ahead.
(23) When Nancy Reagan went to a Sears mall store,
      she was disappointed to find that the store had
      no designer room.

We might call such *the*-phrases *counterepithetic*.

6. Vagaries of the Head-Anaphor Relation

The head of an anaphorically used *the*-phrase need not
specify a unique individual, but may specify several, or
perhaps a whole set of, individuals:

(24)   A couple was sitting on a bench. The man stood
       up.
(25) ·Two men walked along a road. The taller man
       carried a rucksack.
(26)   In a committee the chair cannot second any
       motion.

It is clear that our treatment can handle these cases.
For instance, the initial sentence in (25) prompts the
choice of two individuals by Myself. If the subgame associated with that sentence of (25) is to be followed by the
subgame associated with the other sentence, the former
subgame must be won by Myself. (Cf. chapter 3 above.)
For this purpose, the individuals chosen must be men
walking along a road. Then there exists a winning
strategy for Myself in the latter subgame, viz., choosing
the taller of the two men as the b mentioned in (**) of
(G. anaphoric *the*), if and only if this man carried a
rucksack. This obviously yields precisely the right
semantics for (25).
But there is more involved here than this. Instead of
any sharply defined syntactic head for an anaphoric *the*-
phrase, there need only be some antecedently handled expressions to introduce the members of the set *I*, so that
there is some structure on it that enables the players to
pick out suitable individuals from it (if the sentence in
question can be used to make a true statement). The following are cases in point:

(27)   In every group, the unit element commutes with
       any other element.
(28)   A freight train went by. The caboose was
       painted green.

This mechanism enables us to make statements about the
subject matter of the antecedent expressions by using a
definite description. The idea is that the use of such a
description can yield a true statement only if the intended
conditions are satisfied. This is illustrated by the following examples:

(29)   Surely there is night life in Tallahassee, but this
       weekend the lady is in Tampa.
(30)   Of course they have a graduate program in
       philosophy. They even managed to find a job for

the student.

For instance, the two clauses of (29) can both be true only if the night life in Tallahassee consists of one lady only. This is of course part of what (29) serves to express.

This phenomenon is, in a sense, a generalization of the epithetic uses of *the*-phrases. In such uses, a *the*-phrase is used to attribute further properties to a previously introduced individual. In the examples just discussed, a *the*-phrase is employed to put other conditions on the state of affairs outlined in the earlier part of the semantical game, viz., conditions that serve to guarantee the truth of what is being expressed by means of the definite description and thereby guarantee the existence and uniqueness that figure in the output sentence (**) of (G. anaphoric *the*). This observation shows that, at least occasionally, the requisite existence and uniqueness are not simply *presupposed* in a use of a definite description, but *asserted* thereby. This provides evidence against Strawson's thesis concerning definite descriptions.

7. The Anaphoric Use of Definite Descriptions As a Semantical Phenomenon

Our series of examples has led us further and further away from cases in which we can find a clearly defined head for the apparently anaphoric *the*-phrase. At the same time, the relation between the head and the *the*-phrase becomes increasingly less syntactical and less clear-cut. For instance, in (29) the relation of "the lady" to the only possible candidate for its head, "night life", is clearly not characterizable in any normal syntactical terms. Yet our game rule (G. anaphoric *the*) - which was originally formulated by focusing on the relation of clearly anaphoric expressions to their heads - handles (29) without any problems and without any qualifications.

These observations call our attention to certain important features of (G. anaphoric *the*), and through it to the nature of our approach to *the*-phrases. First, and most important, what is called the anaphoric relation, i.e., the relation of an anaphoric expression to its so-called head, plays no role in (G. anaphoric *the*)) and therefore no relevant role in our approach. What determines the individual referred to by an anaphoric definite description [i.e., the individual playing the role of the b in (G. anaphoric *the*)] in an optimal strategy for Myself is the whole set *I*. This set is not specified by any one phrase, but typically by several different phrases. Of course, one and only one of them will normally refer to b. That phrase will be the counterpart to the head of an anaphoric expression in the conventional treatments. However, we shall see later that it is not even clear that such a phrase can always be found. And even when it can be found, it is not determined by its *syntactical* relations to the anaphoric *the*-phrase in question. Rather, it is determined semantically via the determination of an optimal strategy for Myself. Hence what in the traditional treatments was the cornerstone of the treatment of an anaphoric *the*-phrase, i.e., its relation to a head, is in our treatment a derivative relation of somewhat dubious status, without any direct explanatory value.

Moreover, the set *I* is not determined in any straightforward way by the syntactical relations of the *the*-phrase in question to other ingredients of (*). The relation of the *the*-phrase to *I* is thus also semantical rather than syntactical.

This implies that in our treatment of anaphoric *the*-phrases the notion of head has lost most of its role. This can be illustrated by means of examples. For instance, we may consider the following pair of examples (adapted from Lauri Karttunen):

(31) If John buys a car or a motorcycle, he will take good care of the vehicle.

(32) If John buys a car and a motorcycle, he will take good care of the vehicle.

Here our rule (G. anaphoric *the*) assigns the right meaning (right truth conditions) to (31) (after the changes to be made in section 9 below). Applied to (32) it leads to the result that (32) is always false. Since this can be read off from the form (32), this sentence is useless for the purposes of discourse. Most linguists would - but not for this reason - probably mark it with an asterisk, i.e., would classify it as an unacceptable string. But more important, what is the head of "the vehicle" in the following sentence?

(33)   If John buys a car or even if he buys a motor-
        cycle, he will take good care of the vehicle.

In fact, the relation of an anaphoric *the*-phrase to its
putative "head" can go wrong in almost any imaginable
way. Here is a brief taxonomy of them:

(i)   Sometimes there is no syntactically privileged
        head at all. (Cf. (29) above.)

(ii)   When there is a plausible candidate, it may be of
        the wrong semantical category. (Cf. (27)-(28)
        above.)

(iii)   In other (acceptable) cases, there are two or
        three potential heads. (Cf. (31) above.)

(iv)   In other cases syntactically analogous to (iii), the
        duality of heads seems to make the sentence
        unacceptable. (Cf. (32) above.)

(v)   In some cases, the head gives more information
        about its referent than the anaphoric *the*-phrase;
        in other cases, less. (Cf. (22)-(26) above.)

At this point, our terminology might seem inappropriate. Anaphora is normally conceptualized in terms of some
head (antecedence) relation. Pronouns offer us the purest
cases of anaphora, and the very term "pro-noun" betrays
this antecedence idea. Since the head relation plays no
major role in our treatment, it might seem misleading to
call its objects *anaphoric the*-phrases in the first place.
But this claim prejudices an answer to an important
question. Maybe anaphoric *the*-phrases don't behave
"anaphorically" at all. But do other so-called anaphoric
expressions, including pronouns, behave in the expected
"anaphoric" way? Our terminology cannot be definitively
judged before this large and weighty question is answered.

8. The Quantifier-Exclusion Phenomenon
in Natural Languages

To reach a fully satisfactory theory of definite descriptions, we have to make a few changes in the crucial game

rule (G. anaphoric *the*). The first change is that we have
to include in *I* all the individuals referred to by proper
names that occur in the initial sentence S of a semantical
game G(S). The need for this change is obvious, and examples are easily found to illustrate it.

The second change is a special case of a widespread
phenomenon often discussed, but in different terms, in the
literature. The case that concerns us here is seen from
examples of the following sort:

(34)   John saw the man.
(35)   Harry Truman was an early riser. Newsmen fre-
       quently talked to the peppery politician during
       his early morning constitutional.
(36)   Every company commander received the battle
       order. The order was acknowledged by the
       officer.
(37)   Every company commander received the battle
       order from the officer.
(38)   Jane remembered her misfortunes. The poor girl
       was in tears.
(39)   Jane remembered the poor girl's misfortunes. She
       was in tears.
(40)   The poor girl remembered her misfortunes. Jane
       was in tears.
(41)   Jimmy doubted the president.
(42)   Jimmy doubted that the president could do that.

In (34) "the man" cannot refer to John, while in (35)
"the peppery politician" obviously refers to Harry Truman.
In (36), "the officer" could refer to a company commander,
whereas in (37) it cannot. In (38), "the poor girl" can
refer to Jane, while it cannot in (39). In (41), Jimmy
can't be the president referred to, whereas in (42) he can
be.

The generalization that is illustrated by these examples
is that an anaphoric *the*-phrase cannot refer to an individual introduced by a word or phrase occurring *in the
same clause as it*. In terms of our approach, this means
that the set *I* must not contain individuals introduced by
expressions that occur in the same clause (are commanded
by all the same sentence markers) as the *the*-phrase "the
Y who Z". "Introduced by" means here either (i) referred
to (as by names) or (ii) introduced by applications of
game rules as a value (reference of a substitution-value)

for. We shall call the phenomenon codified by this change in *I* the *exclusion phenomenon*.

This modification deserves several further comments. First, its force is somewhat hidden by another, altogether different principle that seems to be largely conversational and that says, roughly, that whenever an anaphoric pronoun serves the same purpose as an anaphoric *the*-phrase, the former is to be preferred to the latter. For this reason, there is a shade of awkwardness in having "the poor girl" in (38) refer to Jane. However, this principle seems to be merely conversational, and merely preferential.

Second, the exclusion phenomenon codified by the second change in *I* is much more general, and seems to characterize all anaphoric expressions, e.g., pronouns. This case has been discussed by Bach and Partee.[8] Indeed, one can find parallel examples employing pronouns instead of *the*-phrases that illustrate an analogous phenomenon.

This exclusion phenomenon (in the case of the semantical behavior of pronouns) is described by Bach and Partee as constituting a "striking contrast" to the way variables of quantification behave in formal languages. There is indeed a sharp difference between the two cases, but there is also a partial but striking counterpart to the exclusion phenomenon in formal quantification theory (predicate calculus). There is a natural but rarely discussed variant of the usual formalisms of quantification theory that is closely related to the exclusion phenomenon.[9] It is what Wittgenstein preferred in the *Tractatus*.[10] He put his point as follows:

> Thus I do not write 'f(a,b).a=b', but 'f(a,a)' (or 'f(b,b)'); and not 'f(a,b).$\sim$a=b', but 'f(a,b)'.
> And analogously I do not write '(Ex,y).f(x,y). x=y', but '(Ex).f(x,x)'; and not '(Ex,y).f(x,y). $\sim$x=y', but '(Ex,y).f(x,y)'.
> (So Russell's '(Ex,y).f(x,y)' becomes '(Ex,y). f(x,y). v .(Ex). f(x,x)'.)   (5.531-2)

This way of treating quantifiers and free singular terms nevertheless amounts to a relatively small change in the use of quantifiers. It can be captured in semantical games connected with formal languages by means of the following rules:

(G.E$_{ex}$) When a game has reached a sentence (Ex)F[x], an individual, call it "b", may be selected by Myself, different from all the individuals introduced as values of quantifiers in whose scope (Ex)F[x] occurs in the game and different from the individuals referred to by the individual constants in the initial sentence. The game is then continued with respect to F[b].

(G.U$_{ex}$) The same for the sentence (x)F[x], except that b is chosen by Nature.

We shall call these the *exclusion rules* for quantifiers. The difference between them and the usual (inclusion) rules can be explained intuitively by thinking (as we all do in elementary probability theory) of the choices of individuals connected with quantifiers (in semantical games) as draws of certain "balls" (individuals) from an "urn" (the model with respect to which our formal language is interpreted). Then the inclusion rules codify a quantification theory with replacement, as probability theorists say, whereas the exclusion rules formalize a logic of quantification without replacement. Thus the phenomenon of exclusion marks only an insignificant departure from the usual treatments of quantification theory. It does not constitute a striking contrast between formal and natural languages.

All told, the exclusion phenomenon merely means that in natural languages a partially exclusive interpretation of quantifiers is presupposed. The only thing that prevents us from formulating a precise counterpart to the modified rule (G. anaphoric *the*) for formal languages is that in these languages the requisite notion of clause (syntacticians' S-node) is not defined in a way that would give rise to interesting results.

There are certain apparent exceptions to what has been said above about the exclusion phenomenon and also certain asymmetries between pronouns and *the*-phrases that might seem to belie what we have said. In reality, however, these exceptions prove to be merely apparent. Hence they serve to illustrate forcefully the advantages of a game-theoretical approach.

These phenomena are illustrated by the following examples:

(43)   Jane saw her sister.
(44)   Jane remembered her misfortune.
(45)   Jane remembered the poor girl's misfortune.

Contrary to what we perhaps have led the reader to expect, "her" can mean the same as "Jane's" in (43)-(44), while "the poor girl's" in (45) can't.

An explanation is easily obtained, however. In an earlier paper, Hintikka and Carlson have formulated a game rule for genitives in English.[11] That rule will take the players from (43) to a sentence of the form (46):

(46)   Jane saw Jill, and Jill is $\left\{ \begin{matrix} a \\ the \end{matrix} \right\}$ sister of hers.

Likewise, the same rule will have the effect of replacing (44) by an expression similar to the following:[12]

(47)   Jane remembered the Great Crash of 1929, and the Great Crash of 1929 is $\left\{ \begin{matrix} a \\ the \end{matrix} \right\}$ misfortune of hers.

Now in (46)-(47) "hers" occurs in a clause different from the clause that contains "Jane". Hence, it can pick out Jane.

In contrast, in (45) (G. anaphoric *the*) presumably is to be applied before (G. genitive), and such an order of rule application excludes Jane from being the poor girl mentioned in (45). Thus an explanation of the apparent discrepancies is easily obtained. Notice that this explanation does not make any use of the relation of coreference as a primitive explanatory concept.

The phenomenon we are dealing with here (partially exclusive interpretation of quantifiers) is, in the case of pronouns, closely related to the use of reflexive pronouns. These pronouns are used precisely to enforce the identities that would otherwise (i.e., if ordinary pronouns were used) be excluded.

Now we are also in a position to deal with Mates-type uses of definite descriptions.[13] In this type of example, the choice of b in (G. anaphoric *the*) might depend on earlier choices of individuals by the players, including Nature, and this possibility is built into our treatment.

Relevant examples include the following:

(48)   Every marriage has its problems. Sometimes it's

the husband who's the source of the problems, sometimes the wife.

(49) The best advisor of every young mother is her mother.

9. Inductive Domains

Another change is needed in cases where several subgames are involved in a semantical game. The game rule (G. anaphoric *the*) is predicated on the idea that the members of *I* are, intuitively speaking, the individuals available to the players at the time (G. anaphoric *the*) is applied. If such an application takes place in one of the later subgames, say G, the players have available to them more than those individuals chosen by the players at the earlier stages of the ongoing subgame. They may also have access to certain strategies used by one of the players in earlier subgames. (This is the gist of the subgame idea. See chapter 3 above, and the discussion of example (7) at the end of section 4 above.)[14] What are these strategies? They are functions whose arguments and values are members of our domain of individuals, or functionals whose arguments can be such functions, etc. Hence the definition of *I* in (G. anaphoric *the*) has to be extended further. The new definition will be the following:

(Definition of *I*)   *I* is the smallest set that contains *J* and is closed with respect to the totality of functions and functionals available to Myself at the time when the application of (G. anaphoric *the*) is made, where *J* is the set of individuals chosen by the players up to that point in the subgame in question plus the individuals referred to by proper names (of individuals) in the initial sentence of the semantical game.

Following the terminology of logicians, we shall call this definition of *I* an *inductive* one.

An example where this new definition of *I* comes into play is the following:

(50)   If John gives a Christmas present and a card to
       each boy today, some boy will open the present
       right away.

Here the strategy of the player who is trying to verify the
antecedent of (50) - in the subgame associated with it - is
"remembered" by Myself when (G. anaphoric *the*) is
applied in the second subgame, which is connected with
the consequent of (50). This strategy includes a function
f that maps boys into their presents, if the overall game is
to go into the second subgame. Hence, *I* does not contain
only the individual chosen by Myself in the second subgame to instantiate "some boy". It also contains the f(b),
that is, the gift given to that boy. With this proviso, (G.
anaphoric *the*) assigns the right meaning to (50). In the
second subgame, there exists a winning strategy for Myself if it is the boy b who opens the present f(b) right
away. This is precisely when we would, intuitively,
consider the consequent true in circumstances in which the
antecedent is true, i.e., in circumstances in which there
is a function f that assigns to each boy a gift given to him
by John.

10. Anaphoric Definite Descriptions and
Pronominal Anaphora

There is obviously a close parallel between anaphorically
used definite descriptions and anaphoric pronouns. For
instance, the phenomena studied above in sections 8 and
10 are largely parallel to what we find with pronouns.
Likewise, several of the theoretically interesting uses of
the-phrases admit of a pronominal analogue. For instance,
parallel with (29) we have (51):

(51)   Surely there is night life in Tallahassee, but this
       weekend she is in Tampa.

Likewise, parallel with (31) we have (52):

(52)   If John buys a car or a motorcycle, he will take
       good care of it.

Parallel with (3) we have (53):

(53)   Nobody has stolen your missing diamonds, for a

thief would have had to scale a slippery 50-foot wall. Moreover, he would have had to elude detection by an extemely sophisticated security system.

Furthermore, analogous to the interesting phenomenon of "pronouns of laziness" we have "definite descriptions of laziness", illustrated by the following example:

> (54)   Any man who gives his paycheck to his wife is wiser than any man who gives the check to his mistress.

It is not unnatural to expect that the underlying mechanism of "definite descriptions of laziness" is the same as that of "pronouns of laziness".

These significant parallels suggest a theory of pronouns that would be analogous to our theory of definite descriptions in their anaphoric use. This theory would codify the suggestion made above in section 7 that maybe anaphoric pronouns, like anaphoric definite descriptions, don't, after all, behave "anaphorically" in the usual sense of the word, that is, don't rely essentially on the head-anaphor relation. Even though we believe in the viability of such a theory, we shall not try to develop it here.[15] It is nevertheless worth noting that such a theory would amount to viewing pronominal anaphora as a basically semantical phenomenon, and would therefore differ from most of the existing accounts of pronominal anaphora. Here we shall merely point out one theoretically interesting application of the analogy.

In an earlier paper, Hintikka and Carlson have discussed pronouns whose head is a quantifier phrase.[16] Their problem is illustrated by the following example:

> (55)   If Bill owns a donkey, he beats it.

They use the subgame idea, and point out that in the second subgame the only plausible candidate for the reference of "it" is, intuitively speaking, the donkey mentioned in the antecedent. This line of thought is seriously incomplete, however, in that it does not give explicit rules for picking out the individual. Hence their results remain tentative, because the crucial referential mechanism of pronouns is left without a real analysis.

Our results here serve to fill this gap. First, we may observe that (55) has an analogue for definite descriptions:

(56) If Bill owns a donkey, he beats the donkey.

By using the subgame idea, (56) can be handled in the same way as (55) is treated by Hintikka and Carlson. In the second subgame, Myself "remembers" the strategy used by Nature to verify the antecedent in the first subgame. That strategy consists of the choice of an individual that is to serve as the value of "a donkey". The players go to the second subgame only if the individual so chosen by Nature is a donkey owned by Bill. This means that *I* consists of this one donkey alone. Hence we can see from (G. anaphoric *the*) that the only individual available to Myself for the role of b is this donkey. Accordingly, there exists a winning strategy for Myself in the second subgame if and only if it is beaten by Bill. This obviously assigns the right meaning to (56).

Thus (G. anaphoric *the*) (together with the subgame idea) enables us to deal with (56) in the way Hintikka and Carlson handled (55), but without reliance on any informal principles. This suffices to vindicate the theoretical significance of the ideas presented by Hintikka and Carlson.

Of course, their ideas are supposed to apply to pronominal anaphora rather than to anaphoric uses of *the*-phrases. Hence, they are seen to be literally true only if anaphoric pronouns can be treated in the same way as anaphoric definite descriptions. To what extent this is the case remains to be examined. However, most of the theoretical interest of the paper by Hintikka and Carlson remains intact even if their ideas should only apply to anaphoric *the*-phrases. For instance, their explanation of why the indefinite article in (56) has the surface force of a universal quantifier is obviously applicable also to (55). If we allow only intrasentential anaphoric relations, the acceptability of the following examples parallels the acceptability of similar examples considered by Hintikka and Carlson in which "it" stands in for "the donkey":

(56) If Bill owns a donkey, he beats the donkey.
(57) *If Bill owns every donkey, he beats the donkey.
(58) Bill beats a donkey if he owns the donkey.

(59)   *Bill beats every donkey if he owns the donkey.

(57) is unacceptable, or at least much less acceptable than (56). Also, (58), unlike (56), has a reading on which the indefinite article is an existential quantifier rather than a universal quantifier. All these phenomena parallel the data Hintikka and Carlson tried to explain, and they are explainable in our present theory without any gaps left at the mercy of informal considerations.

NOTES

[1] We take this "paradigm of philosophy" (Ramsey) to be familiar to the reader. Russell's classic statement of it is found in "On Denoting", *Mind* n.s. 14 (1905), 479-93, reprinted in (among many other places) Douglas Lackey, editor, *Essays in Analysis*, Allen & Unwin, London, 1973, pp. 103-19. A selection of the subsequent literature is brought together in E. D. Klemke, editor, *Essays on Bertrand Russell*, University of Illinois Press, Urbana, Illinois, 1970.

[2] We have discussed the situation in our joint paper, "Different Uses of the Definite Article", *Communication and Cognition*, forthcoming. There it is shown how to understand the Russellian as well as the generic use of *the*-phrases as variants of the anaphoric use.

[3] A distinction is often made between deixis and anaphora. (See, for example, John Lyons, *Semantics*, vols. 1 and 2, Cambridge University Press, Cambridge, 1977.) The former is the type of reference by which things in the nonlinguistic, e.g., perceptual, situation are referred to, while the latter is the type of reference by which things in the linguistic situation are referred to. We shall in effect argue later in this chapter that this distinction is much less clear than usually assumed. There is a tacit "deictic" element even in typical cases of "anaphora".

[4] See Russell, "On Denoting", pp. 114-15 of the Lackey reprint.

[5] For the rule (G. genitive), see Jaakko Hintikka and Lauri Carlson, "Pronouns of Laziness in Game-Theoretical Semantics", *Theoretical Linguistics* 4 (1977), 1-29, especially pp. 7-8.

[6] See chapter 3 above; also see Jaakko Hintikka and

Lauri Carlson, "Conditionals, Generic Quantifiers, and Other Applications of Subgames", in Esa Saarinen, editor, *Game-Theoretical Semantics*, D. Reidel, Dordrecht, 1979, pp. 179–214, especially pp. 183ff.

[7] There are nevertheless certain further subtleties about the role of proper names in the game rule (G. anaphoric *the*), but we shall overlook them here.

[8] Emmon Bach and Barbara Partee, "Anaphora and Semantic Structure", in Jody Kreiman and A. E. Uteda, editors, *Papers from the Parasession on Pronouns and Anaphora*, Chicago Linguistic Society, Chicago, 1980, pp. 1–28.

[9] It is discussed by Jaakko Hintikka in "Identity, Variables, and Impredicative Definitions", *Journal of Symbolic Logic* 21 (1956), 225–45, and in chapter 1 of his *Logic, Language-Games, and Information*, Clarendon Press, Oxford, 1973.

[10] Ludwig Wittgenstein, *Tractatus Logico-Philosophicus*, Kegan Paul, London, 1921.

[11] Hintikka and Carlson, "Pronouns of Laziness". In that paper (G. gen) is formulated to be applicable to sentences of the form

$$X - Y's \ Z - W,$$

where Y is a proper name. But an extension to pronouns is mentioned there that is different from what we do here: "We can nevertheless extend (G. gen) to situations in which 'Y's' is replaced by the genitive of a pronoun. Then in the output of (G. gen) 'Y' must be replaced by its antecedent." In this paper we don't replace the pronoun "hers" by an intrasentential antecedent. The context can provide other possible antecedents in certain cases. In (43), for example, it need not be Jane's sister that Jane saw.

[12] For the sake of argument, we are treating "The Great Crash of 1929" as if it were a proper name.

[13] See Benson Mates, "Descriptions and Reference", *Foundations of Language* 10 (1973), 409–18.

[14] Cf. also Hintikka and Carlson, "Conditionals, Generic Quantifiers, and Other Applications of Subgames".

[15] Such a development is in progress in our joint paper "Towards a Semantical Theory of Pronominal Anaphora" (in preparation).

[16] Hintikka and Carlson, "Conditionals, Generic Quantifiers, and Other Applications of Subgames".

Chapter 7

"IS", SEMANTICAL GAMES,
AND SEMANTICAL RELATIVITY

1. The Frege Trichotomy

If there is a doctrine shared by almost all analysts of the
semantics of natural language these days, it is the distinction between different senses of "is": the "is" of predication, the "is" of identity, and the "is" of existence.
The "is" of predication is often called the copula. Some
writers add an alleged "is" of class inclusion as the fourth
reading. The most forceful philosophical proponent of the
polysemy of "is" is undoubtedly Bertrand Russell. In *The
Principles of Mathematics*[1] he writes:

> The word *is* is terribly ambiguous, and great care is
> necessary in order not to confound its various mean-
> ings. We have (1) the sense in which it asserts Being,
> as in "*A* is"; (2) the sense of identity; (3) the sense
> of predication, as in "*A* is human"; (4) the sense of "*A*
> is a-man" ... which is very like identity.[2] In addition
> to these there are less common uses ... where a rela-
> tion of assertions is meant ... which ... gives rise to
> formal implication.

Russell goes on to refer to De Morgan's *Formal Logic*
(1847, pp. 49-50) for an earlier treatment of the distinction. In fact, De Morgan there distinguishes from each
other "the 'is' of applicability", "the 'is' of possession of
all essential characteristics", and "the 'is' of identity", but
not the "is" of existence.

The importance that Russell assigns to the trichotomy is
seen from *Our Knowledge of the External World,*[3] where it
is introduced as "the first serious advance in real logic
since the time of the Greeks". What Russell is now emphasizing is the contrast between "Socrates is mortal" and
"All men are mortal", in other words, between predication
and class-inclusion.

In 1914 Russell no longer refers to De Morgan's trichotomy as a precursor of his distinction. He now shows a

much firmer grasp of the main gateway of the trichotomy
into modern discussion, ascribing it to Frege's and Peano's
work.

It is indeed true that the respective formalisms of Frege
and Peano are probably the original sources for the distinction in recent philosophy. However, the distinction is
for Frege not only a feature of a convenient formalism but
reflects important semantical and even ontological (categorical) differences, even though Frege did not think that
we can explicitly discuss semantical matters of this sort.
The trichotomy is such an integral part of Frege's main
achievement - the modern conception of a system of logic -
that in this chapter I shall call it the Frege trichotomy.[4]

Through the formalism of Frege and Peano, and even
more through the notation of the *Principia* of Russell and
Whitehead, the trichotomy became an important constituent
of the contemporary concept of first-order logic. (Among
the aliases of this basic part of logic there are "lower
predicate calculus", "quantification theory", "elementary
logic", etc.) In first-order logic, the "is" of identity is
typically expressed by "=", the "is" of existence by the
existential quantifier, and the "is" of predication by predicative juxtaposition, as in "P(a)". These are entirely
different ingredients of first-order language both semantically and syntactically.

Hence, anyone who uses first-order logic as a canonical
notation for semantical purposes is committed to the trichotomy. The same goes for its immediate extensions.
Accordingly, philosophers, logicians, and linguists as di-
vergent as Quine, Davidson, Chomsky, and Lakoff are in
the same boat with respect to the Frege trichotomy.[5]

2. Game-Theoretical Semantics: General Ideas

In view of the ubiquity of the Frege trichotomy, it is of
interest to see that, given certain not implausible assumptions, it is demonstrably false. The most important assumption apparently needed for the demonstration is the
soundness of the approach to English semantics - or at
least to the semantics of a fragment of English - that has
been called game-theoretical semantics.[6] For our present
purposes, we have to know only some of the main aspects
of that approach.

Game-theoretical semantics is a genuine semantical

theory because it allows us to define the crucial notion of truth[7] for each sentence of a certain, rather loosely defined, fragment F of English.[8] This fragment contains prominently such quantifier phrases as

(1)   Some Y who Z.

Instead of "some", we can have here "a" (or its phonetic variant "an"), "every", "any", or "each". Instead of "who", we can have "which", "where", "when", etc. Moreover, Y and Z are in (1) assumed to be in the singular, and "who" is assumed to be in the subject position of "who Z"; both these restrictions can be relaxed.

   The truth of a sentence S of F is defined as the existence of a winning strategy for the player called *Myself* in a two-person game G(S) against an opponent called *Nature*. By the same token, falsity means that there exists a winning strategy for Nature. The terms "strategy" and "winning strategy" are used here in the precise senses given to them in the mathematical theory of games.[9] For most purposes, though, their commonsense meanings are fairly accurate clues to their import. However, it is noteworthy that a strategy in our sense is a complete strategy: it is a rule specifying a player's move in every situation that could conceivably arise in a game. (The information that a player has or does not have concerning other moves is of course a part of the specification of the situation.) Thus a play of a game reduces conceptually to the choice of a strategy by each player. These choices fully determine the course of a game, including its outcome.

   Since truth values can be assigned only to interpreted sentences, S must be assumed to belong to a language interpreted with respect to some domain D of individuals. This means that the truth-values of all the atomic sentences of F are determined, and so are those of atomic sentences that also contain proper names of members of D. The task of game-theoretical semantics is thus twofold: (1) to extend the concept of truth from atomic to nonatomic sentences; (2) to clarify the concept of atomic sentence.

   This enables a game-theoretical semanticist to define what it means for Myself (Nature) to win a play of the game: it means for the game to end with a true (false) atomic sentence. Among the atomic sentences of our fragment F of English we include those that contain proper names of members of D in addition to the vocabulary of F itself. This concludes our definition of truth in game-theoretical semantics. For truth (falsity) was defined as the existence of a winning strategy for Myself (Nature). A winning strategy for a player is of course one that guides that player to a win against any choice of a strategy by the opponent. And we just defined what it means for a player to win.

Of course, in natural languages the notion of an atomic sentence is less clear than it is in formal languages. As we just saw, it enters into our semantical games through a definition of the end points of a game. The game G(S) begins with S, and each move takes the players from a sentence S' of English to another one S", which typically is simpler than S'. Atomic sentences are the stopping points that allow no further application of our rules.

In dealing with atomic sentences, we thus face three problems:

(i)   We have to make sure that the end-point sentences are so simple that their truth values are determined by the interpretation of the non-logical words of our fragment of English.[10]

(ii) We have to make sure that game rules eventually lead to atomic sentences.

(iii) We have to make sure that no game rules apply to sentences whose truth values are determined by the interpretation. Otherwise, infinitely self-repeating loops might come about.[11]

3. Game-Theoretical Rules for Quantifiers

Here I shall discuss only problem (iii), and that only partially. In order to see what form the problem takes, we have to consider some actual game rules or at least special cases of such rules. Here are a few such special cases:[12]

(G. some)   If the game has reached a sentence of the form

X – some Y who Z – W

an individual may be chosen (from D) by Myself. Let the proper name of this individual be "b". (If it does not have a proper name, the players give it one.) The game is then continued with respect to

X - b - W, b is a Y, and b Z.

(G. a(n)) The same as (G. some) except that "a(n)" takes the place of "some".

(G. every) If the game has reached a sentence of the form

X - every Y who Z - W,

a member of D may be chosen by Nature. Let the proper name of the individual chosen be "b". (If it does not have a proper name, the players give it one.) The game is then continued with respect to

X - b - W, if b is a Y and b Z.

(G. any) The same as (G. every) except that "any" takes the place of "every".

(G. each) Analogously for "each".

These game rules can perhaps be best appreciated by thinking of each G(S) as an attempt on the part of Myself to verify S against Nature's falsificatory efforts. The attempted verification or falsification proceeds by examples. In applying each quantifier rule, one of the players chooses an individual from D that that player hopes will lead to the right outcome, i.e., to a win for the player who makes the move. This hope concerns the outcome of the rest of the game, which is typically played beginning with

X - b - W.

The other part of the output of our quantifier rules serves

merely to guarantee that the chosen individual is of the right kind. This is what the clause

> b is a Y and b Z

is designed to secure. Whether it is combined with the rest as a conjunct or as the antecedent of a conditional depends merely on which player makes the move.

4. Other Game Rules

The rules so far listed are supposed to handle phrases beginning with English quantifier words, such as the words "some", "a(n)", "every", "any", and "each". Over and above these rules, we also need rules for propositional connectives, such as "and", "or", "if", etc.[13] The following are approximations to such rules:

(G. and)   If the game has reached a sentence of the form

$$X_1, X_2, \ldots, \text{and } X_j,$$

where the X_i ($i = 1, 2, \ldots, j$) are clauses, Nature may choose an X_i, and the game is continued with respect to it.

(G. or)   If the game has reached a sentence of the form

$$X_1, X_2, \ldots, \text{or } X_j,$$

where the X_i ($i = 1, 2, \ldots, j$) are clauses, Myself may choose a disjunct X_i, and the game is continued with respect to it.

In (G. and) and (G. or), it must be required that the X_i chosen contains only such anaphoric pronouns as have proper names as their grammatical antecedents (head-noun phrases) when these antecedents are in a different conjunct or disjunct. Each of these pronouns in the chosen X_i is then replaced by its antecedent. An analogous requirement is needed in the following rule:

(G. if)   If the game has reached a sentence of the form

If X, Y

or of the form

Y if X

either Y or neg[X] is chosen by Myself, and the game is continued with respect to Myself's choice.

In (G. if), neg[X] expresses the process of forming the (semantical) negation of a sentence X in English. It is not studied in the present chapter. (See chapter 4 above.)

A much more realistic game rule for conditionals is formulated in Jaakko Hintikka and Lauri Carlson, "Conditionals, Generic Quantifiers, and Other Applications of Subgames".[14] (See also chapter 3 above.)

Other rules will deal with phrasal uses of "and" and "or". The following are approximations to such rules:

(G. phrasal and)   If the game has reached a sentence of the form

(*) $X - Y_1, Y_2, \ldots,$ and $Y_j - Z,$

where the Y_i (i = 1,2,..., j) are phrases rather than clauses, Nature may choose a Y_i, and the game is continued with respect to

(**) $X' - Y_i - Z',$

where $X' - Z'$ is identical with $X - Z$ except when the phrase "Y_1, Y_2, ..., and Y_j" occupies the subject position of some clause in (*). In that case $X' - Z'$ is like $X - Z$ except that the finite verb of the clause in question is in the singular.

One more proviso is needed here, viz., that in (**) all the pronouns that in (*) had the phrase "Y_1, Y_2, ..., and Y_j" as their grammatical antecedent are changed into their corresponding singular forms.

   (G. phrasal or)   Formulated analogously.

   (G. not)   If the game has reached a sentence of the
               form

               neg[X],

               the two players switch roles (as defined by
               these game rules and the rules for winning
               and losing), and the game is continued with
               respect to X.

Most of the details of propositional game rules are
irrelevant for our present purposes.

   Numerous further game rules are obviously needed to
extend the fragment of English that is taken care by these
rules. The following is an example of such rules. It is
calculated to handle predicatively used adjectives (in Peter
Geach's sense).[15]

   (G. pred)   If the game has reached a sentence of
                the form

                (*)   b is a(n) X Y,

                where b is a proper name and X is a
                predicatively used adjective, then (*) may
                be replaced by

                (**)   b is a(n) Y and b is X,

                and the game is continued with respect
                to it.

5. The Semantics of Simple Predications

One remarkable thing about our quantifier rules is that
"any" always marks Nature's move, i.e., is always a universal quantifier, and "a(n)" always marks a move made
by Myself, i.e., is always an existential quantifier. How
these words apparently switch their meanings is discussed
by Jaakko Hintikka and Lauri Carlson elsewhere.[16] This

claim of univocity is highly nontrivial, running contrary to the views of many linguists.[17]

From the rules listed above it is seen that each quantifier rule effects a simplification by eliminating one relative clause. Each application of a propositional rule eliminates one connective word ("and", "or", "if", etc.). Moreover, all quantifier rules other than (G. a(n)) eliminate one quantifier word in favor of "a(n)". Hence we have to look at (G. a(n)) to see how an infinite regress – or, rather, a closed loop – can come about, and how it can be avoided. Let us see how (G. a(n)) works in the simplest case, i.e., as applied to a sentence to which no other rules are applicable.

Let us assume that the game has reached the following sentence:

(2)   Jack is a boy.

The only rule that is applicable here is (G. a(n)), with X = "Jack is", Y = "boy", Z = ϕ, and W = ϕ. A choice of an individual by Myself in accordance with (G. a(n)) will lead us to a sentence of the following form:

(3)   Jack is John Jr., and John Jr. is a boy.

This arose from (2) by plugging "John Jr." in for "a boy" in (2), and conjoining the result with "John Jr. is a Y", i.e., with "John Jr. is a boy". It follows that the first "is" of (3) is the same "is" as is found in (2), while the second "is" of (3) is the kind of "is" that is found in the output sentence of all the quantifier rules mentioned above. Since the second conjunct of (3) is of the same form as (1), this second "is" of (3) must likewise be identical with the "is" of (2). It follows that *all three occurrences of "is" in (2)-(3) are identical in meaning*.

The following scheme illustrates the situation:

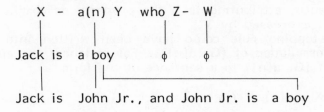

Here the solid lines indicate the identity of the component expressions, and dotted lines indicate substitution.

6. Comparisons with the Fregean View

Now the only possible way of handling the first "is" of (3) in the Frege-Russell trichotomy is to call it an "is" of identity. Almost equally clearly, an occurrence of "is" such as the second one in (3) has to be interpreted as an "is" of predication. For this "is" is an instance of the kind of "a(n)" that occurs in the output of our quantifier rules. And such an "is" is eminently calculated to serve as a vehicle of predication. As was noted above, the clauses in which such an "is" occurs specify the kinds of individuals to which the players have to restrict their choices if they want to have any hope of winning.

There is another, concurrent reason for considering the second "is" of (3) as an "is" of predication - in so far as the received trichotomy is applicable here. It results from the problem of avoiding loops, which was mentioned at the start of my argument. Since the second conjunct of (3) - the output of our application of (G. a(n)) to (2) - has the same form as (2), an infinite loop threatens us here. The obvious way out is to have a stopping rule that says that sentences of the form

(4)   b is a(n) Y

are to be treated as atomic sentences, where "b" is a placeholder for proper names, Y does not contain any relative clauses or attributively used adjectives, and no rule except (G. a(n)) is applicable. But in view of the considerations presented above concerning atomic formulas, it follows that the interpretation of "b" and of the non-logical words in Y suffices to determine the truth-value of (4). And this obviously means taking (4) to be a predicative sentence, attributing to b the property or complex of properties expressed by Y.

This stopping rule could have been written into the original formulation of (G. a(n)). For instance, the applicability of (G. a(n)) to a sentence of the form

X - a(n) T Y who Z - W

can be made contingent on either T's, W's or Z's being ≠
φ.

The stopping rule of course spoils the particular argu-
ment I used that depended on a transition from (2) to (3).
However, a slightly more complicated parallel argument is
readily constructed by starting from a sentence such as
"Jack is a bright boy" or "Jack is a boy who lives in
Boston" that satisfies the condition that T ≠ φ or Z ≠ φ.

Moreover, (2) clearly has to be understood as being an
existential statement like any other sentence of our fragment containing the English indefinite article, its existential force being carried by the combination of words "is
a". This, in turn, comes close to saying that the "is" of
(2) is an "is" of existence. By parity of cases, the same
holds for the latter of the two instances of "is" in (3).
One and the same rule (G. a(n)) applies to both (barring
only our inessential convention that serves to cut off
closed loops of applications of game rules). This rule
lends "a(n)" the force characteristic of an existential
quantifier in English. Hence they both carry an existential force, even though this force is partly due to the
semantical interplay of the words "is" and "a", and can
therefore be considered as instances of the "is" of existence.

But we just saw that all the different occurrences of
"is" in (2) and (3), which according to the Frege trichotomy carry different senses of "is", must be considered
synonyms. Hence Frege and the Fregeans are simply
wrong: we cannot always separate from each other the "is"
of identity, the "is" of predication, and the "is" of
existence.

The identity of the allegedly different senses of "is"
extends to the fourth one, the "is" of class inclusion.
This use of "is" is illustrated by the following sentence:

(5)   A whale is a mammal.

All we have to assume here is that "a whale" is to be understood here *de re*. Then (6) can be paraphrased as follows:

(6)   If an animal is a whale, it is a mammal.

Sentences of this sort are discussed at length on the basis
of game-theoretical semantics by Jaakko Hintikka and Lauri

Carlson.[18] The treatment outlined there turns on handling the phrase "is a" in (5) and its descendant, the second occurrence of this phrase in (6), in the same way as anywhere else. Moreover, the first "is a" in (6) is treated on a par with its other occurrences. Hence the alleged "is" of class inclusion can be treated in game-theoretical semantics. The meaning of "is a" that it involves turns out to be identical with the other senses of this phrase that we have encountered. (Not only is it possible to treat "is a" in (6) as other uses of these words are treated in the Hintikka-Carlson theory; their approach depends essentially on treating "is a" in (6) in the same way as in its other occurrences.) If there is a new semantical phenomenon in (6), compared with my earlier examples, it is the conditional nature of the proposition expressed by (6), not the presence of any new sense of "is" or "is a".

7. The Frege Trichotomy Fails

All told, we can see that, according to game-theoretical semantics, the Frege trichotomy or quadripartition is not only dispensable but positively mistaken. What must be considered nearly paradigmatic instances of the "is" of identity and the "is" of predication must be considered synonymous, and the same goes largely for their relation to the "is" of existence and the "is" of class inclusion. Frege and Russell, Quine and Davidson, as well as Chomsky and Lakoff, are thus all proved wrong.

What this means is that the currently most popular framework of semantical representation is shown to be incorrect. This result cuts deep into the central concepts of semantics. One of the most important of these is the concept of ambiguity. A word that Frege and company claimed to be ambiguous has turned out to be univocal after all in game-theoretical semantics. And this word is not any old recondite philosophical term; it is the verb probably most central for the concerns of logicians, philosophers, and linguists: the verb "to be".

8. "Is" in Game-Theoretical Semantics

What has been said requires a number of further comments. First, I am of course not denying that there are differences between different uses of "is". For instance, there will be among my atomic sentences two (in fact, more than two) different kinds of sentences containing "is". They will have the following forms:

(7)   b is a(n) Y

and

(8)   b is X.

This observation does not have any force, however, as an attempt to establish a difference in meaning between the "is" in (7) and the "is" in (8). The obvious difference between (7) and (8) is that the former sentence contains a common noun and the latter an adjective. This suffices to explain the surface difference between the two without postulating different meanings of "is".

It may be that the deeper logic and semantics of the contrast between (7) and (8) is of interest and that it requires further discussion. It may for instance be suggested that the logic of the difference between (7) and (8) is, in the last analysis, the same as the underlying logic of Aristotle's famous distinction between essential and accidental predication. (Notice that I am not suggesting that the grammatical distinction between common nouns and adjectives is a reliable symptom of the Aristotelian contrast.) However, this does not yet establish a semantical difference between the two occurrences of "is".

It is true that in game-theoretical semantics there is no single rule that applies to "is". Its several uses are taken care of by means of rules that depend on the presence of other words in a sentence. Many such rules have yet to be formulated. For instance, we have not so far included in our fragment continuous-tense sentences of the form "John is running." Depending on the word that triggers an application of a game rule, different rules may serve to handle "is" in different contexts. In this sense, on the game-theoretical account there are semantically different uses of "is". However, it does not follow that such differences coincide with the Fregean trichotomy. On the contrary, we have seen that game-theoretical semantics forces us to declare as synonyms some of the paradigmatic occurrences of "is" claimed by the Fregeans to instantiate the several senses of "is".

A glimpse of the game rule (G. pred) shows that the same can be said of the occurrences of "is" in (7) and (8). In (G. pred), the two occurrences of "is" in its output sentence are both naturally considered as descendants of the "is" in the input sentence of (G. pred). (It is a very sound general methodological principle to assume that no game rule may introduce new lexical material into a sentence, with the sole exception of such "auxiliary" elements as propositional connectives and the indefinite article.) Hence the two occurrences of "is" in the output sentence (**) of (G. pred) are both synonymous with the "is" of (*) in (G. pred), and therefore synonymous with each other. The occurrences of "is" in (7) and (8) are therefore semantically identical, for they can be descendants of the same "is" in a more complex sentence.

The fact that nonpredicative adjectives (or occurrences of adjectives) will have to be treated differently does not militate against my point. On the contrary, the proper treatment of such adjectives will serve to extend further the point I have been arguing for. This proper treatment can here be only illustrated, not discussed systematically; one reason for this is that no uniform treatment of the different predicative uses of adjectives is possible. What I have in mind can be seen from examples like the following:

(9)   John is a tall basketball player,

which perhaps transforms into something like

(10)   John is a basketball player, and John is taller than most basketball players.

Here the "is" in (9) generates not only the first, but also the second "is" of (10). This latter "is" is not quite like any of the senses of "is" we have so far dealt with. It comes closest to the "is" of predication, but expresses a *relation*, rather than an individual's having a property. Now we can see that uses of "is" can also be considered synonymous with the other ones we have inspected.

Similar observations can be made concerning other constructions involving "is". For instance (11),

(11)   Jack is Virginia's admirer

can be treated game-theoretically so as to be transformed

into (12):

(12)   Jack is John Jr., and John Jr. admires Virginia.

This treatment presupposes that the "is" in (11) and the "is" in (12) are synonymous. For the step involved in the transition from (11) to (12) means a choice by Myself of an individual, namely, John Jr., whose name is substituted for the genitive phrase. This phrase is then unpacked in the way illustrated by (12). Here a use of "is" to express a certain relationship turns out to be semantically the same as a garden-variety occurrence of an "is" of identity.

It is important to realize, furthermore, that the difference between the game-theoretical account and the Fregean one is not merely notational. The most obvious weakness of the Frege-Russell theory is that it must be supplemented by an account that has never been produced. If the English word "is" is ambiguous, how do competent speakers tell to which sense to turn on the different occasions of its use? Instead of answering this question directly, the received Frege-Russell approach develops an independent canonical notation (formalism) into which everything relevant can be translated - or so it is claimed. The principles of such a translation[19] have never been spelled out, however, and the whole enterprise has therefore remained on the level of "miraculous translation", to borrow a happy phrase from Merrill Hintikka.

The game-theoretical account attempts to make explicit the contextual criteria of those differences between different kinds of occurrences of "is" that the Fregean treatment labels "different senses of is". We have already seen that on the game-theoretical account they will have to be distinguished by reference to the grammatical context of the word "is". For it is this context that determines which game rule is to be applied, which in turn determines the meaning of the sentence in question.

If one says this, however, one easily creates the impression that there is no deep difference between the game-theoretical treatment and the received one. One may create the impression that the game-theoretical treatment merely spells out something that Frege and Russell left tacit, viz., the precise criteria that tell us when to expect which meaning in natural languages. This impression would be a mistake. The arguments I have offered are calculated to establish much more than the incompleteness

of the Frege-Russell account.   When the different kinds of
occurrences of "is" are studied in game-theoretical semantics, we obtain much more than a statement of the conditions on which different game rules are applicable in the
presence of "is" in a small fragment of English.   We obtain
also the important insight that the different occurrences of
"is" that help to trigger different game rules nevertheless
have to be treated alike, i.e., synonymously.   Thus the
game-theoretical treatment not only goes further than the
Frege-Russell one: it yields distinctly different results
concerning the ambiguity or univocity of "is".

This point is worth spelling out more fully.   One
method of studying the fate of the Fregean trichotomy in
game-theoretical semantics is to study the translation
method from English to first-order notation that we can
obtain from the game rules.   Here I shall study the translation only on the oversimplified assumption of perfect
information.   The translation rules are interesting also in
that they bring out more explicitly the sense in which our
game rules are rules of semantical analysis.

Each game rule can be correlated with a translation
rule.   These translation rules operate in the same order as
the game rules, that is, from the outside in.   They serve
to transform an English sentence S into a sentence t(S) in
the notation of first-order logic.   In general, let the
translation of X be t(X).   Then we can for instance formulate the following translation rule parallel to (G. some):

$$t(X - some\ Y\ who\ Z - W)\ =$$

$$(Ex)[t(X - b - W)(x/b)\ \&\ t(b\ is\ a\ Y)(x/b)\ \&$$
$$t(b\ Z)(x/b)],$$

where "b" is a new proper name, (x/b) is the operation of
replacing "b" by "x" everywhere in an expression, and
"x" a new individual variable.   Other game rules also have
parallel translation rules.

The applicability of these rules is rather severely
limited, however, in that informational independencies between different quantifiers (or other operators) and uses
of the subgame idea complicate the situation radically.   For
instance, in the presence of subgames, a different translation into logical notation is more natural, and indeed can
be used to show that a translation into first-order notation
is sometimes impossible.   (See chapters 3 and 4 above.)

What is relevant to the subject matter of this chapter is that in none of those rules do we have to worry about the difference between "=", "(Ex)", and predicative juxtaposition. The only translation rules for which the difference is relevant are the translation rules for endpoint (atomic) sentences. There we need rules of the following kind:

$$t(b \text{ is } X) = t(X)(b)$$

$$t(b \text{ is a } Y) = t(Y)(b)$$

$$t(b \text{ is } c) = (b = c)$$

$$t(b \text{ is}) = (Ex)(b = x).$$

(Here "b" "c", etc., are proper names, X is an unanalyzable (primitive) adjective, and Y unanalyzable (primitive) common noun.) Obviously, t(X) and t(Y) will be upper case letters.

For relational words we need rules of the following sort:

$$t(b \text{ } Z \text{ } c) = t(Z)(b,c),$$

where Z is an unanalyzable transitive verb (in the third person singular, present tense).

One thing these translation rules show is that game-theoretical semantics is no worse off than formalized first-order semantics in one important respect. Game-theoretical semantics is sometimes accused of failing to say anything very much about the truth or falsity of its primitive (atomic) sentences. This accusation is not altogether unjustified. More work has to be done concerning the semantics of our end-point sentences. However, my observations show that in this respect game-theoretical semantics and first-order logic are completely on a par. The primitive sentences of my fragment of English are translated into atomic first-order sentences of first-order language, allowing us to say everything of the former that is usually said of the latter.

My observations also show quite convincingly that in game-theoretical semantics the Frege ambiguity is indeed dispensable. The only place where a trichotomy of uses comes into play is in interpreting atomic sentences. There the allegedly different meanings are separated from each other by context, as was already intimated above. There is therefore no need to postulate different senses of "is". The undeniable discrepancies between different uses of the word "is" can be fully accounted for in terms of its context. Differences in *use* don't here imply differences in *meaning*.

9. Semantical Relativity

Of course, I have been arguing for a much stronger conclusion. Our rules for semantical games show that the allegedly different occurrences of "is" can sometimes be descendants of one and the same occurrence of "is", with which they are therefore synonymous. Thus we not only need not distinguish the different Fregean readings; we must not distinguish them from each other. All these supplementary arguments thus reinforce my main conclusion: the alleged ambiguity of "is" is mistaken. The Frege trichotomy is simply wrong.

This conclusion might seem to rest on dubious assumptions. The main questionable assumption is apparently the correctness of game-theoretical semantics as providing for us the true framework of semantical representation.

My conclusions nevertheless do not all depend, when they are rightly understood, on the ultimate superiority of game-theoretical semantics over its rivals. I have tried to sharpen the issues and answers concerning the semantics of "is" by presenting my observations as a refutation of the Frege trichotomy. However, many of my conclusions follow from much weaker assumptions than the unique correctness of game-theoretical semantics. They ensue as soon as it is admitted that game-theoretical semantics is a possible framework of semantics, albeit perhaps not the only one. I am hence assuming only the possibility of game-theoretical semantics, not the impossibility of its rivals. What our observations will then establish is not the incorrectness of the Frege trichotomy but its relativity to one particular semantical theory, one possible framework of semantical representation. The adherents of the Frege trichotomy are thus not so much guilty of a fallacy as of an idiosyncracy.

Ultimately, I would like to argue for the exclusive correctness of game-theoretical semantics. However, this is a bigger task than I can undertake in one chapter. In any case, plenty of striking conclusions follow from the weaker assumption of the viability of game-theoretical semantics.

10. Historical Precedents

One interesting conclusion is a historical one. The relevance of game-theoretical semantics as a realistic alternative to more familiar conceptualizations is enhanced when we realize that it is much closer to many traditional theories of logic than is Frege's trichotomy. It is especially close to traditional treatments of verbs for being. Many of these older treatments of "is" and its synonyms go back ultimately to Aristotle. It is a truly remarkable fact that Aristotle, whose favorite philosophical method was to distinguish different senses of crucial words or phrases from each other and who in his doctrine of categories distinguished between no fewer than ten different meanings of "is", never once came within a mile of the Fregean trichotomy. On the contrary, Aristotle asserts, in so many words, that "man" and "existing man" are identical in meaning (*Metaphysics* IV, 2, 1003 b 26-34). Indeed, the upshot of the careful recent studies of τὸ εἶναι by Charles Kahn and others[20] seems to be that the allegedly different existential and predicative senses of τὸ εἶναι were never distinguished from each other by Aristotle or by any other ancient major Greek philosopher.

Concerning the relation of the "is" of identity to the "is" of predication, their identity is implied by Aristotle's repeated statements to the effect that "a man" and "one man" mean the same. (Cf., e.g., *Metaphysics*, loc. cit.) This is confirmed by Aristotle's treatment of such fallacies as "Socrates is not Plato, Plato is a man, hence Socrates is not a man".[21] Far from using them as an occasion to distinguish between the "is" of identification and the "is" of predication, Aristotle deals with them by reference to a distinction between essential and accidental predication. The idea is that since "is not Plato" is an accidental attribute of Socrates, different attributes may in turn belong to "what is not Plato" and to Socrates. This Aristotle perceives as the reason why the putative inference is not valid. In other words, he in effect considers the difference between the "=" and the copula of the Fregean framework as an instance of his own distinction between essential and accidental predication, respectively. There

can scarcely be clearer proof that Aristotle did not distinguish the "is" of identity and the "is" of predication
from each other, whatever other distinctions between the
several uses of τὸ εἶναι he might have made.

It is also of interest to note that whatever temptation
there may be to draw the fallacious inference is due
primarily to taking "is" to be an expression of identity.
There is, e.g., no temptation to accept an otherwise parallel inference like "Socrates is not a donkey, a donkey is
an animal, hence Socrates is not an animal".

It is also fairly clear – even though the point cannot be
elaborated here – that what are inaccurately and patroniz-
ingly called Aristotle's "existential presuppositions" in his
syllogistic theory are due to the inseparability of the different senses of τὸ εἶναι in Aristotle.

Game-theoretical semantics is thus much closer to
Aristotle's views on the logic of being than is the received
view.   The same goes for the views of several other major
historical figures, e.g., most of the medievals, Leibniz,
and Hegel.   Some of the most salient aspects of the early
history of the alleged distinction between different senses
of "is" and its counterparts in other languages are discussed by Benson Mates in his extremely interesting paper
"Identity and Predication in Plato".[22]

11. Natural-Language Inferences

I also submit that the problems (the fallacies) that Aristotle had to cope with and that were mentioned above are a
small price to pay for a treatment of many valid natural-language inferences that is much more uniform than the
treatment based on the Fregean trichotomy.   In order to
see this uniformity, we may consider, e.g., the following
inferences:

(13)   Tully is Cicero.
       Cicero is a Roman.
       Hence, Tully is a Roman.

(14)   Socrates is a Greek.
       A Greek is a man.
       Hence, Socrates is a man.

In expressing (13)-(14) in the language of the Fregean

trichotomy (or fourfold distinction), they will receive different forms, assuming for the sake of simplicity that in our notation predication can be replaced by set membership.

(15)   Tully = Cicero.
       Cicero ε Romans.
       Hence, Tully ε Romans.

(16)   Socrates ε Greeks.
       Greeks ⊆ men.
       Hence, Socrates ε men.

This translation does not help to make the validity of (13)-(14) immediately transparent. The inferences (15)-(16) are valid only in virtue of certain connections between "=", "ε", and "⊆" (i.e., in virtue of assumptions involving more than one of them) that have to be spelled out and recorded, if the notation used in (11)-(12) is to try to display the validity of these logical inferences.

   In contrast, the game-theoretical treatment shows at once the validity of (13)-(14) and - more interestingly - also explains why in (13)-(14) the surface form so strongly suggests that they are valid. For instance, consider the semantical game connected with the consequent of (13) on a model in which its antecedents are both true. Then I clearly have a winning strategy in this (consequent) game. For I can then win in the game G(Tully is a Roman) by choosing, in accordance with (G. a(n)), Cicero (alias Tully) as the individual whose name is to be substituted for the quantifier phrase "a Roman". Similarly, we can explain the obviousness of (14). This explanation, in effect, relies on the properties of the "is" of identity to account for the validity of (13)-(14).

   But what about the other side of the coin? What about problems of the kind already noted by Aristotle? In the sphere of the elementary inferences - syllogistic or comparable inferences - very simple principles go a long way towards handling inferences in natural languages, as well as failures of such inferences. We do not need to puzzle over the interrelations of different logical notions. Those properties of our single unitary "is" that mostly belong to its sometime role of expressing identity give us a great deal of the requisite power, as long as we remember that different occurrences of the same existential-quantifier phrase, like "a man" or "a boy", must be thought of as picking out different individuals. Furthermore, we must assume that what holds of every X holds of the individual that on some occurrence of "an X" or "some X" is thought of as being picked out by these phrases. Thus the following inference is fallacious because different choices of individuals are associated with "a man" in the major premise and in the conclusion:

(17)   Socrates is not Plato.
        Plato is a man.
        Hence: Socrates is not a man.

Likewise, the following inference fails because of the same property of existential-quantifier phrases:

(18)   Socrates is a man.
        Plato is a man.
        Hence: Socrates is Plato.

The validity of the following inference follows from the transition from "every X" to "an X" indicated above:

(19)   Every Greek is a man.
        Every man is an animal.
        Hence: Every Greek is an animal.

On the suggested account this will have something like the form

        Every Greek = a man.
        Every man = an animal.
        Hence: Every Greek = an animal.

What messes up this sweetness and light are the generic uses of the indefinite article. It was already indicated that such uses can be handled game theoretically in a powerful and illuminating manner. It would take us too far afield to explain this treatment here. In spite of its naturalness, it spoils the uniformity of my treatment. But, since such generic uses are somewhat of the nature of exceptions, this does not spoil the basic simplicity of the proposed theory.

In general, the most natural treatment of the traditional syllogistic will take the form of some sort of calculus of equations of both identities and nonidentities between quantifier phrases. It cannot be investigated here whether any of the existing treatments of syllogistic satisfies this desideratum. As was indicated above, the task of developing an account of syllogistic along equational lines is made difficult by the generic uses of some quantifier words. Even if some existing account manages to treat syllogistic as a calculus of equations, it is unlikely to be satisfactory in that it is unlikely to place the treatment into a larger framework of a similar treatment of the whole of first-order logic. The main partial exceptions to logicians' failure to develop a general formalism that would function the same way as natural-language inferences involving quantifiers are perhaps the ε-calculus of Hilbert and Bernays[23] and Montague's treatment of quantifiers.[24] (The first of these was claimed to be a better model of natural-language inferences than the usual predicate calculus decades ago by Paul Ziff.)

12. Logical Form vs. Semantical Relativity

The alternative treatments of (13)-(14) suggest another conclusion. Another concept, over and above the concept of ambiguity, that is seen to be relative to an underlying method of semantical representation is that of *logical form*. For, we may ask, What is the logical form of, e.g., (2)?

(2)   Jack is a boy.

In the logical form of Frege and Russell, the "is" in (2) must be represented either as the "is" of identity, the "is" of predication, or the "is" of existence, i.e., as "=", "X(x)", or "(Ex)". In so far as we can speak of the logical form of (2) according to game-theoretical semantics, it cannot be any one of these. The surface form of (2) is in fact a better representation of its logical form than its several possible translations into conventional logical symbolism, a game-theoretical semanticist will tell you.

Of course, we can develop a regimented shorthand for game-theoretical semantics comparable to the usual notation, and use it for the purposes of semantical representation. However, this new formalism will differ from all of the usual logical languages. The logical form of (2) is, therefore, relative to one's underlying semantical theory.

One can say more than this, however. It is all right to say that the concept of ambiguity is itself ambiguous, as we in effect did above. But it is not possible to say that logical form varies according to one's semantics. The notion of logical form was introduced for the very purpose of uncovering, underneath a multiplicity of various grammatical forms, a unique structure that correctly displays the meaning (or at least the semantical structure) of a sentence. Hence the semantical relativity we have uncovered destroys the rationale of the concept of logical form.

Even if we can argue for the absolute superiority of one particular mode of semantical representation, the notion of logical form would not automatically be saved thereby. For the meaning of such a superiority could be merely a Duhemian preference for one overall theory of language, that includes not only semantical but also syntactical considerations. This would violate an important assumption underlying the concept of logical form, viz., the independence of logical form from the shifting syntactical dress of one's sentences. It is, for instance, entirely foreign to the spirit of the concept of logical form that game-theoretical semantics (and hence the "logical form" it assigns to sentences) should be preferred to Fregean semantics partly because in it semantical form and syntactical surface form are closer to each other than in a Fregean approach.

This point is connected with the fact that historically the main function of the concept of logical form has been to isolate the particular syntactical features of the sentences in question that determine their semantical properties. In this sense, so-called logical form is merely a reflection of the semantical properties of sentences on the syntactical level. If these properties are conceptualized in a new way, our ideas of logical form must change correspondingly. This is in fact just what happens in game-theoretical semantics. This dependence of logical form on underlying semantics is another aspect of the semantical relativity I have argued for.

Hence the possibility of the game-theoretical approach to natural-language semantics and the resulting semantical relativity have most important consequences for our ideas of semantics and of *Sprachlogik*.

13. "The Language of Thought" vs. Semantical Relativity

The semantical relativity we have uncovered tells especially poignantly against theories of "the language of thought", that is to say, against theories that postulate an internal language or an internal method of message representation that is supposed to underlie language understanding.[25] Even if the proponents of such an internal language can allow for sociolinguistic relativity in the style of, say, B. L. Whorf, they are in trouble with the kind of relativity we are talking of here. For what is the translation of (2) into an English-speaking person's "language of thought"? Are there three possible translations, or only one? How does such a speaker decide which "is" occurs in (2)? Does "the language of thought" embody the Fregean tri- chotomy or not? In the case of a number of well-known adherents of private languages of thought, an affirmative answer is strongly suggested by their liberal use of the notation of first-order logic and its variants. But there is no doubt that the game-theoretical treatment is closer to the intuitions of the man in the street - or anywhere else where the artificialities of logic and recent linguistics have not yet spoiled semantical intuitions. The man in the street would, for instance, never say that "is" is ambig- uous. Does that prove that he is mistaken about the most fundamental and most pervasive features of the method of semantical representation on which his understanding of English is based? How can the postulated privileged private language be relevant to an English speaker's linguistic skills if the speaker is so fundamentally wrong about his own private language? And if the private lan- guage of the language-of-thought theorist does not embody the Fregean trichotomy, it is a great pity that he has not noted the fact and relieved the great majority of philoso- phers and linguists from their mistaken reliance on first- order logic. In brief, the semantical relativity we have discovered (relativity to a framework of semantical representation, not necessarily to a culture) makes all theories of "languages of thought" extremely implausible.

The "language of thought" view implies a broader meth- odological thesis that our observations now show to be false. It appears in one of its most explicit forms in the beginning of J. J. Katz's book *Semantic Theory*.[26] This thesis says that the task of semantics is to account for competent speakers' intuitions of synonymy, ambiguity, number of readings, and other semantical relations between expressions, in the same way as we are in syntax explaining, on Chomsky's view, competent speakers' intuitions of grammaticality. Whatever one can say of syntax, we have seen enough to show that in semantics this methodology does not work. Since such crucial notions as ambiguity and synonymy are relative to a framework of semantical representation, people's alleged intuitions concerning them likewise depend on some semantical theory tacitly presupposed. These intuitions can be changed by persuading an informant to adopt a new mode of semantical representation.

Nor is this merely a speculative possibility. How else can we account for the discrepancy between the intuitions of the majority of contemporary logicians and those of the man in the street - as well as those of virtually all logicians from Aristotle to De Morgan? Furthermore, "is" is not the only word that illustrates this point. There is, for instance, a less massive but nonetheless quite striking disagreement between traditional grammarians, who generally assumed the univocity of "any", and recent linguists, many of whom claim that it sometimes serves as a universal quantifier and sometimes as an existential one, and hence is ambiguous. (Cf. chapter 3 above.)

14. Revolt against Frege

The results of this chapter are lent additional interest by the fact that my criticism of the Fregean trichotomy is only one aspect of a much broader revolt against Fregean conceptions of logical system and logical form. Indeed, van Heijenoort is absolutely right in saying that Frege's most influential contribution was the introduction of our present conception of a logical system.[27] This conception has dominated, with a few exceptions, twentieth-century ideas of logic, *Sprachlogik*, and logical form. In recent years, several different aspects of the Fregean conception have nevertheless been challenged. They include, among other things, what might be called his categorical scheme, i.e., the assumption that the world is articulated into individuals, their properties, relations, and functions, plus possibly higher-order properties, relations, and functions. Recently the category of individuals has been dispensed with in the Scott semantics for λ-calculus,[28] and the sufficiency of Frege's list of basic categories has been made questionable by the intensive recent interest in such natural-language phenomena as mass terms[29] and comparatives.[30] Their semantics seems to require new basic categories. Likewise, Frege's tacit assumption that comparisons between language and reality are effected in one fell swoop has been challenged by game-theoretical semantics and its by-products, such as Rantala's theory of urn models[31] and the theory of branching quantifiers.[32]

Several other recent developments in logical semantics can likewise be understood as departures from the Fregean paradigm. The present criticism of the Frege-Russell treatment of "is" can in this spirit be thought of as another aspect of an ongoing revolution against Frege, now directed against the transcategorematic part of Frege's scheme of a logical system rather than against his selection of categories. This is so radical a departure that time may be ripe for a new overall conception of a semantical framework.

15. Questions and Semantical Relativity

That our rejection of the Fregean trichotomy is not an isolated step is further confirmed by the fact that several of its consequences can also be reached by a largely independent line of investigation. This line of thought is the analysis of English wh-questions sketched in my *The Semantics of Questions and the Questions of Semantics*.[33] On this analysis, a direct question amounts to a request to bring about a certain epistemic state of affairs. This state of affairs is described by the desideratum of the question. For instance, the wh-question

(20) Who volunteers to chop the wood?

has as its desideratum

(21) I know who volunteers to chop the wood.

Earlier,[34] I proposed to analyze (21) as being tantamount to

(22) (Ex) I know that (x volunteers to chop the wood).

In a more compact notation, (22) can be rendered as

(23)   (Ex) K_I (x volunteers to chop the wood).

(Here and in what follows, "x" is assumed to range over persons.) The present theory says that (21) has intrinsically two different representations in the usual language of epistemic logic, viz, (23), which can be written

(24)   (Ex)[x volunteers to chop wood &
           K_I(x volunteers to chop wood)],

and

(25)   (x)[x volunteers to chop wood →
           K_I(x volunteers to chop wood)].

This ambidextrous (ambi-quantificational) character of wh-words is, according to my theory, integral to their semantical nature. Of course it may be that one of the two representations is filtered out by contextual (prag-matic) factors. For instance, (23) is the natural force of (21) if it is known that, in asking (20), the questioner is merely looking for one person to chop the wood for today's dinner. In contrast, (25) is the force of (21) if the ques-tioner is preparing the assignments for household chores for the next three months, and needs full lists of who prefers to do what.

The same effect can be illustrated by other examples. For instance, if I say (26),

(26)   Dr. Welby knows who among his patients has pneumonia and who merely a common cold.

I am saying much more than that the good doctor can make the right diagnosis in one case of each kind; I am saying that he can tell the difference in each case. In other words, I am assuming the universal-quantifier "reading".

In contrast, it can be true to say (27),

(27)   Janet knows how to get from Heathrow to Oxford.

even if she does not know all the reasonable ways of doing so. In other words, the natural force of (27) is that of an existential-quantifier sentence.

This two-quantifier theory has several highly interest-ing applications that help confirm it. For instance, it ex-plains (together with obvious conversational assumptions) the alleged skill-sense of "knowing how" and other "knows" + wh-locutions. This is in fact illustrated by (26). For if we are told that (26) is the case, how else can we possibly expect to explain Dr. Welby's diagnostic success except by postulating the requisite skills in him? In general, the skill-sense of "know how" comes about as a combined result of the general universal-quantifier sense of the "knows" + wh-construction and of certain obvious conversational expectations. This is witnessed by the fact that other "knows" + wh-constructions can on occasion acquire a similar skill-sense. Such senses are illustrated by the following examples:

(28) Howard knows when to keep his mouth shut.
(29) Bill surely knows who to flatter.

Furthermore, the theory of wh-words as two-barrelled quantifiers helps to explain such varied phenomena as the uniqueness presuppositions which wh-questions often possess,[35] the missing wh-constructions with epistemic verbs without success grammar,[36] and our frequent preference of the universal reading for wh-questions.[37] Last but not least, I have used the dual-reading hypothesis to explain the different representations that a multiple wh-question can have in English.[38] It usually has even more than two semantical representations in the notation of epistemic logic.

But does the duality of their semantical representations make wh-questions ambiguous? The fairly obvious answer is no, it does not. Virtually no competent speaker of English would ever claim that wh-questions are ambiguous. These intuitions are accounted for by game-theoretical semantics, which assigns only one semantical representation to wh-questions, simple or multiple.[39]

Thus English wh-questions present to us essentially the same situation as "is".[40] Whether certain sentences are ambiguous depends on the framework of semantical repre-sentation. In game-theoretical semantics, wh-questions have only one representation, while in the usual notation of epistemic logic they have more than one reading.

This strongly supports the general conclusions we

reached in sections 9 and 12-13 above, especially the semantical relativity described there. In the case of
wh-questions, our conclusion may seem somewhat less
impressive than our observations concerning "is", for the
ambiguity of wh-questions has been maintained by few
logicians or linguists. However, in another respect the alleged ambiguity of wh-questions is even more striking than
that of "is". For it is not possible to find any one well-
formed sentence of English containing "is" that is ambiguous because of the Frege trichotomy, even though in different sentences "is" is supposed to have different
meanings. In contrast, each wh-question and each desideratum of a wh-question has in principle more than one
reading when we rely on epistemic logic, even if conversational and other pragmatic factors often filter out some of
them. The different readings of the desiderata of
wh-questions can even be written out explicitly in the
notation of epistemic logic. This makes even more remarkable the fact that in game-theoretical semantics they are
entirely unambiguous. The so-called different readings
differ only in that a different player makes the move connected with the wh-word. This leeway in the application
of the game rules does not affect the number of readings,
however.

16. "Is" Again

In much of this chapter, game-theoretical semantics has
been treated merely as one possible framework of semantical representation and semantical analysis. Consequently, the treatment of "is" that is obtained from game-
theoretical semantics and that dispenses with the Frege
trichotomy has been considered as only one possible theory
of the semantics of "is". There is much more to be said
of this matter, however. There is good independent evidence that "is" has to be treated, in any case, as not ex-
hibiting the Frege-Russell ambiguity. In this last section
some such evidence will be briefly discussed.

First and foremost, there does not seem to be a single
English sentence that in fact has several readings because
of the alleged ambiguity of "is". (Certain apparent
counterexamples to this claim will be discussed and refuted
below.) Hence, on any theory, however many senses of
"is" are postulated, the differences between different uses

of "is" can always be explained by reference to the
context. After all, it is the context that always suffices,
if my claim is right, to resolve the alleged ambiguity.
Hence it is surely simpler and theoretically more rewarding
to attribute the apparent ambiguity to differences between
kinds of contexts, than to the multiplicity of the lexical
meanings of "is". Like Laplace, we can say of the latter,
"I don't need that hypothesis." Earlier it was pointed out
that the way in which the distinction between "=", the
copula, and "(Ex)" comes about in translating from a fragment of English to the notation of first-order logic does
not assign any explanatory role to the trichotomy. It is
not needed in any game rule, only in translating the end
points of games (atomic sentences) from English into
first-order notation. And in the primitive (end-point)
sentences the context distinguishes the different uses
anyway. Thus independent evidence strongly suggests
that the answer game-theoretical semantics gives is correct
and the one the Frege-Russell view yields incorrect.

There are linguistic phenomena, however, that have
been alleged to instantiate, or at least show the reality of,
the distinction between the "is" of identity and the "is" of
predication. Seeing how they can be accounted for without resorting to the Frege-Russell trichotomy will clarify
further my theory and illustrate its potentialities. Here I
shall discuss only two such phenomena.

(a) The following sentences are ambiguous:

(30)   What Descartes discovered was a proof of his
        existence.
(31)   What Bill told John is a secret.

For example, (31) can be paraphrased by either (32) or
(33):

(32)   Bill's message to John is a secret one.
(33)   The answer to the question, What did Bill tell
        John? remains a secret.

It has, in effect, been suggested[41] that the difference between the two readings of (31) is that between the "is" of
identity and the "is" of predication. More specifically,
(32) is a paraphrase of the reading with "=", (33) a para-

phrase of the copulative reading.

I disagree with this way of looking at (30) and (31). The difference between their two readings can be explained, and has to be explained, on other grounds. The true explanation is closely related to the distinction between free relative clauses and indirect questions. The two are semantically different since they are subject to different rules of semantical interpretation, e.g., game rules.[42] The problem is caused by the fact that in certain contexts the two can look just alike. For example, if the crucial clause "What Bill told John" is taken to be a free (headless) relative clause, (31) means the same as (32); if it is taken to be an interrogative clause, (31) means (33).[43]

That this explanation does not turn on "is" in any way is seen from the fact that it is needed - and it works - also in contexts where there is no occurrence of "is". The following are cases in point:

(34)   Descartes discovered what Fermat knew.
(35)   Maisie knows what Henry believes.

These are ambiguous in the same way as (30)-(31). Their ambiguity can be accounted for in the same way as was just done for (30)-(31). For instance, it can be explained why (35) is ambiguous between

> Maisie knows the item(s) of information that Henry only believes.

and

> Maisie knows the answer to the question, "What does Henry believe?"

This account is still somewhat crude. No one has formulated precise semantical rules for "secret" or "proof". However, I have given explicit game-theoretical rules for several different constructions with "knows". They explain automatically why and how (35) is ambiguous. We have a rule for the construction "knows" + direct object, and another for the construction "knows" + wh-clause. When the grammatical object is a free relative clause, it may happen that both rules apply, creating an ambiguity. Such is the case with (35), which is parallel to some of the examples I dealt with in *The Semantics of Questions*.

There is every reason to expect that game rules for "secret", "proof", and "discovers" are sufficiently like those for "knows" to enable us to account for (30), (31), and (34) in the same way as (35). However, in the case of "proof" this contrast between two readings becomes a lexical ambiguity between proof in the sense of conclusive argument and proof in the sense of a conclusive item of evidence. In some other languages, these two senses are expressed by different lexical items (cf. Finnish "todistus" and "todiste"). Hence we can explain all the alleged counterexamples without resorting to the assumption that "is" is ambiguous.

(b) The simple sentence

(36)   Mary is a physicist.

can be a reply to either of the following two questions:

(37)   Who is Mary?
(38)   What is Mary?

It has been surmised that this shows that the "is" of (36) can be either "=" or the copulative "is".[44] (Curiously enough, this does not seem to make (36) ambiguous.)

In my theory of questions in *The Semantics of Questions*, I show that these facts can be accounted for without assuming any ambiguity of "is". The desiderata of (37) and (38) are, respectively,

(39)   I know who Mary is,

and

(40)   I know what Mary is.

These can be represented in the notation of epistemic logic as follows:

(41) $(Ex)K_I(\text{Mary is } x)$
(42) $(EX)K_I(\text{Mary is } X)$,

where "x" is an individual variable ranging over persons,

and "X" a variable ranging over kinds of persons. This shows that the difference between (37) and (38) is a difference of subdomains over which the wh-quantifiers "who" and "what" are ranging. Such differences obviously have to be accommodated in game-theoretical semantics in any case. I do not have to discuss here the question whether distinctions between such subdomains of quantification go together with differences in the meaning of "is". For a comparison of (41) with (42) shows that in the special case at hand, viz., our contrast between (37) and (38), this question is simply the question (all over again) whether we have to distinguish the "is" of identity from the "is" of predication. Both desiderata (41) and (42) are formulated most naturally in terms of "is". The question whether the distinction between "who" and "what" implies a distinction between different senses of "is" is simply the question whether there is a difference in meaning between the "is" in (41) and in (42) of the kind Frege and Russell postulated.

Even if there should turn out to be some difference in meaning between the "is" in (39) and in (40), it is not clear that this coincides with the Fregean distinction. The difference between the ranges associated with the different wh-words is essentially Aristotle's distinction between the senses of "is" in different categories, as Charles Kahn has convincingly shown.[45] This category-distinction is different from the Frege-Russell distinction, however, and ought not to be confused with it. For Frege,

(43)   Socrates is a man

and

(44)   Socrates is white

both embody predicative uses of "is". For Aristotle, the difference between (43) and (44) is that between the categories of substance and quality.

Further examples can easily be given to illustrate the dispensability of the Fregean distinction between the allegedly different meanings of "is" for all serious theoretical purposes.[46]

NOTES

[1] Bertrand Russell, *The Principles of Mathematics*, Cambridge University Press, London, 1903; reprinted, George Allen and Unwin, London, 1937; see p. 64, note.

[2] Russell departs here from the typical trichotomists and partially anticipates recent treatments of quantifier phrases. On the received view, Russell's sense (4) has usually been assimilated to the "is" of predication. For a discussion of some more recent views, see, e.g., Jaakko Hintikka, "Quantifiers in Logic and Quantifiers in Natural Languages", in S. Körner, editor, *Philosophy of Logic*, Basil Blackwell, Oxford, 1976, pp. 208-32. A couple of years later Russell changed his mind on this point.

[3] George Allen and Unwin, London, 1914, p. 50.

[4] Frege's achievement in creating the modern concept of a formal system – as well as his reasons for not discussing semantical matters systematically – are brought out very clearly by Jean van Heijenoort, "Logic as Language and Logic as Calculus", *Synthese* 17 (1967), 324-30. Cf. also Jean van Heijenoort, editor, *From Frege to Gödel*, Harvard University Press, Cambridge, Mass., 1967. Frege discusses the different senses of verbs for being in "Uber Begriff und Gegenstand", p. 194 of the original (pp. 43-44 of the Geach and Black translation). Cf. also "Dialogue with Pünjer on Existence", in Gottlob Frege, *Posthumous Writings*, The University of Chicago Press, Chicago, 1979, pp. 53-67, and Leila Taiminen, "On Frege's Concept of Being", forthcoming.

[5] None of these analysts of language has in so many words committed himself to first-order logic as his only canonical notation for semantics. In practice, nevertheless, each of them has relied heavily – indeed well-nigh exclusively – on first-order logic. The only one of these four scholars whose predilection for standard quantificational logic is not conspicuous is Noam Chomsky. For evidence, I can now conveniently refer to his book, *Essays on Form and Interpretation*, North-Holland, Amsterdam, 1977, especially his essay "Conditions on Rules of Grammar" contained therein. For instance, on p. 197 Chomsky says that his analysis "is pretty much along the lines of standard logical analysis of the sentences of natural language".

Donald Davidson's allegiance to quantificational languages is motivated purely pragmatically, as shown by his

note "Action and Reaction", *Inquiry* 13 (1970), 140-48.
There he points out that his position is even compatible
with a relativity of logical form to the underlying logical
theory. This point seems to anticipate some of the conclusions I will defend later in the present chapter. The
important but subtle differences between Davidson and myself in this respect need a longer discussion than I can
launch here. (Cf. especially section 12 below.)

Unsurprisingly, early Wittgenstein maintained the ambiguity of "is"; see *Tractatus Logico-Philosophicus*, Kegan
Paul, London, 1922, proposition 3.323.

[6] See the papers collected in Esa Saarinen, editor,
Game-Theoretical Semantics, D. Reidel, Dordrecht, 1979,
where further references to the literature are also provided. Chapter 1 of the present volume gives a concise
overview. Cf. also Jon Barwise, "On Branching Quantifiers in English", *Journal of Philosophical Logic* 8 (1979),
47-80.

[7] Game-theoretical semantics is accordingly truth-conditional, as I believe every satisfactory semantics must be.
Our game rules correspond to the recursive clauses of a
Tarski-type truth-definition. In both, the notions of
truth and falsity are largely taken for granted insofar as
they apply to atomic sentences, and the main problem is to
extend them to other sentences. But the way this extension is accomplished is different in the two cases. In
Tarski-type semantics, the recursive clauses that effect
the extension apply from the inside out, whereas in game-
theoretical semantics the rules have to be applied from the
outside in. This has several important consequences, including the ability of game-theoretical semantics to cope
with failures of compositionality (also known as the Frege
Principle). For such failures, see chapter 10 below.
Also, Tarski-type truth-definitions assume, as it were, the
possibility of surveying the whole domain D at a glance (in
effect, of quantification over D), whereas in game-theoretical semantics we further analyze the specific process that
connects the language in question with the reality it can
be used to describe.

[8] This fragment is not characterized here explicitly, for it
does not matter for the theoretical conclusions of this
chapter precisely what is or is not included in it.

[9] For this theory, see, e.g., R. Duncan Luce and Howard
Raiffa, *Games and Decisions*, John Wiley, New York, 1957.

[10] This is a much taller order than it might first appear to

be. Sentences that are "semantically atomic" in the sense that their truth-values are determined by the interpretation of the nonlogical words they contain can be far from simple, structurally speaking. Unless something more is said, we must for instance allow some "semantically atomic" sentences to be in the passive voice.

It seems to me that the perfect complement to game-theoretical semantics as applied to English is Joan Bresnan's recent theory of certain aspects of the lexical component of English grammar. (For this theory, see Joan Bresnan, editor, *The Mental Representation of Grammatical Relations*, MIT Press, Cambridge, Mass., 1982, especially Bresnan's own contributions; Joan Bresnan, "A Realistic Transformational Grammar", in Morris Halle et al., editors, *Linguistic Theory and Psychological Reality*, MIT. Press, Cambridge, Mass., 1978, pp. 1–59. For Bresnan's theory provides us with an account of the connections between different semantically atomic sentences that enables us to formulate their precise truth conditions.

[11] It is important to realize that these are not problems that absolutely have to be solved in order for game-theoretical semantics to be viable. For there is nothing intrinsically meaningless or unsatisfactory about infinite games.

[12] In the game rules, "X", "Y", etc, are linguistic rather than logical symbols, referring to linguistic expressions and at the same time acting as placeholders for them, as linguists are wont to expect their symbols to behave.

[13] We also need ordering principles to tell the players in what order the several game rules have to be applied.

[14] In Saarinen, *Game-Theoretical Semantics*, pp. 179–214, and also in Avishai Margalit, editor, *Meaning and Use*, D. Reidel, Dordrecht, 1978, pp. 57–92.

[15] See Peter Geach, "Good and Evil", *Analysis* 17 (1956), 33–42, and cf., George O. Curme, *A Grammar of the English Language*, D. C. Heath, Boston, 1931–35.

[16] Hintikka and Carlson, "Conditionals, Generic Quantifiers, and Other Applications of Subgames".

[17] Cf., e.g., Edward S. Klima, "Negation in English", in J. J. Katz and Jerry Fodor, editors, *The Structure of Language*, Prentice-Hall, Englewood Cliffs, N.J., 1964, pp. 246–323 (see especially p. 279 and the references given there in note 12); see also Robert P. Stockwell, Paul Schachter, and Barbara Partee, *The Major Syntactic Structures of English*, Holt, Rinehart and Winston, New

York, 1973, chapter 5.

[18] See Hintikka and Carlson, "Conditionals, Generic Quantifiers, and Other Applications of Subgames".

[19] A translation of this kind is part of the program of generative semanticists; cf. George Lakoff, "Generative Semantics", in Danny Steinberg and Leon Jakobovits, pp. 232-96. Their theories cannot be considered satisfactory, however. Among other failures, they cannot explain any exceptions to the general ordering principles mentioned in my earlier papers.

[20] See Charles Kahn, *The Verb "Be" in Ancient Greek*, D. Reidel, Dordrecht, 1973; cf. also G. E. L. Owen, "Aristotle in the Snares of Ontology", in R. Bambrough, editor, *New Essays on Plato and Aristotle*, Routledge and Kegan Paul, London, 1965, pp. 69-95.

[21] See *De sophisticis elenchis* 166 b 28-37, 168 a 34-b10; 169 b 4-6; 179 a 33-37.

[22] Benson Mates, "Identity and Predication in Plato", *Phronesis* 24 (1979), 211-29. An earlier version of this paper appeared in Swedish translation under the title "Om Platons argument 'den tredje människan'" in (no editor given) *En filosofibok tillägnad Anders Wedberg*, Bonniers, Stockholm, 1978, pp. 66-84. Even though Mates does not mention it, his onetime colleague Michael Frede had expressed somewhat similar interpretational ideas in his *Habilitationsschrift* entitled *Prädikation und Existenzaussage* (Hypomnemata, vol. 18), Vandehoek & Ruprecht, Göttingen, 1967.

[23] David Hilbert and Paul Bernays, *Grundlagen der Mathematik*, vols. 1-2, Springer, Berlin, 1934-39.

[24] Richmond Thomason, editor, *Formal Philosophy: Selected Papers of Richard Montague*, Yale University Press, New Haven, Connecticut, 1974, chapter 8.

[25] See Jerry Fodor, *The Language of Thought*, Thomas Y. Crowell, New York, 1975; and cf. Peter Geach, *Mental Acts*, Routledge and Kegan Paul, London, 1957.

[26] J. J. Katz, *Semantic Theory*, Harper and Row, New York, 1972, pp. 3-7.

[27] See van Heijenoort, "Logic as Language and Logic as Calculus".

[28] See Dana Scott, "Models for Various Type-Free Calculi", in Patrick Suppes et al., editors, *Logic, Methodology, and Philosophy of Science IV*, North-Holland, Amsterdam, 1973, pp. 157-87; Dana Scott, "Lambda Calculus

and Recursion Theory", in Stig Kanger, editor, *Pro-
ceedings of the 3rd Scandinavian Logic Symposium*, North-
Holland, Amsterdam, 1975, pp. 154-93. Cf. also Joseph E.
Stoy, *Denotational Semantics*, MIT Press, Cambridge,
Mass. 1977, and the further references given there.
29 See, e.g., F. J. Pelletier, editor, *Mass Terms*, D.
Reidel, Dordrecht, 1979, and the bibliography given there.
30 See, e.g., Renate Bartsch, *Adverbialsemantik*,
Athenäum, Frankfurt am Main, 1972, chapter 14; Renate
Bartsch and Theo Venneman, *Semantic Structures*,
Athenäum, Frankfurt am Main, 1972, chapter 12.
31 See Veikko Rantala, "Urn Models: A New Kind of
Non-Standard Model for First-Order Logic", *Journal of
Philosophical Logic* 4 (1975), 455-74.
32 See note 6 above.
33 *Acta Philosophica Fennica*, vol. 28, no. 4, North-
Holland, Amsterdam, 1976.
34 See, e.g., *Knowledge and Belief*, Cornell University
Press, Ithaca, N.Y., 1962.
35 See my *The Semantics of Questions*, pp. 76-79.
36 Ibid., pp. 72-74.
37 This follows from one of the conversational postulates
discussed by Paul Grice, viz., the one that enjoins a
speaker from making a weaker statement when he is in a
position to make a stronger (and relevant) statement.
Hence, the main phenomenon adduced by Lauri Karttunen
as a reason for preferring his theory of questions
(presented in Henry Hiż, editor, *Questions*, D. Reidel,
Dordrecht, 1978, pp. 165-210) receives a most natural explanation on my theory, too.
38 See *The Semantics of Questions*, chapters 6, 8-9.
39 This is not to say that speakers who have been brain-
washed into relying on the framework of epistemic logic
might not claim that English wh-questions are ambiguous,
at least multiple questions. All that they would prove,
however, is how easily affected and therefore frequently
misleading our so-called intuitions are.
40 For the theoretical issues involved here, see *The Semantics of Questions*, chapters 1-2.
41 This example seems to originate from Emmon Bach's unpublished note "Anti-pronominalization", Department of
Linguistics, The University of Texas, January 15, 1969.
42 See *The Semantics of Questions*, pp. 115-19 and 147-49.
43 See C. L. Baker, "Notes on the Description of English
Questions", *Foundations of Language* 6 (1970), 197-219,

for tests that can be used to distinguish free relative clauses from indirect questions, and for references to the linguistic literature relating to the distinction.

[44] Emmon Bach, "In Defense of Passive" (unpublished).

[45] Charles Kahn, "Questions and Categories", in Hiz, *Questions*, pp. 227–78.

[46] This last section owes much to Steve Weisler's criticisms and comments. (One thing it does not owe to him are whatever mistakes it contains.)

Chapter 8

SEMANTICAL GAMES AND ARISTOTELIAN CATEGORIES

1. Game-Theoretical Semantics for Formal Languages

In earlier papers, I have sketched an approach to logical and linguistic semantics that embodies some of the same ideas on which Wittgenstein's notion of language game is based.[1] One of these ideas is that in order to appreciate the semantics of a word (or any other primitive expression of a language) we should study its function in the rule-governed human activities that serve to connect the language (or the fragment of a language) with the world. What Wittgenstein called "language games" can typically be considered such linking activities. In the languages (or parts of languages) that I will study in this chapter, certain activities of this kind are construed as games in the strict sense of the mathematical theory of games. They are called "semantical games", and the semantics based on them is called *game-theoretical semantics*. Its basic ideas are explained most easily by reference to formal but interpreted first-order languages. Such a language, say L, can be assumed to have a finite number of primitive predicates that are interpreted on some given fixed domain D. Their being interpreted on D amounts to saying that any atomic sentence formed from one of the predicates of L plus the appropriate number of proper names of the elements of D (whether the names are in L or not) has a definite truth-value, true or false. One of the main tasks of any semantics for first-order formal languages is to extend this assignment of truth-values to the rest of the sentences of L.

This can be done by defining certain two-person games G(S), one for each sentence S of L. The players are called *Myself* (or *I*) and *Nature*. The game G(S) can be thought of as an attempt on the part of Myself to verify S against the schemes of a recalcitrant Nature. This motivates the games rules, which may be formulated as follows:

(G. v)   In G(A v B), the first move is made by Myself, who chooses A or B. Accordingly, the rest of the game is G(A) or G(B).

(G. &)   In G(A & B), the first move is made by Nature, who chooses A or B. Accordingly, the rest of the game is G(A) or G(B).

(G. ∿)   G(∿A) is played in the same way as G(A) but with the roles of the two players (as defined by these rules) exchanged.

(G. E)   In G((Ex)F(x)), the first move is made by Myself, who chooses an element of D. If it has a proper name in L, the players use this name. If not, the players give it a proper name, and go on to use it. Let this name be (in either case) "b". Then the rest of the game is G(F(b)).

(G. U)   Similarly for G((x)F(x)), except that Nature chooses b.

(G. A)   If A is an atomic sentence, the game G(A) is won by Myself if A is true, by Nature if A is false.

We may think of these semantical games as zero-sum games: what is won by Myself Nature loses, and vice versa.

Comments:
   (i) Since each move in a given game removes one occurrence of the logical symbols ∿, v, &, (E_), (_) from the sentence considered, the game will come to an end in a finite number of steps in a situation in which (G. A) is applicable. Hence (G. A) suffices to define winning and losing for all games (so far considered).
   (ii) Even when the game has reached a sentence A, the two players need not know A completely. In order to allow for the possibility of incomplete information, we must require that some moves are made on the basis of incomplete (at the time) knowledge of A.
   (iii) The given initial sentence S can now be defined to be *true* if there exists a winning strategy for Myself in G(S). S is *false* if there is a winning strategy for Nature.
   (iv) In the simplest first-order languages, this truth definition is equivalent with the usual Tarski-type def-

initions, as one can easily ascertain. Beyond these simple cases, there are, nevertheless, many possibilities of further applications of game-theoretical semantics that are not amenable to traditional treatments, or are not treated equally easily by old methods. Among such extensions of our simple games, one can mention the following:

(a) A game-theoretical truth-definition can be used in games on urn models,[2] and not only on classical (invariant) models.

(b) My game-theoretical approach can be extended by means of the idea of a subgame.[3] In this direction, game-theoretical semantics converges with the functional interpretations first proposed by Gödel.[4]

(c) Game-theoretical truth-definitions can be used even in infinitely deep logics, i.e., in logical languages where atomic formulas cannot always be reached from a given sentence by a finite number of steps of analysis.[5]

(d) Informational independence of different quantifier moves (failure of perfect information) gives us an opportunity to develop a semantics for branching (more generally, partially ordered) quantifiers.[6]

2. Game-Theoretical Semantics for Fragments of Natural Languages

Game-theoretical semantics is thus a powerful and flexible tool in the semantics of formal languages. This prompts the question whether it can be used in the study of natural languages as well.

It follows from what has been said that game-theoretical semantics will apply to natural languages at least in so far as they can be translated into, or paraphrased in, formal first-order languages. The number of eminent philosophers, logicians, and linguists who have in fact sought to use first-order logic as their main semantical framework shows that even this kind of indirect applicability to natural-language sentences (viz., via their translations into the language of predicate logic) is not without interest. However, such an indirect application merely moves our difficulties into a new *locus* by turning them into translation problems. Hence it is of great interest to try to develop a game-theoretical semantics for natural languages directly, without taking the trouble of first trying to translate natural-language sentences into the canonical notation of formal quantification theory.

There may be reasons to think of the language to which the new game rules are applied as a regimented ("formalized") variant of English. If so, this regimented discourse is quite different from any traditional logical formalism, and much closer to the surface forms of English than the usual canonical notations of logical symbolism.

Game-theoretical semantics can in fact be extended to natural languages like English fairly directly. Much of the extension is obvious. Perhaps the most important non-trivial change is that, in the game rules for natural-language quantifiers, it is whole quantifier phrases, not bound variables, that proper names are now plugged in for. This necessitates amplifications in the game rules that serve to take care of the quantifier phrase itself. For instance, a special case of a game rule (G. some) for the English quantifier word "some" will be as follows:

(G. some)   If the game has reached a sen-
[special case]   tence of the form

                 (*)   X - some Y who Z - W

                 an individual may be chosen by Myself.
                 If the proper name (preexisting or
                 freshly coined) of this individual is "b",
                 the game is then continued with respect
                 to

                 (**)   X - b - W, b is a Y, and b Z.

It is assumed in this special case that Y, and Z, and X - W are singular and that "who" occupies the subject position in the clause "who" Z. It is obvious in principle how these simplifying assumptions can be dispensed with.

Much more has to be said about the anaphoric relations that hold in (**), in relation to those holding in (*). Since I believe that no viable general theory of anaphora has been presented by anyone, the need of such further explanations need not cause any special embarrassment to a game-theoretical semanticist.

It is especially instructive to compare (G. E) and (G. some) with each other. Both involve a substitution of a proper name, but the *substituens* is different in the two

cases: a formal variable in (G. E) but a complete quantifier phrase in (G. some). This throws some light on the
differences in the ways that the semantics of formal and
natural languages work.

The corresponding special case of the game rule for
"every" might be run as follows:

(G. every)   If the game has reached a sentence of
[special case]   the form

                (*) X - every Y who Z - W,

                an individual is chosen by Nature. If
                the proper name (preexisting or freshly
                coined) of this individual is "b", the
                game is continued with respect to

                (**) X - b - W, if b is a Y and b Z.

With this one change, the game-theoretical treatment of
quantificational and truth-functional discourse can be extended from formal to natural languages.

One feature of the resulting theory is worth pointing
out here. There is typically in the game-theoretical semantics for a natural language one game rule for each semantically primitive word or phrase. (This is the case
even more clearly in the game-theoretical treatment of
formal languages.) An important exception is "is". Insofar as a special provision has to be made for the purpose
of treating "is", it does not take the form of a game rule
but rather a stipulation concerning how the outcomes of a
play of one of our games is to be treated semantically.
These outcome sentences may take several different forms,
many of which involve "is", e.g.,

    b is A.   (e.g. "Jack is blond.")
    b is an X.   (e.g. "Jack is a boy.")
    b is.   (e.g. "God is.")
    S is a Y.   (e.g. "Red is a color.")

This feature of the behavior of "is" in game-theoretical
semantics is likely to be connected with its status as an
auxiliary in grammar. It is also important in that it shows
that "is" belongs to that part of semantics that deals with
what in the game-theoretical treatment are atomic sentences

and their ingredients. We might call this subsystem of semantics the *referential* system as distinguished from the *structural* subsystem that deals with the semantics of nonatomic sentences. The former subsystem has been sadly neglected in recent philosophical and logical discussions. One by-product of the study of "is" in game-theoretical semantics might thus be to call attention to this neglect.

One way of carrying out the extension of game-theoretical semantics from formal to natural languages systematically would be to cast game-theoretical semantics for natural languages in the form of a formal model of such languages, somewhat in analogy with Montague semantics. Even though I shall not try to carry out such a development here in any detail, the project of doing so offers us a useful viewpoint from which to see the issues that will be taken up in the rest of this chapter.

It is important to note that I am not proposing to translate natural languages into the canonical notation of the received formal logic. Such translations may perhaps ensue from a game-theoretical treatment of natural languages, insofar as it is successful. However, these possible translations are at best by-products of the game-theoretical treatment, not a tool it can use. In other words, the formal model itself that I am envisaging is a direct model of a natural language. Its primitives, including quantifier words, are those of English, and its expressions have in principle the same surface forms as those of a class of English expressions. The game rules apply to these regimented English expressions, not to their possible translations into logical notation - of any sort - and so do the semantical notions that can be defined in terms of the semantical games sketched above.

In this chapter, I shall for the most part restrict my attention to the English counterparts to formal logicians' existential and universal quantifiers, and disregard all the so-called nonstandard quantifiers, such as "many", "few", "most", "several", "the", etc. I believe that essentially the same things can be said of all quantifiers, standard or nonstanard.

3. The Alleged Ambiguity of "Is" according to Frege and Russell

One of the most important consequences of the basic ideas of game-theoretical semantics relates to the Frege-Russell claim that words like "is" are ambiguous. Frege and Russell claim, in effect, that "is" and its cognates are ambiguous in several ways. They distinguish between the following different meanings, each with a different formalization in the usual formalization of first-order logic (lower predicate calculus):

(i)   the "is" of identity, as in "Jack is John Jr," or Jack = John Jr.;

(ii)   the "is" of predication (the copula), as in "Jack is blond," or Blond(Jack);

(iii)   the "is" of existence, as in "God is," or (Ex) (God = x);

(iv)   the "is" of class-inclusion (generic "is"), as in "Man is an animal," or (x) (Man(x) → Animal(x)).

What is more, Frege and Russell built this ambiguity (as we can see from (i)-(iv)) into that marvelous creation of theirs, modern (elementary) logic, variously known as first-order logic, quantification theory, or lower predicate calculus. Anyone who uses this logic as his or her framework of semantical representation is thus committed to the Frege-Russell ambiguity thesis.

In an earlier paper I have shown that this ambiguity claim is false if game-theoretical semantics is the right semantics of the relevant aspects of English.[7] No one doubts that there are different *uses* of "is". But this does not imply that we are dealing with a real ambiguity. The different uses do not represent different *meanings* or *senses* of the verb "is" in game-theoretical semantics. Not only is the Frege-Russell ambiguity dispensable in my semantics; it can be shown that there are cases in which the Frege-Russell distinction just cannot be made in game-theoretical semantics. Indeed, these cases comprise most of the typical uses of "is". In this sense, game-theoretical semantics offers a counterexample to the Frege-Russell ambiguity thesis. Even if we do not want to commit ourselves to saying that game-theoretical semantics is the last and final truth in the semantics of natural languages, it offers a possible and indeed eminently viable semantical framework, alternative to the received ones in which the auxiliary verb "to be" does not exhibit the Frege-Russell ambiguity.

This conclusion has both linguistic and philosophical implications. For instance, no major philosopher before Frege (or possibly before John Stuart Mill and De Morgan) seems to have maintained the Frege-Russell ambiguity claim. Conventional formal logic, which goes back to Frege and which is based on the Frege-Russell thesis, is thus an entirely unsuitable tool in discussing pre-Fregean philosophers' views on existence, predication, identity, and being.

Linguistic repercussions of the demise of the hegemony of the Frege-Russell thesis include a reevaluation of our frameworks of semantic representation and a critical look at the notion of ambiguity itself. Furthermore, my revisionary result is not without relevance to the grammatical theory of auxiliaries, even though I am not in this chapter dealing with it directly. For one thing, if the Frege-Russell thesis is correct and the auxiliary verb "is" is radically ambiguous, there is little hope of construing the linguistic category of auxiliaries as a universal of any sort or even as a uniform grammatical category, at least insofar as semantics is concerned. Those linguists who are maintaining that there is a well-defined grammatical category of auxiliaries in natural languages like English should therefore welcome heartily my refutation of Frege and Russell *qua* theorists of English auxiliaries.

4. Game-Theoretical Semantics As a Many-Sorted Theory

But what can we say of the ambiguity or nonambiguity of "is"? I have so far only suggested that it does not exhibit the alleged Frege-Russell ambiguity. But maybe it is ambiguous in other ways. In order to discuss this subject, we have to go back to the basic ideas of game-theoretical semantics.

There are indeed further insights to be derived from a closer analysis of the special case of (G. some) formulated above. In it, the selection by Myself of an individual b enabled the players to move from (1) to (2):

(1)   X - some Y who Z - W
(2)   X - b - W, b is a Y, and b Z.

In this case, the entity selected obviously has to be a human being. In the case of other wh-words, the choice is to be made from other classes of entities. For instance, if instead of (1), the players were facing

(3)   X - some Y where Z - W,

where the relative clause can be thought of as being formed from an expression of the form

Z - in V,

the choice d would have to be a spatial location, and the output sentence would be

(4)   X - d - W, d is a Y, and Z in d.

What can we say of this kind of move in general? How are the players supposed to know what class of entities to make their selection from? The first answer that I will suggest is that it is by and large shown by the wh-word ("who" in (1), "where" in (3), and analogously in other cases). This is obviously the natural first guess on any view. According to this view, each different wh-word (plus certain phrases containing such words, e.g., a preposition + a wh-word) comes, apart from a number of exceptions that have to be discussed separately, associated with a different range for the quantifier that that wh-word basically is. Among these different wh-words (and expressions with the same function) there are the following:

(5)   (i)   who
       (ii)   that, which
       (iii)   when
       (iv)   where
       (v)   why
       (vi)   how
       (vii)   equal to which, greater (smaller) than
                which
       (viii)   like which

Speaking of wh-words here requires an explanation.
(5) is a list of different relative pronouns, different words
with a comparable function, and certain phrases that
behave similarly. Most of them are identical in form with
certain corresponding question words and phrases. The
latter are what is properly referred to as "wh-words" and
as "wh-phrases". However, in some cases there are discrepancies. For instance, the question word corresponding to "that" (and "which" in some of its uses) is "what",
and the wh-phrase corresponding to "like which" is "like
what". In some cases, there is a question phrase to which
no relative-pronoun-like expression naturally corresponds.
A case in point seems to be "how much", even though
some of its uses resemble those of relative pronouns.
(Witness, e.g., sentences like, "Some reliable indication of
how much money John paid to blackmailers is obtained from
his bank-account balances.") These differences between
relative pronouns (and their cousins) and wh-words will
nevertheless be disregarded in this chapter.

It requires a separate investigation to decide which
phrases involving wh-words (e.g., preposition + wh-word)
require a separate domain of values to be chosen in our
semantical games. Some such prepositional phrases require
further qualifications in our formulation of rules like (G.
some) in the first place. I shall not discuss them here,
however.

Apart from such complications, I have found a rough
one-to-one correlation between the different wh-words
(plus a number of other phrases involving wh-words) and
the widest ranges that quantifiers in English can have.
(Narrower ranges can be established by relativizing our
quantifiers to some class expressible in our language.) To
have a word for these maximal quantifier ranges, I shall
take a hint from Plato and call them *maximal genera*. (Cf.
Plato's *megista gene*.)

5. Predicative Correlates of the Maximal Genera

This correlation between the different maximal genera and
the different wh-words and phrases is paralleled by a
distinction between different substitution-instances of our
Y (see (1) above). In order to see this, note what can
happen to a quantifier phrase like the following:

(6)   some Y - wh-x Z,

(where wh-x is a wh-word) when its several elements are allowed to disappear. Notice, first of all, that the relative clause "wh-x Z" may be absent. (Indeed, the rule (G. some) must be modified so as to allow for this case.) When this happens, the wh-word cannot any longer be used as a guide to the subdomain (maximal genus) from which the individual b is to be chosen. All we have then to indicate the range of choice is Y. Clearly, the meaning of Y will tell what this range is. As a mechanism to accomplish this, some system of semantical markers can be used. The details are not relevant here. As a special case, we obtain a classification of the simple substitution values of "Y", i.e., of the simplest things that can be said of an entity. This multiple classification will match (at least roughly) the list of different wh-words, for both serve to signal the same thing: the set from which the individual b in (G. some) is to be selected.

This observation is further confirmed by noting what happens when we try to remove Y, too, from the input sentence of rules like (G. some). (This case, too, must be included as a variant form in rules like (G. some).) According to the line of thought I have been following, in this case nothing would remain to indicate the subdomain of players' choices. What actually happens in English is precisely what I have led you to expect. We can omit Y only if the quantifier word occurring in the rule is amplified to provide the missing information about what the domain of players' choices is. In other words, (6) ceases to be grammatical, but becomes grammatical when the quantifier word "some" is replaced by a longer variant. Corresponding to the different wh-words (5), are the following *some*-words:

(7)   (i)   someone, somebody
        (ii)   something
        (iii)   somewhen, sometime(s), someday
        (iv)   somewhere, someplace
        (v)   for some reason, because of
                   something
        (vi)   somehow, someway, (somewise)
        (vii)   somewhat, some amount, some
        (viii)   of some kind

Thus it appears that in deciding which maximal genus choices are to be made from, the players do not rely only or principally on the wh-word that occurs in the quantifier phrase. They rely primarily on the meaning of Y. When Y is not around, the information it normally codifies has to be supplied by the quantifier word itself, which therefore has to be amplified as indicated by (7).

For "every" the corresponding partial list is the following:

(8)	(i)	everyone, everybody
	(ii)	everything
	(iii)	always, every when
	(iv)	everywhere, every place
	(v)	(?)
	(vi)	every which way, every how

Similar lists can be given for "any", "no", etc.

The interesting thing here is not the details of the lists (7) and (8). These lists are rather messy in their details. What is interesting is the parallelism between (5) and (7). Even though this analogy is somewhat rough and ready, it is interesting in that it shows that there is a concurrence between the information concerning the relevant maximal genus that is yielded by the wh-word and that is observable from Y.

The latter source of information is open to the players even when the wh-word in question is one that does not help to decide between the different maximal genera. This happens particularly with the words "which" and "that", the latter of which is obviously a variant of "what". Their peculiarities require a separate investigation. "That" has at least four different uses. They are shown more clearly by their interrogative cousin "what". The interrogative "what" can have at least these four paraphrases:

(i)   What (which) *object*?
(ii) What (which) *animal*? More generally, what (which) living organism?
(iii) What *kind of* object (or organism or person)?
(iv) What *material*?

These observations are interesting in view of comparisons with formal languages of logic. If the view I am currently considering is right, natural languages have only a many-sorted quantification. Moreover, this many-sorted-ness appears irreducible. Unlike many formal languages, natural languages like English do not operate by pooling the different restricted ranges of sortal quantifiers to-gether.

For some purposes, this many-sorted quantification in English can nevertheless be (more or less naturally) re-duced to relativized quantification. For some of the widest ranges of quantifiers, there are nouns that delineate that range. The following is a list of such nouns that parallels earlier lists:

(9) (i)   person
     (ii)   (a)   object
             (b)   animal, organism
             (c)   kind
             (d)   material
     (iii)   time (moment or interval of)
     (iv)   place
     (v)   cause, reason
     (vi)   way
     (vii)   amount
     (viii)   kind, quality

In their interrogative use, many of the quantifier phrases of (5) admit of a paraphrase in terms of the corresponding member of (9), e.g., "who" as "which person", "where" as "in what place", etc. This does not vitiate the character of the quantifier ranges that go together with the wh-words of (5) as the widest ones in English semantics - at least in the semantics of the part of English to which we are here, in effect, restricting our attention.

6. Towards a Formal Model of the Correlated Distinctions, and Its Motivation

What kind of formal model of English semantics is suggest-ed by these observations? I cannot give a full formulation here, but some indications may nevertheless be not only relevant but useful. The main point concerns the struc-ture of the models that are used in the semantical inter-pretation of quantifier phrases. The substitution-instances of Y fall into a number of classes. (These need not be exclusive.) Corresponding to these, we have classes of

primitive terms, which are the different maximal genera
listed in (9). The choice of the wh-word used in a quantifier phrase has to be made accordingly, as indicated by
(5).

Even if this simplified formal model does not reproduce
everything that can be done in natural language, it will
turn out to have considerable interest in its own right as
an object of study. For instance, the limits of its expressive powers would be very interesting to examine more
closely.

The parallelism between (5) and (7) (or (8), or any
one of these analogues) nevertheless needs further discussion. I have not yet fully answered the basic question:
What is the situation of the players when they make a
move like the one from (1) to (2)? How do they know
which maximal genus to choose b from? In principle, there
are two plausible sources of this information in (1). They
are Y, especially the predicates it contains, and the wh-
word. We shall, for the time being, work on the assumption that each Y that is available to us in English (or
rather, the part of English that we are considering here),
entails one of the superpredicates (9). This superpred-
icate determines the range of choice for the players in a
given move. This is the simplified model of English we are
considering here. The adequacy of this model is partly an
empirical question.

There are nevertheless several conceptual issues involved in judging our simplified model. For one thing, its
viability depends on the conceptual question concerning
precisely how the limits of a language (the language or
language fragment under scrutiny - in the present case, a
part of English) are drawn. One of the crucial questions
is whether, in the fragment of English under consid-
eration, there are predicates that are not restricted to one
of the maximal genera marked by (9). Here the boundaries of our language fragment matter crucially. For
instance, philosophers have words in their jargon that
break the division between the widest ranges of English
quantifiers as we have delineated them so far, in some
cases comprehending all of them. Words like "entity",
"being", "individual", "particular", etc., are cases in
point. To have a word for them, I will extend the old
scholastic terminology and call them "transcategorematic"
words.[8] However, for the purposes of this chapter there
seem to be good reasons for us to limit ourselves to frag-

ments of English that do not contain such transcategorematic expressions. First, these expressions, in the use they are cast into here, seem to be rather foreign to spontaneous, ordinary discourse. Whatever frightening uncertainties concerning some strange apparition's status are supposed to be conjured up by the title of the recent horror movie *The Entity*, I doubt that they are of the same transcategorematic kind as those associated with philosophers' use of the same word.

Second, set-theoretical and semantical paradoxes serve as a warning not to assume that a part of discourse remains consistent when it breaks the boundaries of the quantifier ranges that go together with different wh-words and phrases. For this reason, too, such words and expressions should be excluded, at least until further notice. Thus the limitation of the different substitution-instances of Y in (1)-(2) to those that entail one of the expressions of (9) can almost be reached by stipulation.

This is closely connected with a third point. One function of the transcategorematic vocabulary in ordinary language is metalogical and metasemantical. (Notice, for instance, how tempting it is to use such transcategorematic terms as "entity" in explaining our game rules, as I did above.) Now it seems to me amply motivated to deal with the metalogical and metasemantical part of a natural language separately, even if we admit that it is a genuine part of that language. For otherwise we are not likely to obtain any coherent semantical theory. This is what the interesting paradoxes show us. Tarski noted in 1936 that no coherent truth-definition is possible for a natural language in its entirety, for the language in which the definition is to be given is supposed to be the same one, and yet it must be stronger than the given (object) language. Instead of giving up the whole enterprise, as Tarski did, the more constructive response would have been to try to find a hierarchical structure in natural languages, for instance, to locate theoretically significant parts of natural language for which an explicit semantical theory can be developed. It is my tentative suggestion that we can do so by excluding, temporarily, all transcategorematic vocabulary from the fragment we are examining.

This suggestion appears especially natural if we compare game-theoretical semantics with such formal models as Montague semantics. The main novelty of my theory seems to be that it uses a many-sorted logic rather than the usual one-sorted quantification theory. This is an essential improvement, it seems to me, over an aspect of the basic Fregean model with which Montague and others are still in basic agreement. However, it remains to be seen whether it will be able to capture completely the actual subtlety of natural languages. With these qualifications in mind, we thus stick, for the time being, to the analogy between (5), (7), and (9). Or, more accurately, we restrict ourselves to a part of English in which the parallelism holds.

7. Different Uses of "Is"

But what does all this have to do with the different uses of "is"? A double answer is implicit in what has been said. Since the widest ranges of English quantifiers – prominently including existential quantifiers – are the maximal genera that go together with the different wh-words, the categorization of the latter is also ipso facto a categorization of the different uses of existence and of the existential "is" in English. Since identity presumably makes sense only within one and the same class over which we can quantify, these classes will also go together with different uses of the "is" of identity in English. Moreover, since it was suggested that in each case of predication in English – and hence in each case of predicative "is" – we are moving within one of the maximal genera marked by (9), the same classification is inevitably also a classification of different uses of predicative (copulative) "is".

An even more striking partial answer is obtained by going back to (1)-(2) (or to any other parallel instance of (G. some)). In the second conjunct of the output sentence, we have an occurrence of "is" that has no antecedent in the input sentence. It comes about as a result of the application of (G. some). In the Frege-Russell classification, it would have to be an "is" of predication, for the whole function in (G. some) of this "is" is to restrict the choice of b to individuals of a certain kind. We can classify such apparently predicative occurrences of "is" according to the wh-word occurring in the quantifier phrase to which (G. some) is applied. Thus we obtain a rough one-to-one correlation between certain predicative uses of "is" and the different wh-words in English.

The parallelism that we have found between different existential senses of "is" and certain of its predicative uses offers further evidence, albeit indirect, for my criticism of the distinction between those two senses of "is".

Our findings concerning the multiply related, but different semantical phenomena that we have considered may thus be summed up in the form of the following list of correlated distinctions:

(10)   (i)   Different wh-words (and phrases).

        (ii)   Different widest classes of entities that English quantifiers can range over.

        (iii)   Different uses of the existential "is" in English.

        (iv)   Different uses of the "is" of identity in English.

        (v)   Different uses of the predicative "is" in English.

        (vi)   Different classes (mutually exclusive and collectively exhaustive) of simple predicates of English.

Moreover, each member of these multiple classifications goes together with a categorial word from our list (9).

It should be pointed out that in addition to the uses of "is" within each maximal genus there are uses of "is" to relate members of different maximal genera to each other. The following are cases in point:

Jill is blonde.
This statue is of bronze.
Stuart is in Oxford.
It is now ten o'clock in Hong Kong.

Do these coinciding distinctions mark different *senses* or *meanings* of "is" or merely different *uses*? Is "is" ambiguous? Since I believe that ambiguity is relative to a semantical framework, I do not have to give an absolute answer to these question. The distinction is the important thing; how it is labelled is not very important. The operative question, rather, is whether we can develop a transcategorial theory of "is" and its conceptual neighbors. The answer to this question is more likely to depend on our self-imposed restrictions on metalogical notions than on "is" itself.

8. Aristotelian Categories Reconstructed

At this point, a philosophical reader is likely to have a vivid déjà vu experience. For what seems to be emerging as a consequence of the basic assumptions of game-theoretical semantics is nothing but a modernized version of Aristotle's doctrine of categories, not in its details (after all, Aristotle was dealing with a different language), but in all of its leading theoretical ideas. Aristotelian scholars have found the combination of different ideas in Aristotle's different categories intensely puzzling. These different aspects of Aristotle's theory include the following:

(11)   (i)   Different questions one can ask about a given entity, and hence different question words (and certain related phrases) in a language.[9] Some scholars have argued on this basis that Aristotle's theory is based on the structure of the Greek language.[10]

        (ii)   Different highest predicates under one or another of which everything that is has to fall.[11]

        (iii)   Different senses of verbs for being in
        -(v)   their different uses: (iii) existential, (iv) copulative,[12] (v) identifying.

        (vi)   Different widest classes of primitive predicates in the language in question. Indeed, (vi) is closest to Aristotle's explanation of the categories in his *Categoriae*.[13]

Scholars have complained that Aristotle is "confusing" these different senses of "category" with each other.[14] They have also quarrelled at length concerning which of the distinctions (11) (i)-(vi) Aristotle "really" intended. What we have found shows that both these problems are spurious. Aristotle is not "confusing" the different distinctions, for they go together inevitably. For the same reason, it makes little sense to ask which distinction he in fact had in mind. The real problem is to understand what Aristotle is doing in assimilating the different distinctions

(11) (i)-(v) to each other. This question we can now answer. These distinctions in fact go together, for the systematic reasons that we have just uncovered. The distinctions (11) (i)-(vi) match very well the distinctions (10) (i)-(vi), which we were led to make and to assimilate to each other on the basis of our game-theoretical analysis. We have thus found a partial vindication of Aristotle's theory and an explanation of what clearly are its most puzzling overall features. Aristotle is not confusing different distinctions with each other. He is in effect pointing out important interrelations that obtain – on the view we are considering here – between the different distinctions (10)-(11).

Now we can see one reason why the formal model I sketched earlier is so interesting. It is interesting because (among other reasons) it embodies the traditional doctrine of the categories. The limitations of the model will therefore be limitations of the doctrine of categories.

Thus we have reached another interesting – albeit somewhat tentative – consequence of the basic assumptions of game-theoretical semantics, applied in the natural way to the semantics of English. Earlier we saw that one of the metatheorems of game-theoretical semantics is the failure of the Frege-Russell distinction between several allegedly different meanings of "is". Now we have just seen that game-theoretical semantics implies a version of Aristotle's doctrine of categories, incorporating all of the most important – and most puzzling – general theoretical features of the latter.

These observations incidentally also vindicate some of my terminological stipulations. My choices of (a) the old term "transcategorematic" for the use I am making of it and (b) the locution "maximal genera" for the widest quantifier ranges turn out to be historically justified. It is not only Plato who speaks of *megista gene*. Aristotle likewise uses the closely related locutions such as "indivisible concepts" (*ta amera*) and "(true) universals" (*ta katholou*) for his categories.[15]

The similarities between my theory and Aristotle's doctrine of categories are not accidental, and they can be pushed further. For instance, one corollary to what we found is that Aristotle's category of relation is not a class of relations. It has to be a class of predicates (cf. (vi) above), and hence it is the widest class of relational predicates. A closer look at what Aristotle says readily confirms this prediction.

This fact is an instructive instance of a much more general feature that is characteristic of the Aristotelian doctrine of categories. It is not a distinction between entities of different *logical types*. (Cf. item (b) of the list in the next section.) This of course goes against what a modern philosopher who learned his or her logic on Bertrand Russell's knee would think first. Nevertheless an analogous mistake is committed by those philosophers who think of Aristotle's category of relation as the supreme class of relations that we might want to consider.

Furthermore, the problem (mentioned above) of whether the parallel distinctions (9) represent different *meanings* or merely different *uses* of "is" has likewise a counterpart in Aristotle. One of the crucial questions he discusses in his metaphysics is whether the uses of τὸ εἶναι in different categories are merely "homonymous" (equivocal) or whether they have something in common. In order to defend the possibility of his "first philosophy" or "science of being *qua* being" (i.e., metaphysics), Aristotle must argue for the latter option, as he in fact does repeatedly (but not invariably), principally in *Metaphysics* IV. Game-theoretical semantics thus offers a framework for discussing and evaluating this famous (or rather, infamous) doctrine of Aristotle.

Likewise, the contrast in (9) (ii) between (a) and (b) on the one hand, and (c) on the other, can be put to use as a rational reconstruction of Aristotle's distinction between primary and secondary substances. Furthermore, it may be that the logic of the difference between common nouns and adjectives (for the former can be substitution-values of Y in such rules as (G. some)) is related to the logic of Aristotle's distinction between essential and accidental predication.

A terminological and conceptual side glance may be in order at this point. A sharp distinction ought to be made between different uses of the term "category" in recent literature. These different uses (or senses) include at least the following:

(a) *Aristotelian categories*. (My rational reconstruction of them enables us to see more clearly than before what they are all about.)

(b) Categories in the sense of *logical types* (as Russell called them). My reconstruction shows that these "categories" are conceptually different from (a), even though there are interrelations. Or perhaps I should rather speak here of problems concerning the precise relationship of (a) and (b).

Recently I have been suggesting that this notion of logical type is perhaps not quite as sacrosanct as it has been in the logical and philosophical discussion of the last hundred years. At the very least, the selection of types that can be expressed in one's formal languages ought to be enriched. This is also one of the changes Montague tried to bring about in his formal models for natural languages.

(c)   Most definitely (a)-(b) have to be distinguished from the notion of a *grammatical* category, even though it may be thought of that it is one of the aims of linguistic theorizing to bring them all together.

9. The Failure of Aristotelian Categories

We have thus reached an interesting reconstruction of the Aristotelian doctrine of categories within game-theoretical semantics. The historical and systematic interest of this reconstruction is not spoiled by the fact that, in the last analysis, it will be found to be an inaccurate representation of the logic and semantics of natural languages, notwithstanding its initial plausibility. On the contrary, the possibility of critically evaluating Aristotle's doctrine is highly interesting in its own right. Moreover, such criticisms are the more convincing the better justice my reconstruction does to Aristotle's views.

An opening for criticism is due to the fact that my reconstruction of Aristotle is based on simplifying assumptions that now have to be discussed in greater depth. Such a discussion must be based on an analysis of the structure of the quantifier phrases themselves to which our quantifier rules are to be applied. Unfortunately, the semantical and syntactical analysis of quantifiers has been one of the most notorious moot points in recent linguistics. I cannot develop a full-fledged theory of this subject in a single chapter. A few words on the subject are nevertheless in order.

So far, we have considered only a relatively simple structure of English quantifier phrases, viz., the one illustrated by (1). For instance, a quantifier phrase might have the structure (12):

   (12)   some Y who Z.

A familiar case is one in which Y is a count noun. Such nouns presuppose a domain of individuals on which they are defined. As long as we confine our attention to such cases (and perhaps restrict our formal semantical models to them), some version of the Aristotelian doctrine of categories appears to be a virtually inevitable consequence. But is this familiar case really representative? As long as we are working along the same (or similar) lines as the best-known recent formal theories of semantics, such as Montague semantics, it is not unnatural to think that whatever goes into Y consists ultimately of predicates and functions, each defined within some given maximal genus. However, this is not the best available analysis of English quantifier phrases, even when we leave the relative clause "who Z" (and its analogues) out of the picture. As far as the syntactical situation is concerned, I shall here rely on Joan Bresnan's (unpublished) treatment.[16] On Bresnan's analysis, a quantifier phrase (in my sense, but with the relative clause omitted) has a structure somewhat as follows:

   (13)

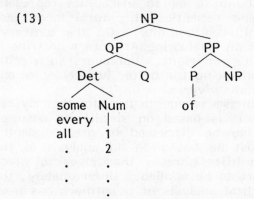

Here Q seems to mark quantity classifiers as, for example, the following:

(14)   Q

            one(s)
            number
            part
            pile
            group
            ton
            .
            .
            .

An example of an unabbreviated NP of this form might be

(15)   every three gallons of fine old wine.

One fact here that is of interest for our present semantical purposes is that the different parts of Bresnan's
analysis correspond (as she herself has pointed out) to the
different roles of quantifier phrases in my semantical
games, at least roughly.   Det specifies which player or
players make a move (and, if both players make a move at
the same time, how their moves are related to each other).
Num specifies how many times the move is repeated. (This
role of Num in (13) is illustrated by the fact that when
the move in question cannot be repeated, Num cannot have
an instantiation, either, e.g., if one tried to use as the
quantifier word in (13), instead of "some", "every", "all",
etc. the definite article "the".)   Finally, the quantity
classifier Q serves to individuate the elements of the
players' domain of search jointly with the PP.
     This analysis of quantifier phrases has a distinct simi-
larity with Aristotle's metaphysics, for Aristotle, too,
brings in ideas of matter and of the form-matter contrast
in discussing the nature of substances.   In (13), it is the
last NP that can indicate what kind of matter we are dealing with.   And instead of a quantity classifier, the Q in
(13) might serve to indicate a certain shape or form, as in
the following examples:

(16)   all three statues of bronze
       some cubes of ice
       few bracelets of pure gold

Hence in this direction the way we have to go beyond the

original oversimplified doctrine of categories has at least
some resemblance with Aristotle's own way of doing so.

However, Bresnan's analysis is calculated to apply more
widely than merely to cases in which the last NP is a mass
term and Q a quantity classifier or a "formal" term. It is
for these additional applications that the list (14) includes
"one(s)". This part of the analysis mentioned above relies
on Perlmutter's hypothesis that "a(n)" is a proclitic
variant of the numeral "one".[17] For example, we have to
derive "a man" from (13) as follows:

(17)

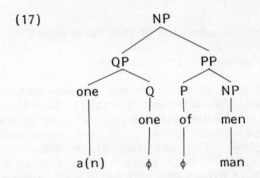

Here, the first bottom line is motivated by Perlmutter's
hypothesis. Bresnan has shown how to motivate the
others as well.

What this means is that the proffered analysis is
calculated to bring under the same roof cases in which the
last NP in (13) is a mass term and those in which it is a
count noun. What distinguishes the two is how they enter
into (13). Thus we have, on the one hand, examples like
(15) or (16) and, on the other, examples like the
following:

(18) Every two of the men,

which is assumed to give rise further to

(19) Every two men.

This suggested treatment, which cannot be discussed
fully here, goes in a quite different direction from most
philosophers' recent attempts to deal with mass terms.[18]
There are some good indications, however, that linguisti-
cally it has to be taken very seriously. At least syntacti-

SEMANTICAL GAMES AND ARISTOTELIAN CATEGORIES

cally, the contrast between count nouns and mass terms has been exaggerated. Perhaps the most striking suggestion of this fact comes from the Finnish language, where count nouns behave in the role of the last NP in (13) precisely in the same way as mass terms, except for the fact that Q has to be empty:

> (20) Kaikki kolme miestä [all three out-of-man (= the singular partitive of "mies")]
> Jokaiset kaksi naulaa sokeria [every two out-of-pound out-of-sugar (both nouns in the singular partitive case)]

Obviously, this whole complex of problems needs further discussion.

Speaking generally, this sketchy analysis of quantifier phrases does not by any means automatically invalidate our reconstructed version of Aristotelian category theory. However, it does open a door to a line of thought that leads us beyond Aristotle's categories and also, in certain respects, beyond the modern logic of quantification. What happens here is that the individuals over which our quantifiers range are no longer taken for granted in all uses of language, but our language can be used to specify how these instances are, as it were, built out of more primitive ingredients. The simplest case is undoubtedly one in which the NP of the PP is a mass term and the Q of the QP (see (13)) is a unit of the mass in question, as in (15). Then (13) shows how our individuals are constructed out of the material specified by the mass term. This observation has in fact a moral for formal models of semantics. If such models are to accommodate mass terms with their characteristic uses, we cannot postulate just one fixed domain of individuals, but must allow for the introduction of new ranges for quantifiers as indicated.

This shows one way in which new ranges of quantifiers can be "manufactured" in ordinary discourse. However, it is really a special case within the general semantical situation. A different case that I have not yet mentioned is illustrated by the following examples:

> (21) any two additive groups of numbers; a continuum of colors; each discrete set of points.

For these phrases, what would be the last NP in (13) is

not a mass term. However, the counterpart to the Q of
(13) is not empty, either. In this intermediate case, new
individuals (values of quantifiers) are not constructed, so
to speak, out of unstructured matter, as in (15) or (16),
but out of entities that already have an individuality of
their own. Yet the outcome is a separate entity that can
be the value of a different kind of a quantifier.

Hence, this represents a different way of manufacturing
conceptually new individuals. It is clear that the result of
such constitution of higher-type entities out of individuals
breaks the boundaries of simple-minded Aristotelian categories. As can be seen from examples like (21), the same
structural terms, playing the role of the Q of (13), apply
in different categories. Yet the outcome entities (groups,
discrete sets, continua, etc.) can be quantified over.
This shows that the Aristotelian scheme of a finite number
of fixed coordinated categories is an oversimplified model
of natural languages.

The new "categories" (ranges of quantifiers not included in any traditional categories) are much more like
logical types than Aristotelian categories. In this direction, traditional (Aristotelian) categories are therefore
beginning to change in the direction of categories in the
modern sense of logical types.

Quantifier phrases like (21) are thus one of the many
vehicles by means of which natural language transcends
the limits of the fragments of natural languages in which
the Aristotelian theory of categories – or some variant
thereof – holds. If transcategorematic words were a
philosopher's or a semanticist's luxury, we could and
should dispense with them in our theory of how honest-
to-Austin ordinary language works semantically. But they
are not used for those esoteric purposes only. As is
suggested by examples like (21), our transcategorematic
vocabulary is used for perfectly substantive purposes.
Hence, any realistic account of natural language must
accommodate them and their use in quantifier phrases.

One way of looking at the Aristotelian idea of form is to
think of it as an attempt to deal with both examples like
(16) and examples like (21). (Whether this was Aristotle's
own purpose will not be discussed here.) This interpretation is encouraged by the idea found in the Aristotelian
tradition that the concept of form is relative: what is form
on one level can be matter for a higher-order entity.

It is nevertheless clear that the notion of form cannot

do the whole job here. It sits most comfortably on the cases where the matter is completely unstructured and the structure imposed on it ("the form") is comparable to a fairly simple geometrical form, e.g., "a cube of ice". The notion of form is much less happy in connection with complex relational structures, such as are exemplified by (21). In some ways, Aristotle's notion of form was supposed to do the job that our modern concept of relation (relational structure) is calculated to do; but it could not quite manage it. It seems true historically that it was primarily the logic of relations and functions that led logicians and other thinkers out of the fly bottle of Aristotelian logic and Aristotelian categories. Now we can see that such an historical development is to some extent reflected in the synchronic facts of natural-language semantics.

However, the line of thought that I have sketched, and that is based on an analysis of quantifier phrases in English, is not the only direction in which some natural languages transcend the confines of Aristotelian categories. Another direction is that of *events*. This direction is messier than the one first considered philosophically. Indeed, it leads at once to the problem of whether events are (or can be) full-fledged basic particulars. There is more potential evidence than has been resorted to by philosophers, however, at least insofar as natural languages (and the ontologies they presuppose) are concerned. Sundry nominalization processes provide such evidence. We cannot examine them in this chapter, however, except for suggesting an historical "application". From this vantage point it is not accidental that Aristotle should have had considerable difficulty in accommodating change and motion in his conceptual framework, and that the overthrow of his philosophy began in the area of the analysis of motion.

It is a shortcoming of the last two sections that they do not develop any game-theoretical treatment of the phenomena registered there. Perhaps the readers of this chapter will rise to the challenge of developing such an account.

NOTES

[1] See chapter 1 above. For earlier work see the papers collected in Esa Saarinen, editor, *Game-Theoretical Semantics*, D. Reidel, Dordrecht, 1979. Chapter 2 above

provides a philosophical motivation for game-theoretical semantics along Kantian lines. For further references see
section I of the bibliography at the end of this volume.
[2] See section II (ix) of the bibliography.
[3] See chapter 3 above and Jaakko Hintikka and Lauri
Carlson, "Conditionals, Generic Quantifiers, and Other
Applications of Subgames", in Saarinen, *Game-Theoretical
Semantics*, pp. 179-214.
[4] See chapter 3 above and also section II (v) of the bibliography for Gödel's paper, and for the literature generated by it.
[5] See sections II (iii)-(iv) of the bibliography.
[6] See sections II (i)-(ii) of the bibliography.
[7] Jaakko Hintikka, "'Is', Semantical Games, and
Semantical Relativity", *Journal of Philosophical Logic* 8
(1979), 433-68 (reprinted as the preceding chapter).
[8] The term "syncategorematic" is sometimes used for this
purpose. Both etymology and medieval usage make it more
natural to speak instead of "transcategorematic" terms.
[9] Cf. Ockham (Michael J. Loux, translator and editor,
Ockham's Theory of Terms, University of Notre Dame
Press, Notre Dame, Indiana, 1974, pp. 8-9); J. L.
Ackrill, *Aristotle's Categories and De Interpretatione*,
Clarendon Press, Oxford., 1963, p. 79; Theodor Gomperz,
Greek Thinkers, vol. 4 (tr. by G. G. Berry), Murray,
London, 1912, p. 39; and Charles Kahn, "Questions and
Categories", in Henry Hiż, editor, *Questions*, D. Reidel,
Dordrecht, 1978, pp. 227-78 (passim).
[10] See Adolf Trendelenburg, *Geschichte der Kategorien-
lehre*, Bethge, Berlin, 1846; Emile Benveniste, "Catégories
de pensée et catégories de langue", in *Problèmes de
Linguistique générale*, Gallimard, Paris, 1966, pp. 63-74;
and Charles Kahn, "Questions and Categories".
[11] See, for example, Hermann Bonitz, *Uber die Kate-
gorien des Aristoteles*, Staatsdruckere, Vienna, 1853.
[12] See, for example, O. Apelt, *Beiträge zur Geschichte
der griechischen Philosophie*, Leipzig, 1891.
[13] Aristotle, *Categoriae*, 1 b 25 - 2 a 10.
[14] See, for example, Heinrich Maier, *Die Syllogistik des
Aristoteles*, vols. 1-2, Tübingen, 1896-1900; and W. D.
Ross, *Aristotle's Metaphysics*, vols. 1-2, Clarendon Press,
Oxford, 1924.
[15] Aristotle sometimes uses the term "genus" in another,
narrower, sense, as a mere correlate to the term "spe-
cies". In this sense, categories of course are not genera.

However, this sense is not relevant to our present problems. See *Posterior Analytics* II, 19, 100 b 1-2.
[16] Since I am not sure that I have understood Bresnan's
view fully, the responsibility for the following discussion
is nevertheless mine and not hers.
[17] David M. Perlmutter, "On the Article in English", in M.
Bierwisch and K. E. Heidolph, editors, *Progress in Linguistics*, Mouton, The Hague, 1970, pp. 233-48.
[18] For a sample of such attempts, see F. J. Pelletier,
editor, *Mass Terms: Some Philosophical Problems*, D.
Reidel, Dordrecht, 1979.

Chapter 9

ON THE *ANY*-THESIS
AND THE METHODOLOGY OF LINGUISTICS

1. General[1]

In earlier publications, I have outlined a largely novel approach[2] to the semantics of certain formal languages and the semantics of certain fragments of natural languages.[3] In this approach, the truth of a sentence S is defined as the existence of a winning strategy for one of the two players, called *Myself*, in a certain two-person game G(S) associated with S.[4] Intuitively, G(S) may be thought of as an attempt on the part of Myself to verify S against the schemes of an actively resistant opponent who is called *Nature*. On the basis of this idea, most of the game rules can be anticipated. For instance, I win if the game ends with a true primitive sentence, and Nature wins if it ends with a false one. For quantifier phrases like "any Y who Z" and "every Y who Z", the game rules can also be anticipated. As special cases we have the following rules:

(G. every) If the game has reached a sentence of the form

> X - every Y who Z - W,

> then a person can be chosen by Nature, say b. The game is continued with respect to

> X - b - W, if b is a Y and b Z.

Further discussion of this rule is, of course, needed here.

(G. any) The same with "any" replacing "every".

(G. each) The same with "each" replacing "every".

The main claims that are being tacitly made in (G. any) are (i) that "any" is unambiguous and (ii) that it always has basically the force of a universal quantifier. This runs counter to many recent treatments of "any" by lin-

guists.[5] Some of the ways to account for apparent counterexamples to my unified treatment are indicated later in
this chapter – and in some of my earlier papers on game-
theoretical semantics.   Other phenomena to be explained
are found largely in connection with negation and with
epistemic notions. They will be dealt with in separate
studies. (See here chapter 4 above.)

For existential-quantifier words we have similar rules,
the main difference being that I make the choice of an
individual:

(G. some)   If the game has reached a sentence of the form

X – some Y who Z – W,

then a person may be chosen by Myself, say
b. The game is continued with respect to

X – b – W, b is a Y, and b Z.

(G. a(n))   The same with "a(n)" replacing "some".

Among the further problems concerning the quantifier
rules that will not be discussed here, perhaps the most
important ones are the following: (i) the way the different
domains of individuals are determined from which the players choose their individuals; (ii) the provisos needed in
the quantifier rules to preserve anaphoric relationships.
The former question is very closely related to the
Aristotelian notion of category.[6]   Some aspects of the
latter problem have been touched upon briefly in an earlier
paper.[7] Both need a great deal of further discussion,
which cannot be undertaken here.

For a logician, game-theoretical semantics is scarcely
news. It is merely a systematization and generalization of
such ideas as Skolem functions, functional interpretations,
game quantifiers, and Henkin quantifiers.

When game-theoretical semantics is applied to natural
languages, we need principles governing the order in
which applicable game rules are to be applied to a given
sentence. There are both general ordering principles and
special ones. The former include the following:

(O. comm) A rule must not be applied to a phrase in a
           lower clause if a rule can be applied to a

phrase in a higher one.

(O. LR)   In one and the same clause, game rules are
               applied left to right.

If the game rules are turned around and their syntactical
components used as rules for sentence generation,
(O. comm) is tantamount to what linguists call the
principle of the cycle.[8]
        General ordering principles can be overruled by special
ones, however. An example of a special ordering principle
is the rule (O. any), which gives the game rule (G. any)
priority over the rules for negation and for conditionals as
well as over modal rules (in the narrow sense of the term
that does not include rules for epistemic notions or other
propositional attitudes). In contrast, the ordering principle (O. every) says that the game rule (G. every) does
not enjoy comparable privileges. Likewise, the ordering
principle (O. each) says that (G. each) has priority over
other quantifier rules as well as over the propositional
rules (G. and) and (G. or). Thus ordering principles
serve to distinguish between the meanings of certain
closely related words, such as "any", "every", and
"each". Later in this chapter, a change will be made in
(O. any).
        Relying on all these different ordering principles, I
have put forward a criterion for the acceptability of "any"
in a certain fragment of English. This criterion I have
dubbed the *any*-thesis. In its simplest form, which needs
qualifications, it says that "any" is unacceptable in an
otherwise grammatical context if an exchange of "any" for
"every" yields an equivalent (and grammatical) sentence.
The purpose of this chapter is to offer some further evidence for the *any*-thesis – and for the ordering principles
it relies on – and to discuss some of its methodological
consequences.
        It may be in order to remove one possible source of
needless puzzlement, and perhaps even misunderstanding,
immediately. The very form of the *any*-thesis challenges
the currently fashionable dogma that (syntactical) well-
formedness (acceptability) and (semantical) meaningfulness
(interpretability) go together. For in order to reject a
string of the form "X – any – Y" as unacceptable on the
basis of the *any*-thesis, we have to compare its meaning
with that of "X – every – Y", which of course presupposes

that it has one.   Hence, I am in effect assuming, in formulating the *any*-thesis in the way I have done, that a
syntactically unacceptable string can have a well-defined
semantical interpretation.   This may seem paradoxical, but
it really isn't.   I shall return to some of the questions
raised by this situation later in this chapter.   Meanwhile,
suffice it to register my strong belief that the current
dogma is simply that, and does not amount to an objection
to my formulation of the *any*-thesis.

2. New Evidence

(i) Some indirect evidence for the *any*-thesis is obtained
from observations concerning the particle "ever".   An account analogous to the *any*-thesis serves to explain its
distribution.

The assumption that corresponds to the *any*-thesis (we
might call it the *ever*-thesis) says that "ever" is unacceptable in an otherwise grammatical context if an exchange of "ever" for "always" yields a semantically equivalent sentence.   Also it is assumed that the game rule (G.
ever) enjoys the same priorities as that for "any" except
that it does not have a priority over modal rules (in the
narrow sense).   This exception somewhat reduces the
variety of examples that can illustrate the phenomena we
are studying here.

Examples are easily forthcoming to illustrate the consequences for these assumptions.   They are all analogous
to the corresponding examples in terms of "any".

The first group of examples illustrates the ordering
principles:

   (1)   I'd be surprised if Scot ever contributes.
   (2)   I'd be surprised if Scot always contributes.
   (3)   Bill doesn't ever smile.
   (4)   Bill doesn't always smile.

The second group illustrates the consequences of the
ever-thesis:

   (5)   *If I ask him, Scot ever contributes.
   (6)   If I ask him, Scot always contributes.
   (7)   *Bill ever smiles.
   (8)   Bill always smiles.

(9)   Nancy doesn't believe that Mary ever lies.
(10)   Nancy doesn't believe that Mary always lies.
(11)   Do you ever read detective stories for relaxation?
(12)   Do you always read detective stories for relaxation?
(13)   *Nancy believes that Mary ever lies.
(14)   Nancy believes that Mary always lies.

All these examples are consistent with the *ever*-thesis, as the reader can easily ascertain.

(ii)   New evidence for the *any*-thesis is available from apparent counterexamples to it.   Insofar as they can be explained away in a natural way, we obtain further confirmation for the thesis.[9] The variety of modes of explanation that we can use also serves as a reminder of how many-splendored and subtle the explanations are that may be used in exploring the surface data of language.
The following is a case in point:

(15)   I'd be surprised if John didn't find any of Bill's mistakes.

The ordering principle (O. any) assigns to the "any" of (15) a wider scope than to either the negation ("not") or the "if".   Hence the expected reading of (15) seems to be

(16)   (x)[(x is a mistake of Bill's →
        $\sim$(John found x)) → I'd be surprised],

which is equivalent with

(17)   (Ex)(x is a mistake of Bill's &
        $\sim$(John found x)) → I'd be surprised.

Yet intuitively (17) does not seem to be the right reading of (15). We definitely seem to prefer another reading that can be captured by the following:

(18)   (x)(x is a mistake of Bill's → $\sim$(John found x))
        → I'd be surprised.

Is this a counterexample to the ordering principles on which the *any*-thesis is based? No, it is not. Indeed, an explanation of why we prefer (18) is implicit in the *any*-thesis itself.   For on the reading (17), (15) would be synonymous with

(19)   I'd be surprised if John didn't find all of Bill's mistakes.

For the "logical form" of (19) is clearly

(20) $\sim$(x)(x is a mistake of Bill's $\rightarrow$ John found x) $\rightarrow$ I'd be surprised,

which is logically equivalent with (17).   Hence the reading (16)-(17) is ruled out by the *any*-thesis itself.

This explanation presupposes two things.   First, it assumes that when the *any*-thesis conflicts with our ordering principles, it wins.   In this sense, ordering principles like (O. any) are not absolute, but can be overruled by other factors.   (Otherwise the other, actually preferred, reading (18) would not be possible.)   This is in keeping with collateral evidence.

Second, we must be able to apply the *any*-thesis to readings of sentences and not to the grammaticality or ungrammaticality of sentences simpliciter.[10]   This is in the spirit of the *any*-thesis, even though its original formulation must be generalized so as to allow for it.   The idea is obvious: when the game rules can be applied to a sentence in several different orders and/or with different informational dependencies (different information sets), thus creating several putative readings, only those readings are acceptable that result in a meaning different· from the otherwise analogous reading of a sentence with "every" instead of "any".

This explanation of the readings of (15) is further supported by the observation that whenever the reading prescribed by (O. any) (the "wide scope" reading) does not conflict with the *any*-thesis, it is perfectly acceptable. This is illustrated by the following example:

(21)   I'd be surprised if nobody failed to point out any of Bill's mistakes.

The reading prescribed by (O. any) is represented by

(22)   (Ex)[(x is a mistake of Bill's)   &
         (z)$\sim$(z pointed out x)] $\rightarrow$ I'd be surprised.

This is indeed a possible, and, to my mind, the most plausible, reading of (21). It is clearly different in meaning from

(23) I'd be surprised if nobody failed to point out all of Bill's mistakes.

(iii) It has been claimed that examples like the following present a problem for my theory:

(24) Sue did not tell everything to anybody.
(25) Sue did not tell anybody everything.
(26) Sue did not tell anything to everybody.
(27) Sue did not tell everybody anything.

My ordering principles imply that (24)-(25) should have the following representation:

(28) $(x)\sim(y)$(Sue told y to x).

Likewise, (O. any) entails that the logical form of (26)-(27) should be

(29) $(y)\sim(x)$(Sue told y to x).

Indeed (28) is clearly the intuitively preferred reading of (24)-(25). Furthermore, (26) has (29) as one of its readings. Finally, (27) is probably taken to say the same as (29) by many educated informants. However, (27) has clearly another reading on which it is not tantamount to (29) but rather to

(30) Sue told nothing to somebody.

Likewise, (26) has a secondary reading that has the same force as

(31) Sue told nothing to everybody.

Even (24) perhaps has a reading on which it is equivalent with

(32) Sue told something to nobody.

The logical form of (30), which is (33), is clearly different from (29):

(33)   (Ex)(y)∿(Sue told y to x).

Likewise the respective logical forms of (31)-(32) are

(34)   (x)(y)∿(Sue told y to x)

and

(35)   (Ey)(x)∿(Sue told y to x).

Since one natural reading of each of (24)-(27) is the one predicted by (O. any), there is no need to explain (28)-(29) on the basis of (O. any). Rather, we must show that (30)-(32) are somehow compatible with (O. any) and the rest of my approach, for they are not the readings that would ensue if we simply disregarded (O. any). Disregarding it would result in the impossible reading

(36) ∿(x)(y)(Sue told y to x).

Where do the readings (30)-(32) come from? In order to answer that question, let me remind you what (O. any) says. It says something about the *order* in which different rules are to be applied. It does not say anything about whether the applications are informationally dependent on earlier ones or not.[11]
Informational independence does occur in natural languages, even though the precise conditions on which the requirement of perfect information fails seem to be quite difficult to capture, and probably are not very sharply defined anyway. Assuming that (O. any) holds but that the two quantifier moves in (27) are informationally independent, we obtain as the semantical representation of (27), in the usual branching-quantifier notation, the following:

(37)   (Ey)
            ⟩(Sue told y to x),
        ∿(x)

which is equivalent with (30). But this is equivalent with (33), that is, with the secondary reading of (27), which is

thereby explained. Notice that, far from giving up the
ordering principle (O. any), we used it in our explanation
of the reading (33) of (27). The only other essential
assumption we made was allowing for the possibility that
the two quantifier phrases in (27) might be informationally
independent of each other. This possibility, we know on
independent grounds, we have to keep in mind for natural
languages anyway. The success of this explanation
therefore enhances the credibility of (O. any) and this
approach.

Likewise, the informationally independent reading of
(26) is, if we assume that "everybody" is informationally
independent of the negation also,

(38) (y)∿
        ⟩(Sue told y to x),
      (x)

which is equivalent with (31).

Furthermore, the reading (32) of (24) can be explained
in analogy with the reading (30) of (27). There is apparently also a weak secondary reading of (25) analogous
to the nonpreferred reading (31) of (26), which is explainable analogously.

Notice that this line of thought is reinforced by the
observation that even the following sentence has a secondary branching-quantifier reading:

(39) Sue did not tell everything to everybody.

The primary reading of (39) is of course

(40) ∿(x)(y)(Sue told y to x),

and its secondary reading is

(41) ∿(y)
        ⟩(Sue told y to x),
      E(x)

which is equivalent to

(42) ∿(Ey)(x)(Sue told y to x).

This is the precise force of the secondary reading that

(39) has intuitively.

All this is evidence for (O. any) and at the same time evidence for the presence of imperfect information in the semantical games associated with many quantifier sentences in natural languages.

(iv) Another apparent counterexample to the *any*-thesis is constituted by questions of the following sort:

(43)   Why did anyone applaud?

On the analysis of wh-questions that I have offered,[12] (43) is tantamount to something like this:

(44)   Bring it about that I know why anyone applauded.

And of course (44) is no more acceptable than the crucial part of it that I have called its desideratum:

(45)   I know why anyone applauded.

Is there thus something wrong with the *any*-thesis? In order to answer this question, we have to understand the force of questions like (43) and the reasons for their acceptability.

First, these apparently anomalous questions are not restricted to questions involving any particular wh-word. For instance, we have the following questions.

(46)   When has anyone taken such nonsense seriously?
(47)   How have you come to think anything like that?

What is common to all questions that contain an apparently anomalous "any" is that they express disbelief or surprise. In other words, (43), (46), and (47) have a force that can also be expressed somewhat as follows:

(48)   Did anyone really applaud? Why?
(49)   Has anyone really taken such nonsense seriously? When?
(50)   Have you really come to think anything like that? How?

Here "anyone" and "anything" are of course perfectly

in order in the yes–or–no questions that constitute the respective first parts of (48)-(50). Thus, we can see what the function of "anyone" or "anything" is in the wh–questions (43), (46), and (47). It is to assimilate them to the yes–or–no questions that occur tacitly as parts, and thereby lend the wh–questions an element of surprise. By using a word in the wh–question that is admissible only in the corresponding yes–or–no question one focuses attention on the latter. This amounts to questioning the presupposition of the wh–question, or otherwise paying special attention to it. Thus, it is obviously a most natural way to signal surprise. This successful explanation employs the *any*-thesis and hence provides further support for it, even though (43), (46), and (47) don't directly fall under the generalization embodied in the thesis.

Once again it can be seen that "ever" behaves in the same way, mutatis mutandis, as "any", as illustrated by examples like the following:

(51)   How did you ever come to think of it?

Its desideratum, namely,

(52)   *I know how you ever came to think of it,

is not acceptable. The apparent acceptability of "ever" in (51) can nevertheless be explained in the same way as the acceptability of "any" in (43), (46), and (47).

(v)   Further apparent counterexamples we have to explain away are those of the following type:

(53)   *Jim did not insult Bill and anyone else.

Why is (53) unacceptable? Assuming (O. any) in the form given above, the logical form of (53) seems to be

(54) $(x)((x \neq Bill) \rightarrow \sim(Jim$ insulted Bill $\&$ Jim insulted $x))$.

It seems that if the *any*-thesis is valid, (54) should be logically equivalent with

(55)   Jim did not insult Bill and everyone else,

for this equivalence is what according to the thesis is
supposed to explain the ungrammaticality of (53). Yet,
(55) has an altogether different representation, which is
not logically equivalent with (54):

(56) $\sim$(Jim insulted Bill $\&$ (x)(x $\neq$ Bill $\rightarrow$
       Jim insulted x)).

What we have here is nevertheless much less a failure
of the *any*-thesis as a further insight into the ordering
principles that govern (G. any). In saying that the
semantical representation of (53) is apparently (54), I
made an assumption that is not sanctioned by my actual
formulation of (O. any) above. I had to assume that
(G. any) has priority over (G. and).[13] Ordinarily this
makes no difference, for (x)(A $\&$ B(x)) is logically
equivalent with (A $\&$ (x)B(x)). However, if the whole
conjunction is governed by an operator whose game rule is
applied later than (G. any), this makes a difference. For
then (G. any) cannot have a priority over this rule,
either. A case in point is precisely (53), where the
governing (outside) operator is negation. Hence, the
logical form of (53) is in reality (56), which is the logical
form of (55). Hence (O. any) explains, after all, the
unacceptability of (53), if it is recognized that (G. any)
does not have priority over (G. and).
   This explanation can be tested by looking at examples
that are like (53) except that negation is replaced by some
other operator with respect to which (G. any) has the
right of way. The following are cases in point:

(57) *It is possible that Bob has beaten Boris and any
      other grandmaster.
(58) If John is happy if anyone contributes, and Bill
      contributes, then John is indeed happy.

Hence my explanation of the unacceptability of (53) is not
ad hoc, but is based on regularities that have to be
heeded in any case.
   It is worth noting that (G. any) has priority over
(G. or). Otherwise, we cannot explain the acceptability of

(59) Jim did not insult Bill or anyone else.

The logical form of (59) is clearly (60):

(60) (x)(x ≠ Bill → ∿(Jim insulted Bill v
      Jim insulted x)),

which requires that (G. any) precedes (G. not) in (59).
This means that (O. any) has to be amplified so as to
recognize the priority of (G. any) over (G. or).

All these different alleged counterexamples to the
any-thesis or to (O. any) can thus be put to the service
of my theory. They also suggest a heuristic moral for a
semanticist: put more faith in general theoretical insights
and less faith in specific examples. Apparent counterexamples should not be given too much weight; frequently
it turns out that they can be explained away at some level
of explanation or other. It is especially instructive to see
that the objections (i)-(v) above were met using entirely
different explanatory strategies. It seems to me in general
that several linguists have recently been far too long on
counterexamples and far too short on genuine theoretical
contributions, and that one of the reasons for this one-
sidedness has been a lack of creative imagination concerning the different ways in which the surface phenomena of
language, including our so-called intuitions, can be
accounted for. Frequently, they are not explained by
means of the basic theory alone, however true it may be,
but by this theory *in conjunction with* various contextual
factors.[14] A theoretical generalization like the *any*-thesis
can serve to account for interesting linguistic phenomena
even when these phenomena are not direct instances of the
generalization. (This is illustrated in different ways by
both (iii) and (iv) above.) Linguists seem far too en-
amoured these days of the narrowest forms of hypothetico-
deductive explanation – especially explanation by direct
generalization from the data.

3. Reply to Chomsky

The most interesting potential consequence of the
any-thesis – in conjunction with certain other assumptions
that are themselves not unproblematic – is probably the
result that says that the set of acceptable (grammatical)
sentences of English is not recursively enumerable
(r.e.).[15] Since the basic strategy of all generative
grammars in explaining the grammaticality of sentences is
to generate them by means of recursive procedures, the

sentences whose grammaticality they can thus explain must
form a r.e. set. Hence generative grammars alone cannot
offer a complete account of grammaticality. This account
was earlier considered by Chomsky as "the fundamental aim
in the linguistic analysis of a language L".[16] Hence my
nonrecursivity result - if it is valid - uncovers a remarkable limitation of all generative grammars. They cannot
alone achieve one of the fundamental goals of linguistic
analysis.

Moreover, it is of interest to note the kind of explanation offered by the *any*-thesis concerning the distinction
between grammatical and ungrammatical strings in English.
This explanation is in semantical terms, for it turns on the
identity in meaning of two sentences (strings) that differ
only with respect to one occurrence of "any" or "every".
This type of explanation differs markedly from those that
used to be envisaged by Chomsky. For according to
Chomsky, "Semantic ... studies of language ... appear to
have no direct relevance to the problem of determining or
characterizing the set of grammatical utterances."[17]

It is instructive to recall these statements by Chomsky
in view of his later pronouncements on the same subject.
In *Essays on Form and Interpretation*, he takes cog-
nizance of the argument that leads to my nonrecursivity
result, but claims - without giving any reasons - that
"other formulations that cover the clear facts as well as
that do not lead to this conclusion".[18] By "other formulations" Chomsky means generalizations different from the
any-thesis, and by "this conclusion" the non-r.e. character of the set of grammatical sentences in English. But
what formulation he had in mind he did not reveal on that
occasion.

This suspense was broken by Chomsky in his Immanuel
Kant Lectures at Stanford University in 1979.[19] His reply
there to my earlier criticisms of generative grammar is
two-pronged.

(i) First, Chomsky claims that my *any*-thesis need not
be accepted, because the facts it accounts for can be
explained in another way. This other way is obtained,
Chomsky says, "if we replace the phrase 'identical in
meaning' in the *any*-thesis with 'identical in form' under a
quantifier rule, which we may think of as mapping of
syntactic representation into a representation in standard
logical notation.... Thus, 'John knows anything' and 'John
knows everything' both map into 'for all x, John knows x',

under the quantifier rule, but 'John doesn't know everything' maps into 'not for all x, John knows x' whereas 'John doesn't know anything' maps into 'for all x, John doesn't know x', since the rule treats 'any' as a wide-scope quantifier. But differences in form are checkable," and hence, according to Chomsky, no nonrecursivity results need follow.

(ii) Secondly, Chomsky denies that any major methodological consequences would ensue even if my results are true and the set of all grammatical sentences in English is not r.e. "There is nothing in 'the concept of language' ... that rules out Hintikka's conclusions," he writes.

I shall discuss these two points in order.

(i)(a)   The alternative to my *any*-thesis that Chomsky proposes depends on a translation or "mapping" of strings of English words into the notation of quantification theory (first-order logic). On the most plausible formulation of the requisite translation rules, however, Chomsky's claim to be able to explain the facts "in the moderately clear cases at least" is simply false. Counterexamples involving moderately, and perhaps even immoderately, clear cases are not hard to find. The following are a sample of some such counterexamples:

(61)   *If Chris trained hard, she has won any match.
(62)   If Chris trained hard, she has won every match.
(63)   *You must pick any apple.[20]
(64)   You must pick every apple.
(65)   *Nobody doesn't like any Sarah Lee product.
(66)   Nobody doesn't like every Sarah Lee product.

To understand these, please note that because "any" has wide scope, (61) and (62) have different formal representations ("translations into quantificational notation"), viz.,

(67)   (x) (Chris trained hard →
       (x is a match → Chris has won x))
(68)   Chris trained hard →
       (x) (x is a match → Chris has won x),

respectively. Hence, by Chomsky's proposed condition, (61) ought to be acceptable, which it is not. This is

explained by the *any*-thesis, for (67) and (68) are logically equivalent (and hence presumably identical in meaning), even though they are formally distinct.

Likewise, "any" has priority over (wider scope than)
"must", whereas "every" doesn't. Hence (63) and (64)
have different mappings into a canonical notation of quantified modal logic. They are

(69) For each apple x, you must (bring it about that
      you) pick x,

and

(70) You must bring it about that, for each apple x,
      you pick x,

respectively. Hence, according to Chomsky's lights, (63)
ought to be acceptable, because (69) and (70) are formally
distinct. Yet, (63) is unacceptable. This is explainable
in terms of the *any*-thesis, for a necessity-type operator
("must") and the universal quantifier are often commuta-
tive. Hence, (69) and (70) are presumably logically
equivalent, which explains the ungrammaticality of (63).

Notice that this ungrammaticality cannot be explained by
giving "every" a wider scope than "must" in (64). For
there are closely related pairs of sentences that can be
accounted for only by assigning "every" the smaller scope,
e.g.,

(71) You must pick any apple that squirrels have not
      damaged.
(72) You must pick every apple that squirrels have
      not damaged.

However the difference between (71) and (72) is to be accounted for in detail, it is clear that in (71) the choice of
the apple is independent of the choice between alternative
courses of events that are brought about by "must",
whereas in (72) the choice is restricted to those that
actually have not been damaged. In other words, the
scope of "every" has to be smaller than that of "must" in
(72) and by the same token in (64).

Analogously, my ordering principles for "any" and
"every" serve to map (65)-(66) on the following representations, respectively:

(73) (x)[x is a Sarah Lee product →
      ∿(Ey)∿(y likes x)]
(74) ∿(Ey)∿[(x)(x is a Sarah Lee product →
      y likes x)]

These representations are formally different, and hence
Chomsky predicts the acceptability of (65). In reality,
however, (65) seems unacceptable, except perhaps on a
secondary reading that turns (65) into a synonym for

(75) Everybody likes some Sarah Lee product.

In my theory, the unacceptability of (65) on the reading (73) is explained. by the logical equivalence of (73)
and (74). The secondary reading (75) of (65) is possible
because game-theoretical ordering principles are not completely black-and-white.
These counterexamples to Chomsky could easily be
multiplied beyond necessity.

(i)(b) It may be that Chomsky does not include these
counterexamples among his "moderately clear cases" because he has in mind other possible mappings from syntactical representations into the quantificational idiom,
mappings that differ from those I presupposed in discussing (61)-(66) and that he thinks will save his alternative
formulation of the *any*-thesis. However, this way out is
not realistic. Not only is the onus of providing actual
translation rules on Chomsky. It is eminently clear that if
anyone should actually try to formulate rules that would
vindicate Chomsky, he or she would run into essentially
the same nonrecursivity phenomena as are uncovered by
my theory. Indeed, it does not help Chomsky at all to
have an effective criterion of acceptability (like the formal-
identity criterion he proposes) applicable to the translations of English sentences into a quantificational notation. Such a criterion would not yield an effective criterion of
acceptability for the original English strings unless the
translation rules themselves were recursive. And if one
starts fiddling with translation rules along the lines just
mentioned (in effect, so as to depart from (O. any) and
other ordering principles I have formulated), there is no
guarantee that the rules turn out to be recursive. Indeed, if the *any*-thesis is extensionally correct in that it
assigns a right classification (grammatical vs. nongrammat-

ical) to each English string of words, there cannot be a
set of recursive translation rules that together with
Chomsky's criterion always yields the right prediction.

Hence the very form of Chomsky's criticism seems to me
inappropriate. The only persuasive criticism would be an
actual example in which the *any*-thesis yields a wrong
prediction.

(ii)   Chomsky   admits   that   my   nonrecursivity   result
would lead "to a modification of theories of language and
grammar". The moot point here is the general methodological significance of the modification. This is to some
extent a matter of perspective. Chomsky is looking at the
situation from the perspective of his own theories of
language and grammar. From that point of view, the new
specific changes that are needed perhaps are not so great.
I agree in fact with Chomsky that generative grammar has
a role not only in an overall language theory, but also in
explanations of grammaticality (acceptability). The pre-
sumable result of the modifications Chomsky mentions is
hence a situation in which generative "grammar does not in
itself determine the class of what we might choose to call
'grammatical sentences'; rather, these sentences are the
ones that meet both some condition that involves the grammar and a condition lacking a decision procedure."

I can agree with Chomsky's statement here. What he is
describing may indeed be a natural aspect of the situation
for Chomsky to emphasize in view of his own current
interests. However, from a more general perspective other
observations may appear more pertinent. One obvious
point is that Chomsky has radically redefined the ends of
grammatical theory as compared with, say, his stance in
Syntactic Structures. A glance at the quotations above
will show what I mean. What in 1957 was called a part of
"the fundamental aim of linguistic analysis of a language"
is now admitted by Chomsky, however tentatively, to be
beyond the powers of generative grammars. The identification of the set of all acceptable sentences now belongs to
the theory of language, which is distinguished by Chomsky
from the theory of grammar. The latter does not,
Chomsky is apparently willing to admit, exhaust the
former. Chomsky denies that my nonrecursivity result provides a clear-cut counterexample to generative grammar.
He is obviously right, in the sense that my result does not
show that generative grammars cannot be important ingre-

dients in an overall language theory. However, equally obviously, my result does provide a clear-cut counterexample to his own earlier claims of the exhaustiveness of generative grammars for some of the main tasks of language theory. Chomsky's partial admission of this point amounts to a major change in his theoretical position.

The reason why this change does not seem more momentous to Chomsky is that he now consistently emphasizes the importance of grammar (and knowledge of grammar) but disparages the rest of language (and knowledge thereof). Such phenomena as are illustrated by the *any*-thesis are referred to by Chomsky as "various forms of ill-definedness of language". The aim of showing the exhaustiveness of grammar for various important theoretical tasks, such as the separation of acceptable and unacceptable strings of a language from each other, is now replaced by the claim of a privileged theoretical position allegedly enjoyed by grammar in relation to the rest of our knowledge of language. A generative grammar is said to be "represented in the mind", and in general it is held by Chomsky to enjoy a high degree of psycholinguistic reality.

I cannot review here Chomsky's positive reasons for these claims. What is relevant is that much of his evidence is comparative. Generative grammars are preferred by Chomsky because they are the best available means of accounting for a wide variety of data. If so, Chomsky's emphasis on generative grammars is very much subject to further investigation. Should we find equally or more powerful explanatory methods that are different from generative grammars, the general methodological importance of the latter would be correspondingly diminished. It is here that the importance of the *any*-thesis - and more generally of game-theoretical semantics - comes in. My results do not show that there is anything intrinsically wrong with generative grammar. However, these results present us with concrete examples of modes of explanation that are in no way inferior to those based on generative grammar and that open entirely new theoretical possibilities. There is nothing "ill-defined" about language because it is subject to the *any*-thesis and hence possesses a non-r.e. set of acceptable sentences. Nor is there anything ill-defined about a logic without axiomatization and without a decision method. On the contrary, there are other extremely interesting applications of the ideas on which the *any*-thesis is based. One of them throws serious doubts on the viability of the kind of logical languages Chomsky is using as his framework for semantical representation of natural languages like English.[21] Much more is thus at stake than Chomsky admits.

For more than twenty years, generative methods have served as the paradigm of linguistic explanation. Gradually, limitations of these methods have become more and more apparent. Chomsky's changes of position are a reluctant recognition of this development, even though he still believes that generative grammars occupy a privileged position. What have been missing in the literature are sharp examples of alternative modes of explanation. The significance of the *any*-thesis (and of the more general ideas on which it is based) is not so much just another reminder of the limitations of generative methods. There are plenty of such reminders that are quite independent of game-theoretical semantics. Each of them alone can undoubtedly be taken care of in Chomsky's theoretical framework by adding a new epicycle here or there. Their cumulative effect is nevertheless beginning to tell against the hegemony of generative methods. What are perhaps needed are completely new explanatory paradigms that altogether break the old molds of thinking.

There is, in any case, plenty of indication that the new types of linguistic explanation offered by game-theoretical semantics deserve closer attention. For instance, we can compare the *any*-thesis to Chomsky's alternative hypothesis with respect to psycholinguistic reality. In deciding intuitively which occurrences of "any" are acceptable, we (as competent speakers of English) are, both on my account and on Chomsky's, comparing a string, say "X - any - Y", with a corresponding string containing "every", viz., "X - every - Y". Which are we likelier to have in mind (to use Chomsky's expression), the translations of these two into the notation of quantification theory, or their respective meanings? The answer would be obvious even if there were no independent reasons to doubt the psycholinguistic reality of the quantificational idiom.

I also find it difficult to understand Chomsky's comments on the relevance or irrelevance of the *any*-thesis to the problem of the autonomy of syntax.[22] The type of account of grammaticality that the *any*-thesis offers is in direct contradiction to what he himself said in 1957 of the role of semantical studies in explanations of grammaticality. (See the quotation above.) Yet Chomsky claims that the *any*-thesis would actually support what he has called a "parameterized version" of the thesis of the autonomy of syntax.[23] By such a version of the autonomy thesis, Chomsky means a version that allows some semantical input into a grammar, but only such input as can be localized by the choice of certain parameters. For instance, those parameters might include the meanings of certain lexical elements or certain semantical relations between them.

The only reason given by Chomsky why the *any*-thesis would support a parameterized autonomy thesis is that our overall linguistic theory would then make "reference at some point to a notion of 'related word' that has a semantic element". This is not the only parameter needed here, however. In the *any*-thesis, reference is made to the *synonymy* or *nonsynonymy* of the strings "X - any - Y" and "X - every - Y". How much semantics does that involve? The synonymy or nonsynonymy in question depends essentially on the differences between the ordering principles (O. any) and (O. every). These in turn depend on the game rules with respect to which (G. any) and (G. every) behave differently. These rules define the meanings of the words they are associated with. At the very least, these include "and", "if", negation, and modal words. Moreover, negation can be a matter of the lexical meanings of one of a large number of words. (Perhaps we can also say that the fact that some other game rules behave in the same way with respect to (G. any) and (G. every) is a reflection of the meanings of the elements the rules are calculated to deal with.) All told, the *any*-thesis involves, over and above a part of the general semantical notion of meaning identity, the meanings of a large number of the most central words in our logical and nonlogical vocabulary. In view of this interaction of meaning and the *any*-thesis, it seems odd for Chomsky to say that the *any*-thesis supports a parameterized version of the thesis of the autonomy of syntax, even though Chomsky points out aptly that this thesis deals with matters of more or less, not with complete independence or complete dependence. The number (and importance) of the interrelated semantical "parameters" that the *any*-thesis involves is in fact so large that the effect of the thesis depends on large chunks of the most central parts of semantics. In brief, what the *any*-thesis supports should be called a parameterized *dependency* thesis rather than a parameterized autonomy thesis. In this direction, too, the *any*-thesis has far more sweeping consequences than Chomsky is willing to countenance.

Perhaps linguists should also have a closer look at the interrelations of syntax and semantics with the view to evaluating the role of generative methods in this field. As was mentioned above, Chomsky still - after all his admissions - seems to think of generative grammar as the core of language theory. The possible reason why generative grammar "does not in itself determine the class of what we might choose to call grammatical sentences" is, according to Chomsky, that the strings generated by the grammar may have to meet some additional conditions. These additional conditions seem to be looked upon by Chomsky as something messy and theoretically less central than generative grammar. Indeed, it is in this connection that Chomsky refers to the "various forms of ill-definedness of language".

But which ingredient of our linguistic theory is *really* the messy one? Let's look again at the quantifier rules (G. every) and (G. some), and analogous rules for other quantifier words. By concentrating on their syntactical component alone and by turning them around, we can think of each of them as containing a generative syntactical rule. For instance, (G. every) would tell us to construct

> X - every Y who Z - W

from something like

> (a)   X - x - W, if x is a Y and x Z,

where "x" is a dummy proper name, or possibly (as in a generalized transformation) from the three strings

> (b)   X - x - W; x is a Y; x Z.

(Of course, several further explanations are needed here.) One part of these rules governs the formation of the relative clauses that figure in the original input sentences. Of course, if we take this syntactical function of the game rules seriously, we need further restrictions on them, which seems to lead us straight into the notorious mess of formulating the precise conditions of relative-clause for-mation.[24] Yet for my semantical theory, the restrictions are neither here nor there. My game-theoretical treatment works completely independently of how precisely the re-strictions are formulated. Semantical rules are the excep-tionless smooth component here, while the generative syn-tactical restrictions appear as a messy additional ingre-dient. The extra restraint they impose on acceptable sen-tences moreover seems to be of secondary importance only, because violations of this restraint do not automatically impair the semantical interpretability of the strings in question.

One feature of the resulting situation, in any case, is that a much wider class of strings of words is semantically interpretable than is syntactically admissible. This should be enough to dispel all feelings of awkwardness that might result from the formulation of the *any*-thesis above. As was pointed out at the end of section 1 above, its formulation presupposes that certain strings are intel-ligible (in the sense of being semantically interpretable), though ungrammatical. Now we can see that the *any*-thesis is not the only context where semantical intelligi-bility extends much wider than syntactical acceptability.

This relation between meaningfulness (semantical inter-pretability) and syntactical well-formedness raises serious doubts about Chomsky's continued insistence on generative grammar as the most important element of all linguistic theory. How can generative grammar help us to under-stand competent speakers' mastery of meanings of certain strings that are rejected by the grammar?

Notice that this understanding cannot be thought of in general as being obtained by analogical extension from well-formed sentences, as most linguists seem to think. This might seem to work for the strings rejected by the *any*-thesis, for there the parallel construction in terms of "every" is normally well formed. This explanation does not work in general, however. For instance, the inter-pretability of those quantifier-phrase sentences that are ill-formed because the relative clauses they contain violate familiar but elusive restrictions cannot be explained ana-logically. Hence the semantical interpretability of many syntactically ill-formed strings is not a secondary phenom-enon parasitic upon the notion of syntactical acceptability, but a fact of life for linguists that demands an ex-planation.

The *any*-thesis is unusual only because, for the phenomena it deals with, the more widely defined semantical relationships happen to have a role in delineating the narrower class of acceptable sentences.

Thus the following overall picture suggests itself as a more plausible alternative than Chomsky's. A relatively small class of unqualified generative rules produces a set of strings for which a semantical interpretation is defined. These syntactical rules are presumably closely related to the corresponding semantical rules. However, the class of strings for which the semantical rules yield a reading is wider than the class of well-formed sentences. The latter class is obtained through a variety of further restrictions, some of them conditions on the sequences in which syntactical rules can be applied, some others possibly holistic, to be formulated in terms of the output string rather than in terms of generative rules. Still others might be based on the semantical properties and relations of the generated strings.

The interplay of semantics with syntax in the *any*-thesis is thus not a marginal phenomenon, if this picture is correct. It seems to me to illustrate a much more widely observed phenomenon. It is not the semantical rules on which the *any*-thesis is based that create certain "forms of the ill-definedness of language". It is the further restrictions on semantically interpretable strings that are messy, if not always ill-defined. This restriction is perhaps more vivid when it is semantically based, but can be messy also when it is syntactical.

A related phenomenon is found in the field of multiple questions.[25] There, "accidental" syntactical factors don't limit the class of acceptable sentences, but rather limit the class of acceptable readings. It is again the syntactical component that gives rise to a messy situation - so messy that no reasonable generative explanation seems feasible.

NOTES

[1] The research reported here was supported by a Fellowship from the John Simon Guggenheim Memorial Foundation for 1979-80 and by The Florida State University. I have greatly profited from comments by Steven Weisler on an earlier draft of this chapter and also from the comments of two anonymous referees for *Linguistics and Philosophy*.

Most of the putative counterexamples in section 2 that can be turned into evidence for my theory were suggested to me by Lauri Carlson, whose help has been important in other ways as well. Donald Provence first brought examples like (58) to my attention. All these contributions and others that I may have forgotten are gratefully acknowledged.

2 But not completely novel. Over and above the partial anticipations that belong to logicians' folklore and that will be mentioned below, Risto Hilpinen has unearthed a neat anticipation of the main idea of game-theoretical semantics in C. S. Peirce. See Hilpinen, "On C. S. Peirce's Theory of Propositions: Peirce as a Precursor of Game-Theoretical Semantics", *The Monist*, 65 (1982), 182–88.

3 Most of my earlier papers in this direction are reprinted in Esa Saarinen, editor, *Game-Theoretical Semantics*, D. Reidel, Dordrecht, 1979. Cf. also my monograph, *The Semantics of Questions and the Questions of Semantics* (Acta Philosophica Fennica, vol. 28, n. 4), North–Holland, Amsterdam, 1976; and see the other chapters of this book for more recent developments.

4 The notions mentioned here are explained more fully elsewhere. To find such explanations, please consult the index of Saarinen, *Game-Theoretical Semantics*. See also chapter 1 above, and the index to this book.

5 See, e.g., Edward S. Klima, "Negation in English", in Jerry A. Fodor and Jerrold J. Katz, editors, *The Structure of Language*, Prentice–Hall, Englewood Cliffs, N.J., 1964, pp. 246–323; or Robert P. Stockwell, Paul Schachter, and Barbara Hall Partee, *The Major Syntactic Structures of English*, Holt, Rinehart and Winston, New York, 1973, especially ch. 5.

6 Cf. Charles Kahn, "Questions and Categories", in Henry Hiż, editor, *Questions*, D. Reidel, Dordrecht, 1978, pp. 227–78; also, see chapter 8 above.

7 Jaakko Hintikka and Lauri Carlson, "Pronouns of Laziness in Game-Theoretical Semantics", *Theoretical Linguistics* 4 (1977), 1–29.

8 Charles J. Fillmore, "The Position of Embedding Transformations in a Grammar", *Word* 19 (1963), 208–31; and cf., e.g., Noam Chomsky, "Conditions on Transformations", in Stephen R. Anderson and Paul Kiparsky, editors, *A Festschrift for Morris Halle*, Holt, Rinehart and Winston, New York, 1973, pp. 232–86, reprinted in *Essays on Form and Interpretation*, North–Holland, Amsterdam,

1977, pp. 80-160.

[9] Turning putative counterexamples into support for my theory not only enhances its credibility by increasing the number of its confirming instances. One does not have to be a Popperian to believe that being able to withstand serious challenges, e.g., in the form of prima facie counterexamples, is a good index of the veracity of a theory. After all, it is seen even from Bayes's notorious formula that a priori unlikely evidence supports a theory more strongly than a priori likely evidence, ceteris paribus.

[10] The possibility of this generalization was first pointed out to me by Lauri Carlson.

[11] For the notion of informational independence and its connection with branching quantifiers, see Saarinen, *Game-Theoretical Semantics*, especially Jaakko Hintikka, "Quantifiers vs. Quantification Theory", pp. 49-79.

[12] See my book *The Semantics of Questions*, especially chapters 2-3.

[13] The rule (G. and) in its simplest form is formulated in the papers included in Saarinen, *Game-Theoretical Semantics*. A special case of (G. and) says that when the game has reached a sentence of the form

X and Y,

where X and Y are clauses, Nature chooses one of the conjuncts X and Y, whereupon the game is continued with respect to it. Pronouns or other anaphoric expressions in the chosen conjunct are to be replaced by their head if this head is in the other conjunct. Normally, this head has to be a proper name. (The problem of extending (G. and) to uses of "and" to connect terms (NPs) will not be discussed here.) Giving, as I shall do, (G. and) priority over (G. any), is of course a significant change in (O. any).

[14] The methodological precepts proposed in the first chapter of my book *Models for Modalities*, D. Reidel, Dordrecht, 1969, still seem to me to be pertinent.

[15] This consequence is spelled out most explicitly in my paper, "Quantifiers in Natural Languages: Some Logical Problems", in Saarinen, *Game-Theoretical Semantics*, pp. 81-117, especially pp. 104ff.. It is to be noted that the arguments I give there for the conclusion that the set of all grammatical (acceptable) sentences of English is not recursively enumerable rest on certain assumptions that

are, according to my own lights, not beyond doubt. However, as we shall see, Chomsky is not challenging these admittedly problematic premises.

[16] Noam Chomsky, *Syntactic Structures*, Mouton, The Hague, 1957, p. 13.

[17] Ibid., p.17.

[18] Noam Chomsky, *Essays on Form and Interpretation*, North-Holland, Amsterdam, 1977, p. 202.

[19] Published as *Rules and Representations*, Columbia University Press, N.Y., 1980. See here pp. 123-27.

[20] The question of the acceptability of (63) should not be confused with the question of the acceptability of such closely related sentences as

  (i)   You must not pick any apple that is red.
  (ii) You may pick any apple.

I have offered an explanation for their grammaticality in Saarinen, *Game-Theoretical Semantics*, pp. 142-45.

[21] See chapter 7 above.

[22] It is very interesting to see, as we have just seen, that Chomsky himself is trying to deal with the recalcitrant phenomena by means of a rule that depends on a mapping to *semantical* representations. An unwary reader of, say, *Syntactic Structures* would have expected him to try to show how the syntactical derivation of the unacceptable strings is impossible. I find this aspect of Chomsky's new proposal commendable. However, an attempt to give a syntactical account of the phenomena that the *any*-thesis serves to explain soon leads to grave difficulties. The main semantical peculiarity of "any" is that it interacts with its environment, even beyond the clause it occurs in. An attempt to account for such phenomena syntactically is bound to lead to a conflict with the cyclic principle, which uin effect rules out interaction with such external elements in the application process of syntactical rules.

[23] See Chomsky, *Essays on Form and Interpretation*, pp. 72-73; and see 57-58.

[24] Indeed, one can hardly avoid here the conjecture that the requisite restrictions do not depend on the transformational situation as much as on the perceptual distance of the output sentence from some underlying pattern of a "normal sentence".

[25] See my book *The Semantics of Questions*, especially chapters 8 and 11.

Chapter 10

THEORIES OF TRUTH AND LEARNABLE LANGUAGES

By far the most interesting and successful recent theories of meaning have been truth conditional. The paradigm of such theories is usually taken to be Tarski's recursive characterization of truth for certain formal languages.[1] Donald Davidson has both practiced truth-conditional theorizing in the semantics of natural languages, and has pleaded for the general importance of truth-conditional semantics.[2] What is even more interesting and more unique to him, Davidson has sought to give a deeper motivation - perhaps a foundation - for truth-conditional semantics of the kind pioneered by Tarski. This deeper foundation Davidson has sought in the requirement of the *learnability* of the language in question.[3]

This attempted link between semantics and language learning is perhaps not completely new. For instance, Wittgenstein used to illustrate his semantical claims by reference to how certain parts of language are learned or could be learned. Furthermore, highly interesting work has recently been done in mathematical linguistics on the precise formal conditions of learnability for various explicitly defined languages.[4] However, Davidson seems to be unique in using learning-theoretical ideas to support a Tarski-type approach to the semantics of natural language. He does not claim that the learnability of a language implies the existence of a Tarskian truth-theory for it, but he clearly thinks that this is the most natural form of a truth theory for a learnable language. Even if learnability does not necessitate the availability of a truth characterization, it makes such a characterization eminently natural, Davidson thinks.[5] In the form of a slogan, theories of meaning for learnable languages are supposed to become so many theories of truth for these languages.

The mediating link between learnability and a recursive truth-theory is what Davidson calls the *Frege Principle*, which says that the meaning of a complex expression is a function of the meanings of its constituent parts.[6] Since we are dealing with truth-conditional theories of meaning,

259

in this chapter we can equally well consider the corresponding referential principle that says that the extension
(reference) of a complex expression is a function of the
extensions (references) of its constituent parts. Linguists
know the Frege Principle as the *principle of compositionality*.[7] Learnability is supposed to bring us close to the
Frege Principle, and the Frege Principle is expected to
make feasible a Tarski-type truth-definition.

I disagree sharply with this overall conception of
Davidson's. Accordingly, what I shall argue in this chapter is the following. First, I shall suggest that learnability alone does not make compositionality very natural.
Second, I shall argue, in terms of a list of examples, that
compositionality fails in natural languages in a wide variety
of ways. Third, a number of supplementary issues of a
partly historical character are discussed. They lead by
stages to an overall evaluation of Davidson's approach to
linguistic semantics. Fourth, I shall briefly suggest that
what the learnability requirement principally motivates is a
theory of truth different from Tarski's and independent of
the requirement of compositionality. As you can see from
this summary, I am not rejecting the idea of truth-conditional semantics, even though I believe that philosophers
and linguists usually think of such semantics in seriously
oversimplified terms.

Why should the learnability of a language make us expect that the Frege Principle holds for it? Davidson does
not present an explicit argument, but something along the
following lines is what he seems to have in mind.[8]
Learnability presupposes that the meaning of a given complex expression, say E, can be gathered from a finite
number of clues in E. Moreover, these clues have to be
syntactical, based either on the vocabulary of E or else on
the structure or structural features of E. In either case,
the meaning of E is identifiable on the basis of its several
constituent features or components. In this sense, the
meaning of E is recoverable from the contributions of its
several constituent components or parts.[9] But such a
contribution of a constituent part e to the meaning of the
larger whole can safely be identified with its meaning, the
meaning of e – or so it seems.[10] (After all, the meaning
of any expression is supposed to be its use in language.)
Hence the meaning of the whole is determined by the
meanings of its components, that is, the Frege Principle is
valid.

The crucial step in this train of thought is the identification of the meaning of a component part e with its contribution to the meaning of the larger complex expressions E in which it can occur. This amounts to a reification of use into meaning. Its fashionability notwithstanding, this hypostatization needs a closer scrutiny. It is largely to safeguard this step, it seems to me, that Frege introduced the other principle frequently associated with him, according to which a word or other simple grammatical constituent has meaning only in a context.[11] As Wittgenstein later put it: "Only propositions have sense; only in the context of a proposition does a name have a meaning" (*Tractatus* 3.3). It should be clear why it was in effect resorted to by Frege here. If a constituent part e could have a meaning also in isolation, there would not be any general guarantee that its meaning in the context of a complex expression E should be identical with its meaning in isolation, and the argument just sketched would be fallacious. Frege attempted to escape this problem by denying that it can arise.

A brief historical comment may be in order here. Frege admittedly never considers (as far as I know) his second principle as a response to a challenge directed against his first principle (compositionality). However, a closer examination of what he in fact does serves to vindicate my way of explaining Frege's procedure. It is seen, for instance, from the beginning of sec. 62 of the *Grundlagen* what the second Frege principle was supposed to do. It was calculated to enable Frege to say that any contribution to the meaning of a sentence by a word can be considered as the meaning of that word (in the sense that this contribution of the word is what its definition must specify). This freedom would be severely limited if we could assign to the word some fixed reified meaning already in isolation. This is what Frege is doing in the passage referred to. Hence the motive I have ascribed to Frege is a special case of his real motivation. Accordingly, I am not violating the spirit of what Frege is doing.

Frege's attempted way out is inadequate, however. What is at issue in the difficulty just mentioned is much more than merely a possible difference between meaning in isolation and meaning in context. The real, general problem is that the meaning of e might vary, even when it is thought of as e's contribution to the meaning of a complex expression E in which e occurs. Imbed e in a different context E', a critic might aver, and its role in determining the meaning of that whole will be different. Then there would not be any such thing as *the* contribution of e to the respective meanings of the different complex expressions in which it can occur, and the hypostatization employed in my experimental argument cannot succeed. The second Frege principle deals with this problem only in the special case in which the second context E' is the empty one, with e occurring in splendid isolation. Even if the principle were correct, it would therefore solve only a small part of the real problem.

Simply saying, as Frege in effect does, that we can always identify the meaning (sense) of a component expression with its contribution to the thought expressed by the sentence in which it occurs, does not make it possible. We can still ask whether the contribution is the same in different contexts. The general principle Frege is relying on here would, for instance, enable him to say that "is" has a unique sense, viz., its contribution to the different thoughts it can help to express, even though Frege himself, on certain other grounds, treats "is" as being ambiguous.

Hence we can see a serious flaw in Davidson's argument, or, rather, in the argument sketched here as a possible rational reconstruction of his line of thought. Learnability alone does not suffice to motivate the Frege Principle. It is only in conjunction with another assumption that learnability can serve to motivate compositionality. This further assumption is a kind of context-independence of meaning. The meaning of an expression must not depend on the context in which it occurs. For the purposes of the present chapter, I shall call this assumption the *context-independence thesis*. If this thesis does not hold, we face the problem just indicated; and the role of e in determining the respective meanings of the complex expressions in which it can occur cannot be reified into any one entity with which the meaning of e itself can be identified.

The assumption of context-independence is closely related with another thesis, of which it can even be considered a variant. This new thesis says that the proper direction of semantical analysis is from the inside out in a sentence or other complex expression. I shall call this the *inside-out principle*.[12] Its connection with the context-independence principle is clear. If the meaning of e depends on the context E(e) in which it occurs, the meaning of E(e) cannot be analyzed from the inside out. For if we tried to do so, we would run into an impasse: the meaning of e could not be decided on the basis of its "inside", for by assumption it depends on the context, i.e., on what there is "outside" it. Hence we could not process it semantically by proceeding always from the inside out.

Another assumption among the interrelated principles we have to consider here is one that asserts that syntactical and semantical rules operate in tandem. I shall call it the *parallelism thesis*.[13] It says that to each syntactical formation rule, telling us how a complex expression E is constructed from simpler ones, say e_1, e_2, ..., e_i, there corresponds a semantical rule that tells how the meaning of E (the semantical object associated with E) depends on the meanings of those of the simpler input expressions, e_1, e_2, ..., e_i.

I suspect that the parallelism thesis has been instrumental in encouraging semanticists to believe in the inside-out principle. If you accept the parallelism thesis and believe that the rules of syntax work from the inside out (this is what characterizes all generative grammars), you very easily slip into thinking that the rules of semantical interpretation do the same, i.e., that the inside-out principle holds. This would be a mistake, however. The parallelism thesis is quite distinct in its implications from the inside-out principle and from the context-independence thesis. The parallelism thesis implies the inside-out principle only together with certain further assumptions. The most important of them is the assumption that when E is formed from certain simpler strings e_1, e_2, ..., e_i, these will not be constituent parts of E, for they may be changed when E is built up out of them. We shall call the assumption that forces e_1, e_2, ..., e_i to be actual parts (constituent components) of E the *invariance thesis*.

The invariance thesis can be said to hold in virtually all formal languages. It also holds of many of the simpler syntactical generation rules for natural languages. It is, for instance, related rather closely to what is known among grammarians as the *cyclic principle*. This principle deals with the case where e_1, e_2, ..., e_i are clauses (subordinate sentences) and E a higher sentence. There is no general a priori reason, however, why the invariance thesis should be valid.

In envisaging possible failures of the invariance thesis
even when the parallelism thesis holds, we are not dealing
with a mere abstract possibility, either, but with a kind of
behavior that is exemplified by what happens in an actual
semantical theory.   In my game-theoretical semantics the
meaning of a complex expression E is typically analyzed in
terms of the meanings of certain simpler expressions E_1,
E_2, ..., E_i.   These simpler expressions are obtained from
E through certain game rules, and their syntactical relation to E is determined so closely that we can (at least for
the sake of argument) think of E as being constructed
from E_1, E_2, ..., E_i.   Nevertheless, these expressions are
not always themselves parts (constituent components) of E
in any natural sense of the word.   Hence, game-theoretical
semantics can be said to violate the invariance thesis, even
though it can be hoped to preserve a form of parallelism
between syntax and semantics.[14]

Another assumption needed for obtaining the inside-out
principle from the parallelism thesis is that the meaning of
E must be completely determined by the meanings of the
expressions E_1, E_2, ..., E_i from which it is constructed.
For otherwise the meaning of E is not a function of the
latter.   It is far from clear that this stronger thesis holds
of all the formation rules of fairly simple formal languages.
A striking counterexample to it will in any case be found
later in this chapter; see counterexamples (v) discussed
below.   This requirement will be called the *determinacy
thesis*.

If learnability alone implies any of the assumptions we
have discussed, it implies the parallelism thesis.   This
thesis seems to come fairly close to Davidson's purpose
when he says that the meaning of each sentence can be
established on formal grounds alone.[15]   For this reason, it
is of interest to see that parallelism alone does not imply
the Frege Principle without substantial additional assumptions.

The main dependencies among the assumptions I have
just examined can be summed up in the following schema:

$$\text{learnability} \rightarrow \left. \begin{array}{l} \text{parallelism} \\ \text{invariance} \\ \text{determinacy} \end{array} \right\} \rightarrow \text{compositionality}$$

The possibility of maintaining the parallelism thesis
without thereby subscribing to compositionality has impli-

cations for recent developments in linguistic semantics. The gradual rejection of deep-structure semantics around 1970 by some transformational grammarians entailed a prima facie rejection of compositionality. The rules of semantical interpretation did not any longer show how the meanings of composite expressions are determined by the meanings of those component expressions from which they can be built by phrase-structure rules. Instead, interpretive semanticists went close to the other extreme by making the rules of semantical interpretation operate partly on the surface structure. The connection between syntactical rules of generation and semantical rules was largely severed.

My observations above suggest that this revisionism may have gone too far. In order to give up compositionality – and I agree with the interpretivists that we have to do that – we don't have to give up the parallelism between syntactical and semantical rules. Indeed, this parallelism is our best bet in approximating Tarski-type truth conditions without being committed to compositionality. Once again game-theoretical semantics offers us a concrete example of my point, in that it shows how at least a partial parallelism can coexist with the failure of compositonality.

The dependence of the Frege Principle on the context-independence thesis shows where we can look for counter-examples to compositionality in natural languages. Whenever the meaning (interpretation) of an expression depends on the wider context in which it is embedded, a violation of the Frege Principle is in the offing. This guiding idea has proved most useful in locating counter-examples to compositionality in English, some of which will soon be outlined. Conversely, these examples will illustrate and otherwise throw light on the context-independence principle. In this respect, the examples below that deal with the behavior of "any" and with backwards-looking operators are especially instructive.

Another method of finding counterexamples to compositionality is suggested by the determinacy thesis. It might seem that this thesis is trivially valid. For when E is constructed from e_1, e_2, ..., e_i, nothing is added to them. They are merely combined or given a structure in a certain way (assuming invariance). This structure must be indicated syntactically, and hence it must be represented by one of the constituent features e_1, e_2, ..., e_i.

This attempted vindication of determinacy fails, however. If the determinacy thesis and the Frege Principle are to have any real bite, a postulation of the "constituent parts" they speak of (here, the constituent features e_1, e_2, ..., e_j) must have independent syntactical motivation. They must in some straightforward sense be *syntactical* parts of E. But there are many properties of English sentences that are not indicated by any clear-cut syntactical marks. Some of them will turn out to have important semantical functions, and hence give rise to failures of determinacy. I shall later present examples of such breakdowns of determinacy. The best example is probably the behavior of branching (partially ordered) quantifiers in formal as well as natural languages. As I have remarked in earlier papers,[16] in natural languages like English, informational independence is usually not indicated by any single grammatical feature. Even in formal languages, there is no "logical constant" to mark informational dependencies and independencies. Hence we have here a failure of determinacy: whether or not the different quantifier phrases of a sentence E are independent of each other is not determined by any number of constituent parts of E.

The following is a survey of some of the most conspicuous failures of compositionality. Of these counterexamples, (i)-(iii) can be traced to contextual dependence, whereas (iv)-(v) illustrate the breakdown of determinacy.

(i) I have shown earlier that the English quantifier word "any" interacts with its environment.[17] In a game-theoretical treatment, this is shown by the fact that the game rule (G. any) for "any" has priority over a number of other rules (even when these other rules apply to expressions in higher clauses or further on the left). These rules include game rules for negation, modal concepts, and "if". Accordingly, we can expect to find counterexamples to compositionality in these contexts. This expectation turns out to be fulfilled. It is especially interesting to see what happens in a context that contains intensional concepts over and above negation. The following is a list of examples of the failure of the Frege Principle that are due to the semantical context-dependence of "any":

(1)   Chris can win any match.

(2) Jean doesn't believe that Chris can win any match.
(3) Chris will beat any opponent.
(4) Chris will not beat any opponent.
(5) Anyone can beat Chris.
(6) I'd be greatly surprised if anyone can beat Chris.
(7) Any businessman can become a millionaire.
(8) The sentence "Any businessman can become a millionaire" is true if any businessman can become a millionaire.

Of these, (3)-(4) require a comment. It is not clear that (3) can be taken to be a constituent part of (4). Not very much turns on this question. However, how else can you generate a negated sentence except from the corresponding unnegated one? (But see chapter 4 above.)
I shall return to (7)-(8) later.

(ii) Another class of linguistic phenomena that exhibit semantical context-dependence are the ones that Esa Saarinen has sought to deal with in terms of his "backwards-looking operators".[18] Their nature is best seen from formal systems of modal logic. If we think of an outside-in evaluation procedure being applied to a sentence of such a system, you can easily see that such an evaluation procedure is always a one-way journey. We start from a given world, the one at which the sentence is being evaluated, move to one of its alternatives, then perhaps to an alternative to this alternative, and so on. (The game-theoretical semantics I have developed serves to vindicate this intuitive picture.) However, we can never return to worlds considered earlier. The world of conventional modal logic is like the world of Thomas Wolfe: in it, you can't go back home again.
Nevertheless, it turns out that several different phenomena in natural languages presuppose a return to a world considered earlier. The simplest method of treating such phenomena formally is to introduce explicit operators that tell us to return to an earlier world. This is what Esa Saarinen has done in his work on what he calls "backwards-looking operators". They are precisely the return-ticket operators I mentioned. From my description we can also see that those operators depend on their context. They presuppose a kind of "memory" of what happened in

evaluating those parts of the sentence that lie farther outside. Hence they violate the inside-out principle and thereby the Frege Principle.

It turns out that natural languages have few, if any, explicitly indicated backwards-looking operators and that the return to earlier worlds, therefore, has to be accomplished in them by some other means. This does not militate against what I just said of there being counterexamples to Frege in natural language, however. What is left open is merely the question concerning their closest formalization.

The following series of examples, adapted from Saarinen, illustrates these counterexamples:

(9)   A child was born who would become ruler of the world.
(10) Joseph said that a child had been born who would become ruler of the world.
(11) Balthazar mentioned that Joseph said that a child had been born who would become ruler of the world.

Each of these has more ambiguities than its predecessor. The moment of the child's becoming the ruler of the world is in (9) in the future as looked upon from the moment of birth; in (10) that moment can also be in Joseph's future; and in (11) the child's becoming the ruler of the world can even be in Balthazar's future. In other words, the semantical interpretation of the innermost clause varies with its context.

A general historical comment may be in order here. The natural-language phenomena that Saarinen studies by means of his "backwards-looking operators" used to be studied by means of a clumsy device that complicated our metasemantical apparatus by taking the process of semantical evaluation to be relative to *two* parameters: the world being considered at a certain stage of the evaluation, and the world from which the whole evaluation started. This procedure has proved insufficient, and it is in any case ill-advised, for we have precious few clear intuitions about the rules of evaluation based on such double-think. Whether or not Saarinen's treatment is the last word, it is clearly logically superior to the introduction of such awkward epicycles into one's metasemantical framework. Why had such operators not been used before? Clearly because their semantics violates the Frege Principle and hence cannot be handled by means of techniques that are committed to compositionality.

(iii) Probably the most illuminating way of viewing backwards-looking operators is to consider them as allowing anaphoric back reference to worlds considered earlier in the same evaluation process. Since the world in question is usually specified by expressions outside the context in which the backwards-looking operator in question occurs, the operator introduces a violation of the thesis of context-independence and hence a violation of the Frege Principle.

Similar things can be said of several other kinds of expressions with an anaphoric function. Their semantical evaluation depends on taking into account ("remembering") a wider context considered earlier in the evaluation process, sometimes because the head phrase occurs in that wider context and sometimes because the anaphoric expression is for other reasons context dependent.

This suggests a direction in which further counterexamples to the Frege Principle can be expected to be found. This expectation turns out to be justified. The explicit treatment of counterexamples depends on one's theory of anaphora. Here we can use as an example the treatment of anaphoric *the*-phrases outlined in chapter 6 above. Roughly speaking, in this treatment "the X" is assumed to operate as predicted by Russell's theory of descriptions provided that quantifiers are restricted to individuals mentioned earlier in the evaluation ("introduced earlier in the semantical game").[19] In other words, "the X" refers in a Russellian fashion to the one and only X among the ones that the semantical game has so far produced. The context-dependence of this semantics for an anaphorically used definite article "the" is obvious. The following example shows how it leads to a violation of the Frege Principle:

(12)   Even the best mathematician sometimes makes mistakes.

(13)   Thomas, Richard, and Harold were classmates in school. Thomas was the best mathematician, Richard the best cricketeer, and Harold the most amusing story-teller.

It may be objected here that the *the*-phrases in (12) and (13) have a different meaning. The latter is an anaphoric *the*-phrase whereas the former is a purely "Russellian" one, in the sense of behaving in accordance with Russell's original theory of descriptions, where quantifiers range over the whole universe of discourse. Be this as it may, one can also produce examples where one and the same anaphoric *the*-phrase is semantically context-dependent. Here is an example:

The primitive ritual had strict rules. First, three men sang a song. Then the oldest man said a prayer, whereupon they were joined by four other men. After that, the oldest man and the youngest man performed the sacrifice.

Here the two phrases "the oldest man" do not have to pick up the same person.

(iv) A phenomenon of an apparently different kind is the behavior of quantifier scopes in English.[20] Not only is it the case that quantifier scopes are not marked syntactically in English; they are in a very real sense not even determined. Or, rather, they extend arbitrarily far, not only in one and the same sentence, but also in a discourse involving several sentences. You can begin a sentence by saying something about "an old man" and keep on referring to "him" or "the old man" all through the sentence and all through shorter or longer bits of discourse, perhaps throughout an entire book (if you are Ernest Hemingway).

This indefinitely large scope of natural-language quantifiers alone shows or at least strongly suggests that the Frege Principle cannot possibly hold in natural languages like English. For what are the component parts of an English sentence which contains quantifiers? Whatever they are, one requirement is clear: whenever such a part contains a quantifier, it must include the entire scope of that quantifier. But if this scope extends arbitrarily far, there cannot be any such parts at all. The Frege Principle is thus shown to be false or at least inapplicable.

When we try to convert this observation into a specific counterexample to compositionality, however, we face a technical problem. This problem is that the wide scopes of some natural-language quantifiers are as it were merely potential. In order to actualize them, we need pronouns or other vehicles of anaphoric cross-reference. It is in such references back to a quantifier that the scope of the quantifier can be seen. Moreover, we can hope to obtain an obvious counterexample only when the back reference changes the semantical status of the original quantifier. Otherwise we can still in each particular case hope to analyze the situation in keeping with compositionality by including enough of the sentence (or discourse) in the scope of the quantifier. Hence the specific examples one can find here will depend on some other semantical phenomenon over and above the indeterminacy of quantifier scopes.

The following examples can be thought of as exemplifying these remarks:

(14)   Bill owns a donkey.
(15)   If Bill owns a donkey, he beats it.

In (15) the context somehow changes the existential quantifier "a" into a universal one. The mechanism of the change is explained by Carlson and Hintikka elsewhere.[21] Suffice it here to say that the explanation shows that the semantical interpretation of the consequent of (15) depends on what happens in the antecedent. This context-dependence is the reason why the Frege Principle fails in (15).

Even though the phenomenon of indefinite quantifier scopes is relatively hard to cash in in the form of particular examples (for reasons explained above), it is one of the most characteristic features of natural languages. It involves a clear violation of the spirit of the Frege Principle.

(v) It is interesting to see that the Frege Principle can fail even in some formal languages. There are two main types of such failures. Both are dealt with most naturally in game-theoretical terms, and have in fact been so treated by logicians independently of my game-theoretical semantics.

(a) In one, an outside-in game can go on to infinity. The best-known case is what logicians call languages with game quantifiers.[22] They cannot be dealt with by means of Tarski-type recursive truth-definitions because such a definition must start from atomic propositions and work its way up to complex ones, while infinitely deep languages are characterized precisely by the occasional absence of such absolute starting-points. In contrast to this failure of recursive truth-definitions, there is no difficulty in treating such "bottomless" languages game-theoretically. The only novelty that is needed is a definition for winning and losing for certain infinitely long games. But of course they do not present any difficulties to a game theorist.

Among languages of this sort there are, besides the well-known game-quantifier languages, also the languages defined in Hintikka and Rantala in 1976. [23]

(b) The kind of logical behavior exhibited by these infinitary languages is not found in natural languages, with the possible partial exception of certain semantical paradoxes. There is another interesting mode of logical behavior, however, that is much closer to what happens in natural languages. It is the behavior of partially ordered (e.g., branching) ·but otherwise normal first-order quantifiers.[24] As is shown in detail by Jon Barwise, such quantifiers violate the principle of compositionality.[25] They can easily be dealt with game-theoretically, however. In particular, the intuitive reason why they are not subject to the Frege Principle allows a simple explanation in terms of game-theoretical semantics. What makes quantifiers branch instead of being linearly ordered is the fact that the game choices associated with a given quantifier may depend on the choices associated with only *some* of the outer quantifiers (quantifiers within the scope of which the given one apparently occurs), not on *all* of them. (The quantifiers it depends on are the ones occurring earlier in the same branch.) This is a clear violation of the inside-out principle, for it means that the interpretation of a quantifier depends on its relation to "outside" quantifiers (quantifiers occurring outside its own scope). Small wonder, therefore, that branching quantifiers violate the Frege Principle.

Even if partially ordered quantifiers occurred only in formal languages, they would constitute a forceful reminder of the limitations of Tarski-type truth-definitions aimed at by Davidson. They are made an even more telling counterexample to the Frege Principle by their presence in natural languages. I have argued this point at length in earlier papers, and answered critics.[26] By this time, the main point – their occurrence in natural languages – seems to have been established beyond reasonable doubt. The two sample sentences (17)-(18) below are modest examples to illustrate the role of branching quantifiers in English. They both instantiate the following branching-quantifier structure (16), which does not normally reduce back to a linear form:

(16)
$$\left.\begin{array}{l}(x)(Ey)\\(z)(Eu)\end{array}\right\rangle M(x,y,z,u)$$

(17)   Every villager has a friend and every townsman has a cousin who are memebers of the same party.

(18)   Some novel by every writer is mentioned in some essay by every critic.

The most persuasive natural-language examples of branching quantifiers probably deal with so-called nonstandard-quantifier words ("many", "few", "most", etc.), as distinguished from logician's "standard" quantifiers (the existential and the universal one). It has been claimed by Jackendoff (among others)[27] that sentences containing such words frequently have readings that cannot be explained in terms of quantifier ordering. These readings, allegedly inexplicable in logical terms, turn out to be precisely branching-quantifier readings. The following is a simple case in point:

(19)   Few men accomplish as much as many women.

This has (barely) a liberated reading ("there are many women such that for each of them you can find few men who accomplish as much"), a moderately feminist reading ("there are not many men each of whom accomplishes as much as each of a large number of women"), and a rampant male-chauvinist reading ("a small group of men accomplishes as much as many women together"). The first two readings can be obtained by the two possible linear orderings of the two quantifiers "few" and "many". The last reading, however, cannot be so obtained. But it obviously results from making the two quantifiers independent (parallel or "branching"). The possibility of such a reading in ordinary English shows the presence of branching quantifiers in natural languages.

At least one writer has claimed that sentences of the form (19) are not acceptable, presumably because the ambiguity makes it hard to process. I don't see that it is ungrammatical in the least; but even if it is, examples of the following kind serve the same purpose:

In this library, few women read few books.

This can be taken to mean, (i) that there are not many women who read a small number of books, (ii) that there are not many books each of which is read by a small number of women, or (iii) that the total number of both women readers and books they read is small.

In general, simpler branching-quantifier structures are often irreducible in the case of "nonstandard" than in the case of "standard" quantifiers.

(vi) I have argued on an earlier occasion that the behavior of multiple and iterated questions in English cannot be explained in a satisfactory way without assuming that our tacit methods of semantically processing such questions work from the outside inwards.[28] This involves a violation of the inside-out principle and hence a violation of the Frege Principle. The argument is too long to be summarized here. Basically, the problem is to explain why multiple questions have the precise multiplicity of readings they in fact have in English.

What is impressive about these counterexamples to the Frege Principle is that they span many of the most pervasive and most interesting semantical phenomena: quantifier scopes, both relative and absolute; definite descriptions (the definite article); some types of anaphora; multiple questions; generic uses of the indefinite article; and so on. In view of these examples no one can any longer claim that violations of the Frege Principle are marginal or otherwise unimportant phenomena.

It might be thought that one main reason why many philosophers of language believe in the Frege Principle is that they believe in extensionality. There is a historical connection between the two problems in that Frege's formulation of his principle was prompted by his struggles with nonextensional contexts.[29] Moreover, it seems to me very likely that the well-known interpretational merits of extensional languages have led logicians and philosophers of language to favor languages in which the Frege Principle holds. I don't know if Davidson's distrust of modalities and possible-worlds semantics is connected with his adherence to the Frege Principle.[30] Doesn't the mutual substitutivity of two component expressions e and e', occurring in E on the basis of the identity of their references show that the reference of E is determined by those of its parts and that the Frege Principle is therefore valid? No, it does not, for the substitutivity guarantees neither that the semantical contributions of e and e' are context-independent (independent of their environment in E) nor that the contributions of such syntactically well-defined parts are collectively sufficient to determine the meaning (reference) of E. This is the fact illustrated by my earlier examples, several of which pertain to first-order languages in which extensionality holds. For instance, the introduction of branching quantifiers does not destroy extensionality, but it does destroy the Frege Principle.

Conversely, some suitable version of the Frege Principle can very well hold in nonextensional contexts. This question is connected with the historical question: Was Frege a Fregean? In other words, did Frege believe in compositionality? Even though he apparently adhered to the principle, some philosophers these days are assuming as a matter of course that Frege's treatment of oblique (opaque, nonextensional) contexts violated the principle of compositionality.[31] It is quite clear, however, that Frege did not think so. In general, in asking whether the meanings of the component parts e_1, e_2, ...,e_i of a complex expression E determine the meaning of E we have to decide whether we are considering the meanings e_1, e_2,...., e_i have in E or whether we are speaking of the meanings they would have *in isolation*. Accordingly, we obtain two different versions of the Frege Principle. Can we make the real Frege Principle stand out? As I said earlier, Frege denied that we can really speak of the meanings that e_1, e_2, ..., e_i would have in isolation. Hence he must have rejected the second alternative. But if we opt for the first alternative, as Frege did, Frege turns out to be a Fregean after all. For, on Frege's analysis of opaque contexts, the subordinate expressions occurring in such contexts refer to what is normally their sense or *Sinn*. In other respects, the reference of the whole is determined as usual. Hence the reference of the whole depends in a regular way on the references *in that context* of its component expressions, which means that the Frege Principle holds in its most Fregean form.

This analysis can in a sense be vindicated in possible-worlds semantics.[32] There the semantical entity associated with, say, a singular term s as its meaning or sense is a

function from possible worlds to individuals. These meaning functions correspond in possible-worlds analysis to
Frege's notion of "sense". What happens in a context
where we are speaking of, say, John's beliefs is that these
functions are restricted to worlds compatible with John's
beliefs. Now the alternativeness relation associated with
John and with the notion of belief (this alternativeness
relation is the appropriate semantical entity determined by
the word "believes") suffices to pick out that class of all
possible worlds admitted of what John believes. (They are
the worlds bearing this relation to the given one.) Hence
the semantical interpretation of a complex expression is
determined by the semantical entities associated with its
component parts.

However, other versions of the Frege Principle fail to
be satisfied by Gottlob's own treatment. Frege himself in
effect admits that the reference of an opaque expression is
not a function of what the meanings of its parts would be
in isolation. What is even more important, the inside-out
principle is not satisfied by Frege's treatment of opaque
(nonextensional) contexts, even though it can be thought
of as being satisfied by the possible-worlds treatment of
the same contexts (as long as no backwards-looking operators are present).

The two forms of the Frege Principle, therefore, differ
in their relation to the inside-out principle. The one
Frege himself appears to have embraced does not presuppose the inside-out principle, whereas the other form
does. These two forms have not been distinguished sufficiently sharply in recent discussion.

Futhermore, tables can be turned on Frege here.
Frege denied that we can speak of the meanings of component expressions, say e_1, e_2, ..., e_i, *in isolation* from
the context, say E, in which they occur. It is not clear,
however, that we can always speak of their meanings
within that context, either. In order to see that, we can
consider what might happen when the invariance principle
fails, as it fails in game-theoretical semantics. Then the
meaning of a complex expression E might be determined by
the meanings of certain other expressions e_1', e_2', ...,
e_i', obtainable from e_1, e_2, ..., e_i, and E. Then the
procedure for determining the meaning of E might turn
completely on the meanings of e_1', e_2', ..., e_i' and hence
bypass e_1, e_2, ..., e_i altogether. In such circumstances
it might be nonsense to speak of the respective meanings

of e_1, e_2, ..., e_i in the context E. Again, this is precisely what happens in game-theoretical semantics.

It is also seen that this is an additional reason why Frege's attempted way out from possible failures of context-independence is inadequate.

But how does Davidson fare amidst all these failures of compositionality? Not very well, it seems to me. He has consistently used as one of his tools in semantics the famous T-schema of Tarski.[33] In other words, he has required that all the substitution-instances of the following schema be true:[34]

(T)   'p' is true if and only if p

where "'p'" can also be replaced by a structural description of the same substitution-value of "p".

One of the guiding lights of Davidson's semantics is the requirement that any satisfactory theory of meaning must imply as theorems all the substitution-instances of the schema (T). This way of imposing truth conditionality on one's semantics is not very happy, however. As I have pointed out elsewhere,[35] one half of (T) sometimes even fails to be true, as shown by examples like (8) above. Now we can see the deeper reasons for the failure of the schema (T). Its failure is merely one example among many of the failures of compositionality. It is not the most straightforward example, but the role of (T) in Davidson's overall research strategy makes it especially dramatic.

Attempts to defuse this criticism of Davidsonic attempts to apply (T) to natural languages have totally failed, it seems to me. For instance, James C. Klagge[36] imagines that he can escape the trouble by in effect replacing (8) by

(20)   It is not the case that any businessman can become a millionaire or "Any businessman can become a millionaire" is true.

But of course (20) says precisely the same in English as (8).

Klagge tries to avoid this by inviting the reader to insert "just" in front of the first "any" in (20). This would amount to lending "any" an emphatic stress, and would therefore change the situation completely here and everywhere else, as illustrated, e.g., by the haughty debutante's line, "I don't dance with *any* boy." (She could equally well have said, "I don't dance with just any boy.") It is well known that emphatic stress changes scope conventions in general. Hence Klagge's attempted way out here is without any force.

Klagge's other attempted ways out involve mixing logical symbols and English in the substitution-instances of the schema (T). The truth-conditions of such sentences are not fixed either by logic or by the semantics of English, and are hence useless for elucidating the meanings of English sentences. After all, it was the unproblematic pretheoretical truth of its substitution-instances that was supposed to make the use of the schema (T) so useful.

Notice that there are further problems about the applications of the schema (T) to an ordinary language like English. An instance of the schema is grammatical if and only if the following conjunction is grammatical:

(21) 'p' is true if p, and 'p' is true only if p.

Earlier, I registered certain difficulties about the first conjunct. There are problems about the second conjunct too. Strings of the form

(22) 'p' is true only if p

are typically ungrammatical (unacceptable) if 'p' contains the word "any", for reasons I have spelled out elsewhere.[37] Hence (21) is in the same circumstances ungrammatical, too. Thus both halves of the T-schema can fail in English: the one can be false and the other ungrammatical. It turns out that the underlying reason for both is one and the same, viz., the context-dependence of the semantics of "any".

Alex Blum's attempted rejoinder[38] to my criticism is equally beside the point. He proposes to modify (T) by allowing "p" to be replaced by the interpretation in the canonical notation (of a metalanguage) of the sentence whose quote or structural description replaces "'p'". This course would not solve the problems I am concerned with but merely push them around. Instead of being problems about the schema (T), they would now become problems of translating the critical sentences into one's canonical notation. It is not news that Tarski's T-schema works in a suitable canonical notation, for instance, in a formalized first-order language. But the problem of translating natural language into a quantificational notation is a much more formidable one than philosophers currently seem to realize. Even when they manage to translate some particular sentences, their paraphrases almost invariably remain, in Merrill B. Hintikka's apt phrase, "miraculous translations": they do not have any real grasp of the general principles or rules their translation relies on.

Indeed, Davidson has made it clear that he considers the use of T-schema a way of avoiding the problem of miraculous translation and relying on our pretheoretical understanding of a familiar language as a stepping-stone to a semantical theory. This purpose would be completely destroyed if applications of T-schema themselves rely on immaculate translation, as they will do on Blum's suggestion. Thus by restoring the validity of the T-schema, Blum is destroying its usefulness for the very purpose it is calculated by Davidson to serve.

Much more important than the failure of any one particular argument or device of Davidson's is the overwhelmingly clear fact that the aims of his whole program are too narrow. The failures of compositionality mean, in plain English, that there is a large number of sentences in natural languages like English for which no Tarski-type recursive characterization of truth will work. Nor can this failure be blamed on the fuzziness, ambiguities, or other imperfections of natural language. For, as I mentioned earlier, there likewise are highly interesting formal languages for which a Tarski-type truth definition cannot work. Hence, it seems to me that a radical revision of the whole project is in order.

How is Davidson's program to be revised? I believe that he is right in looking for truth conditions (and conditions of satisfaction). But we have to take a much longer and harder look at the way those truth conditions actually operate than anyone, including Davidson, has so far done. Among the features of this actual mode of operation of truth conditions, it seems to me, there is the fact that they operate from the outside in, which is enough to prove Davidson's aims unrealistic.

How should our truth conditions operate? If a conjecture is permitted, they should operate in parallel with the processes we actually use in understanding our language. And these processes, it seems to me, are basically anticipations of the operations ("language-games") that link our language with nonlinguistic reality. Davidson is indeed right in trying to connect truth conditions and language learning. But what we basically learn are not recursive truth-clauses but the use of our language. The time is ripe, it seems to me, to create an entirely new paradigm for truth-conditional semantics.[39]

Even after we have reached this conclusion, a few supplementary remarks are in order. Indeed, the line of thought represented in this chapter requires two important further explanations.

As I formulated the notion of compositionality above, it refers to the component parts of a complex expression E. What they are is determined by the syntax one is presupposing. Whether or not a given sentence E violates compositionality is therefore relative to one's underlying syntactical theory. In principle, a sentence can be compositional on the basis of one syntactical theory and noncompositional on another.

It follows that in the counterexamples to compositionality that I offered above I was tacitly making certain syntactical assumptions. More accurately, I was tacitly appealing to certain commonsense ideas about the syntactical structure of certain sentences. For instance, I assumed (very roughly speaking) that a sentence like (6) is formed in such a way as to turn (5) into a "component part" (in the intended) sense of (6). In principle, this is not a foregone conclusion. Instead of doing so, we could try to form (6) from "any" and from "I'll be greatly surprised if ___ can beat Chris."

I don't see that there is a knockdown a priori argument to show the impossibility of such alternative generations (or of the correlated analysis of (6) into constituent parts). At the same time, it seems to me that there is an overwhelming abundance of prima facie reasons to prefer the simple-minded generation that I was assuming earlier. If one tries to take on the alternative theory seriously, one soon ends up facing a formidable array of complications. For instance, different quantifier words have to be dealt with in different ways in one's generative rules. It is significant here, it seems to me, that when Noam Chomsky recently had to face the problem of accounting for certain closely related peculiarities in the behavior of "any", he did not try to give an alternative generative account (e.g., along the lines indicated in the preceding paragraph) but preferred a nongenerative account that can

preserve the original simple generation of sentences like
(6).[40] In general, it seems to me that the syntactical
assumptions I have in effect made are not only extremely
plausible ("intuitive"), but can also be argued to be in
agreement with the best syntactical analysis of the
sentences involved.

My line of thought earlier in this chapter is also
critically predicated on certain semantical assumptions. In
order to see this, let us consider the example offered by
such branching-quantifier sentences as (16). It is its
nonlinearity (the informational independence of some of the
semantical rules that have to be applied to it) that makes
it noncompositional. But – it may be objected here – there
is no problem in turning (16) into a linear sentence if we
are willing to go to *second-order* logic. Indeed, as
game-theoretical semantics shows at once, (16) is logically
equivalent with the linear second-order sentence that says
that suitable Skolem functions exist to codify (partially)
my winning strategy in the correlated game:

$$(23) \quad (Ef)(Eg)(x)(z) \quad M(x,f(x),z,g(z)).$$

Indeed, second-order sentences like (23) seem to be very
well suited for the purpose of spelling out the partially
ordered structure of the original quantifiers by means of
different choices of arguments for the Skolem functions
that correspond to the existential quantifiers of the
original sentence.

Now (23) is linear and hence compositional. Therefore
compositionality can be restored in this example in what
looks like a most natural way. What, if anything, is supposed to be wrong with such a vindication of compositionality? Do I have any guarantee that such a restoration of
compositionality is not possible in all the other cases, too?

In order to answer these questions, let us note what
happens in the transition from (16) to (23). In (16), the
semantical object (interpretation) that in the semantical
game starting from (16) is associated with each existential
quantifier is of the logical type of an individual. In (23),
the semantical entity associated with each existential quantifier is something much more complicated and much more
abstract. It is the function that not only specifies an
individual but shows how the choice of this individual
depends on the semantical entities that in the original
sentence (16) are correlated with certain expressions

(universal quantifiers) occurring farther out in (16).

It is obvious that this strategy can be followed in some other cases. (A specific example will be given below, viz., the semantics of the English past tense.) We can hope to restore compositionality by changing our semantics. Instead of correlating with a context-sensitive component e_0 of a sentence E the kind of semantical entity we usually correlate with e_0, we can try to correlate with it a more complex entity that codifies its interaction with the interpretations of those outside expressions e_1, e_2,... to whose presence it is sensitive. Then this more complicated and more abstract entity must refer to the "interpretations" of (i.e., semantical entities correlated with) e_1, e_2, ...

This strategy works in some cases. What is wrong with it? Why can't we use it as a general method of vindicating compositionality? As an answer, let me first note that there is no general reason to believe that a similar maneuver will work in all cases. But even if it did, there would be a price to be paid. It was pointed out above that the specific dodge used there to rescue compositionality from the clutches of branching quantifiers means complicating our semantics. The semantical entities that are assigned to certain component expressions (existential quantifiers) are more complicated and more abstract than they were before the change. Typically, the new semantical entities to which we have to resort in the modified semantics are of a higher logical type than the old ones. (Once again, my point is illustrated by the step from (16) to (23).) These facts alone amount to a serious argument against the change and therefore to an argument against compositionality. What is even more important, the projected change is an obvious step away from psychosemantical realism. When we contemplate the choice of an individual to instantiate an existential sentence, we don't normally have in mind any general strategy (Skolem function) of making such choices in all cases, depending on the individuals selected earlier, nor do we have in mind what we do in similar choice situations. Whether or not universalizability is a sound doctrine in ethics, I don't see any reason to believe that it amounts to good psycholinguistics. The original simpler semantics was clearly closer to what actually happens when we semantically process the sentence in question.

Notice here that if the change is consistently carried

out, we also have to understand normal linearly ordered quantifier sentences as being about Skolem functions, not about the individuals in our domain of interpretation. This seems so artificial as to be almost a parody of realistic semantics, which is supposed to help us to understand how we actually process sentences.

On a more technical level, the unnaturalness of this procedure is illustrated by the uncertainties that are attached to the interpretation of such higher-order variables as the function variables of (23). Are they supposed to range over all extensionally possible functions, or only over some smaller set, such as recursive functions perhaps or functions whose existence can be proved in some suitable axiom system of set theory? [41] Each answer can be argued for, and a choice between them seems extremely hard to motivate in a theoretically interesting way.

Moreover, if this class of functions is wide enough, the resulting second-order logic is not axiomatizable.[42] Then it becomes more than a little questionable how much is gained by developing such a semantical theory, if it is doomed to be so complicated that we cannot systematize (axiomatize) all logically valid sentences.

Similar remarks can be made in other, parallel cases. In general, this kind of attempt to save compositionality in the semantics of natural languages is bound to falter, it seems to me, not on any general impossibility but on the artificiality and abstractness of the resulting putative semantics. Hence the main conclusion of this chapter still stands.

An instructive example is the semantics of the (simple) past tense in English.[43] At first sight, there does not seem to be any problem here. Syntactically, it presumably is codified by a marker attached to a verb V_1. The question is what its semantical interpretation is. This does not appear to be much of a problem, either. No matter how you set up your semantics, what is involved is a step to an earlier moment of time. So what's the problem?

The problem arises that when several different verbs V_1, V_2,..that are all in the past tense occur in one sentence - or even in different sentences - the choices of the relevant past moments of time are rarely independent of each other, but are usually either combined to a single choice of only one past moment of time common to all the verbs, or else they are related to each other. (For instance, the temporal order of the moments chosen has to match the left-to-right order of the verbs.) An outside-in semantical analysis takes such dependences in its stride. However, in a compositional treatment one must assign to each past-tense marker (attached to a verb V_1), a semantical entity that can refer to all the other verbs V_1, V_2, ... that have to be heeded in correlating the different choices of past moments of time with each other (and to the criteria of distinguishing these verbs from others in the same sentence). Once again, this is not only a complication. It is a serious violation of all principles of reasonable semantical theory. In this case, the problem is not only alienation from actual semantical information processing. Rather, it is obvious that we must combine in the more complicated compositional rule at least two entirely different ideas that in a satisfactory semantical theory should be kept separate, viz., a step to an earlier moment of time and the principles of combining or coordinating several such steps. It turns out that the principles governing the latter are quite general, and by no means peculiar to the past tense. Their role in determining the semantical relations of different occurrences of the imperfect tense hence cannot be fully appreciated if they are built into the semantics of this tense. Hence this example also strongly suggests that it is futile to try to enforce compositionality in the semantics of natural languages.

Notice that saying all this is compatible with admitting that in other kinds of semantics a similar modification (serving to salvage the Frege Principle) is more natural than it would be in psycholinguistically motivated natural-language semantics. For instance, for a computer scientist, the foremost concrete realities are not what is involved in particular steps of computation, but the very programs that encode computational algorithms. For a computer scientist, the above argument against attempts to save compositionality through type-theoretical ascent does not carry much weight.[44] Indeed, I am not at all claiming here that compositionality must fail for computer languages.

It seems to me that the type of attempt to vindicate compositionality that we have been considering in the last few pages is in effect employed to a large extent by Montague semantics.[45] One of its characteristic features is Montague's liberal use of higher-order (higher-type) conceptualizations even where lower-order ones are possible. A case in point is his decision to assign to a singular term as its correlated semantical entity, not an individual, but the set of properties this individual has. This obviously has no psycholinguistic motivation whatever. The set of all properties (including, of course, complex ones) that an individual has simply is not the kind of entity that plays any role in our actual semantical-information processing.

Moreover, first-order formulations have other advantages over higher-order ones. In first-order languages we can achieve an axiomatization of logical truths and of valid inferences. In them, we do not as easily get involved in the problems (noted above) of determining the ranges of higher-order variables. Hence some reasons are needed for the emphasis Montague puts on higher-order conceptualizations.

I suspect that one of the unspoken reasons Montague and Montague semanticists have had is precisely to defend compositionality by means of type-theoretical ascent. For reasons different from Davidson's, Montague also started out considering Tarski-type truth-definitions as the paradigm example of satisfactory truth-conditional semantics. Hence he was deeply committed to compositionality. In view of the several different kinds of prima facie violations of compositionality we have registered, the relative success of Montague semantics may therefore appear surprising. The explanation that suggests itself here is that these successes have been obtained partly at the expense of the kinds of disadvantages that we have seen attaching to the type-theoretical ascent as an attempted vindication of compositionality. Critics have occasionally complained about the abstractness and about the lack of psycholinguistic realism in connection with Montague semantics. Now we have found reasons to think that these are not due to accidental features of intellectual taste and theoretical style, but are grounded on Montague's commitment to compositionality.[46]

Attempts to save the Frege Principle are not limited to Montague semantics. One of them is relevant to one of my counterexamples to compositionality above, viz., (ii). It might have been objected to my use of the phenomena discussed there that there can be - and have been - treatments of these phenomena by means of received compositional methods, essentially by means of glorified Tarski-type truth-conditions.[47]

This objection is well taken in that such treatments are certainly possible, at least in some cases. However, they pay a price in the form of complications. Typically, they take a form similar to what is often used, for other reasons, in connection with tenses. Instead of evaluating (determining the truth-value of) a sentence S in a given world w_1, S is at each stage of the evaluation considered also in relation to another world, w_2. In this case, the intuitive meaning of w_1 is fairly natural: it is the world from which the whole evaluations process started. We have to "remember", so to speak, where the evaluation process began. However, this complication is nevertheless a complication. Moreover, it does not alone handle all problems. Sometimes we have to "remember", not only what world the evaluation process started from, but what some of the interim worlds are to which the evaluation process has meanwhile taken us. It has been argued by Esa Saarinen that no fixed finite limit can be set to the number of such reference-point worlds.[48] The specific example presented above in (ii) is calculated to illustrate this impossibility of setting a limit to the number of worlds that can be "remembered". Now we can see that it also serves to illustrate the futility of efforts to save the Frege Principle by complicating one's semantical framework.

At the same time, we can see here how very easy it is to handle context-dependent phenomena in game-theoretical semantics. For instance, all we have to do to cope with so-called actuality operators is give the game rules governing them priority over the other relevant game rules. No complications are needed either in the object language itself (no new operators are needed) or in the semantical framework.

The general strategy of defending the Frege Principle that we have discussed and rejected can be related to Frege's initial line of thought of enforcing compositionality by reifying use into meaning, i.e., identifying the contribution of a component part to the meaning of a complex expression with the meaning of the part. The meaning of the whole is inevitably determined by the interaction of the different parts. How, in view of this interaction, can we separate the contributions of different parts from each other – and from the extra contribution to meaning that comes about through their interaction? I don't see that any general principles can be set up here. What the rejected strategy of defending compositionality amounts to is including essential parts of the interactional contribution in what is usually taken to be the contributions of several components. There can be no general justification for such a procedure, and it is objectionable on general theoretical grounds because it tends to hide distinctions that are vital for a realistic understanding of what goes on in the semantics of our language. In different ways, all these warnings serve to highlight the pitfalls of the initial strategy of reification of use into meaning that I attributed to Frege.[49]

NOTES

[1] Tarski's classical monograph *Der Wahrheitsbegriff in den formalisierten Sprachen* has appeared in English translation in the volume *Logic, Semantics, Metamathematics*, Clarendon Press, Oxford, 1956, pp. 152–278.

[2] Davidson's most important writings along these lines are the following: "Theories of Meaning and Learnable Languages", in Y. Bar-Hillel, editor, *Logic, Methodology, and Philosophy of Science: Proceedings of the 1964 International Congress*, North-Holland, Amsterdam, 1966, pp. 383–94; "Truth and Meaning", *Synthese* 17 (1967), 304–23; "On Saying That", ibid. 19 (1968–69), 130–46; "True to the Facts", *The Journal of Philosophy* 66 (1969), 748–64; "Semantics for Natural Languages", in *Linguaggi nella Societa e nella Tecnica*, Communita, Milan, 1970, pp. 177–88; "In Defense of Conventon T", in H. Leblanc, editor, *Truth, Syntax and Modality*, North-Holland, Amsterdam, 1973, pp. 76–86; "Radical Interpretation", *Dialectica* 27 (1973), 313–28; "Belief and the Basis of Meaning", *Synthese* 27 (1974), 309–24; "Thought and Talk", in S. Guttenplan, editor, *Mind and Language*, Clarendon Press, Oxford, 1975, pp. 7–23; "Reality without Reference", *Dialectica* 31 (1977), 247–58.

[3] Cf., for instance, the title of Davidson's Jerusalem paper of 1966, namely, "Theories of Meaning and Learnable Languages".

[4] See Kenneth Wexler and Peter W. Culicover, *Formal Principles of Language Acquisition*, The MIT Press, Cambridge, Mass., 1980; and Peter W. Culicover and Kenneth Wexler, "Some Syntactical Implications of a Theory of Language Learnability", in Peter W. Culicover, Thomas

Wasow, and Adrian Akmajian, editors, *Formal Syntax*, Academic Press, New York, 1977, pp. 1-60 (with discussion and further references to the literature). The classical results concerning the nonidentifiability of transformational grammars by Stanley Peters and R. W. Ritchie can be understood in the same spirit; see P. Stanley Peters and R. W. Ritchie, "A Note on the Universal Base Hypothesis", *Journal of Linguistics* 5 (1969), 150-52; and "On the Generative Power of Transformational Grammars", *Informational Sciences* 6 (1973), 49-83. It is a pity that Davidson's ideas have never been related to this interesting line of work.

[5] Cf. "Theories of Meaning", p. 387: "I do not mean to argue here that it is necessary that we be able to extract a truth definition from an adequate theory [of meaning] (though something much like this is needed), but a theory certainly meets the condition I have in mind if we can extract a truth definition; in particular, no stronger notion of meaning is called for." Davidson does not discuss the additional assumptions, however, on which we can extract a Tarski-type truth definition from an adequate theory of meaning.

In "On Saying That", Davidson goes so far as to say that "a satisfactory theory of meaning must, then, give an explicit account of the truth conditions of every sentence, and this can be done by giving a theory that satisfies Tarski's criteria; *nothing less should count as showing how the meaning of every sentence depends on its structure"* (my italics; p. 131). This is necessary because "by giving such a theory, we demonstrate in a persuasive way that the language, though it consists in an indefinitely large number of sentences, can be comprehended by a being with finite powers" (ibid.).

The "Tarski criteria" referred to by Davidson here are not Tarski-type truth conditions, but rather the requirement that one's theory of truth imply all instances of Tarski's T-schema. This schema will be discussed later in this chapter.

[6] Cf. Michael Dummett, *Frege: Philosophy of Language*, Duckworth, London, 1973, pp. 152-57, 159-60.

[7] Cf., e.g., Barbara Hall Partee, "Possible Worlds Semantics and Linguistic Theory", *The Monist* 60 (1977), 303-26, especially 306-8; "Montague Grammar and Transformational Grammar", *Linguistic Inquiry* 6 (1975), 203-300.

[8] Even if Davidson should not subscribe to the argument to be presented, it serves to bring out some pertinent aspects of the conceptual situation. The historical accuracy of my "rational reconstruction" therefore is not a major issue here. Davidson has never himself spelled out fully what the connection between learnability and truth conditions is supposed to be. Hence every attempt to discuss the rationale of his views is bound to contain an element of conjecture – or at least extrapolation.

The best way out seems to me to take Davidson literally when he refers to Frege as the originator of the principle and to examine how Frege conceives of it and motivates it.

[9] Cf. Davidson, "Theories of Meaning", p. 387: "We can regard the meaning of each sentence as a function of a finite number of features of the sentence...."

[10] This identification is made explicitly by Frege, as witnessed by *Grundgesetze*, vol. 1, sec. 32 (p. 51 of the original, p. 90 of the Furth translation): "The names ... contribute to the expression of the thought and this contribution of the individual [component] is its *sense*." Statements of the same general import are found in Frege's *On the Foundations of Geometry and Formal Theories of Arithmetic*, edited and translated by E. H. W. Kluge, Yale University Press, New Haven, 1971, pp. 8, 53, 67.

[11] See Frege, *The Foundations of Arithmetic* (translated by J. L. Austin), Basil Blackwell, Oxford, 1950, pp. 71 and 73; and cf. Dummett, *Frege: Philosophy of Language*, pp. 192–96.

[12] Often, the Frege Principle is simply identified with the inside-out principle. Later in this chapter we shall see that such an identification is historically inaccurate, however.

[13] The main function of the compositionality principle (Frege Principle) is often seen in effecting this parallelism between syntax and semantics. Cf., e.g., Partee, "Possible Worlds Semantics", pp. 307–8. Relatively little of the total force of the Frege Principle is needed for this one purpose, however.

The reason that there can be expected to be a close connection between our syntactical and semantical rules should be obvious. The end-all and be-all of my uttering a sentence S is to make Myself understood. What you have to go on in trying to understand is mostly the syntactical from of S. Since the semantical process of interpreting a sentence thus depends crucially on its

syntactical form, it would be very strange indeed if the
rules defining the syntactical form of S were unrelated to
the rules we use in processing S semantically.   See
chapter 4 (sections 8ff.) above for discussion of the importance of the syntax-semantics affinity in game-theoretical semantics.
[14] See the bibliography at the end of this volume, sec. I,
especially, the different papers collected in *Game-Theoretical Semantics*, ed. by Esa Saarinen, D. Reidel,
Dordrecht, 1978.
[15] Cf. "Theories of Meaning", p. 387: "We must be able to
specify, in a way that depends effectively and solely on
formal considerations, what every sentence means."
[16] See my "Quantifiers vs. Quantification Theory",
Linguistic Inquiry 5 (1974), 153-77; reprinted in Saarinen,
Game-Theoretical Semantics, pp. 49-79.
[17] "Quantifiers in Natural Languages: Some Logical
Problems II", *Linguistics and Philosophy* 1 (1977), 153-72;
reprinted in Saarinen, *Game-Theoretical Semantics*, as
sections 10-19 of "Quantifiers in Natural Languages: Some
Logical Problems", pp. 98-115.
[18] See Esa Saarinen, "Backwards-Looking Operators in
Tense Logic and in Natural Language", *Reports from the
Department of Philosophy, University of Helsinki*, no.4,
1977; "Intentional Identity Interpreted", ibid. no. 5;
"Propositional Attitudes, Anaphora, and Backwards-Look-
ing Operators", ibid. no. 6.   The first has also appeared
in *Essays in Mathematical and Philosophical Logic*, ed. by
Jaakko Hintikka, Ilkka Niiniluoto, and Esa Saarinen, D.
Reidel, Dordrecht, 1979, pp. 341-67, and the second in
Linguistics and Philosophy 2 (1978), 151-223.   The first
two are also reprinted in Saarinen, *Game-Theoretical
Semantics*, pp. 215-327.
[19] This idea was first mentioned in Lauri Carlson and
Jaakko Hintikka, "Conditionals, Generic Quantifiers, and
Other Applications of Subgames", in *Meaning and Use*, ed.
by Avishai Margalit, D. Reidel, Dordrecht, 1978; reprinted
in Saarinen *Game-Theoretical Semantics*, pp. 179-214.
[20] This phenomenon marks one of the most interesting and
most neglected differences between formal and natural languages.   I have mentioned it earlier in "Quantifiers in
Natural Languages".
[21] See Hintikka and Carlson, "Conditionals, Generic Quantifiers, and Other Applications of Subgames".
[22] See the bibliography to this volume, section II (iv).

[23] See the bibliography to this volume, section II (iii).
[24] See the bibliography to this volume, section II (i).
[25] See Jon Barwise, "On Branching Quantifiers in English", *Journal of Philosphical Logic* 8 (1979), 47-80, especially appendix 5.
[26] See Hintikka, "Quantifiers vs. Quantification Theory" and "Quantifiers in Natural Languages".
[27] Ray S. Jackendoff, *Semantic Interpretation in Generative Grammar*, MIT Press, Cambridge, Mass., 1972, pp. 305-8). Cf. here also Lauri Carlson, "Plural Quantifiers and Informational Independence", in Ilkka Niiniluoto and Esa Saarinen, editors, *Intensional Logic: Theory and Applications* (Acta Philosophica Fennica, vol. 35), Societas Philosophica Fennica, Helsinki, 1982, pp. 163-74.
[28] *The Semantics of Questions and the Questions of Semantics* (Acta Philosophica Fennica, vol. 28, no. 4), North-Holland, Amsterdam, 1976, especially chapters 6, 8-9.
[29] Cf. Dummett, *Frege: Philosophy of Language*, pp. 186-92.
[30] Carnap's discussion in *Meaning and Necessity*, University of Chicago Press, Chicago, 1956, p. 121-24, comes very close to this identification.
[31] Frege's own formulations sometimes encourage such a view; cf. "Uber Sinn und Bedeutung", pp. 37-38, 49-50 of the original. We read, for instance, on p. 37: "One can legitimately conclude only that the reference of a sentence is *not always* its truth-value."
[32] Cf., e.g., the articles in my books *Models for Modalities* (D. Reidel, Dordrecht, 1969) and *The Intentions of Intentionality* (D. Reidel, Dordrecht, 1975), especially the paper "Carnap's Heritage in Logical Semantics" in the latter.
[33] See especially Davidson, "In Defense of Convention T".
[34] I am employing single quotes in the role of Quinean quasi-quotes (corner quotes) in the T-schema and its derivatives.
[35] See Jaakko Hintikka, "A Counterexample to Tarski-Type Truth Definitions as Applied to Natural Languages", *Philosophia* 5 (1975), 207-12; "The Prospects for Convention T", *Dialectica* 30 (1976), 61-66.
[36] Cf. James C. Klagge, "Convention T Regained", *Philosophical Studies* 32 (1977), pp. 377-81.
[37] See Jaakko Hintikka, "Quantifiers in Natural Languages: Some Logical Problems".

[38] Alex Blum, "Convention T and Natural Languages", *Dialectica* 32 (1978), 77–80.

[39] This is what my game–theoretical semantics is calculated to do. For a survey of it, see chapter 1 above.

[40] See Noam Chomsky, *Rules and Representations*, Columbia University Press, New York, 1980, pp. 123–27; and cf. chapter 9 above.

[41] A special case of this interpretational choice is Leon Henkin's classical contrast between standard and non-standard semantics for higher-order logic. See his paper, "Completeness in the Theory of Types", *Journal of Symbolic Logic* 15 (1950), 81–91.

[42] See here my paper, "Is Alethic Modal Logic Possible?" *Acta Philosophica Fennica* 35 (1982), 89–105.

[43] Cf. chapter 5 above.

[44] This point was made forcefully to me by Michael Arbib (private communication).

[45] See here Richmond Thomason, editor, *Formal Philosophy: Selected Papers of Richard Montague*, Yale University Press, New Haven, 1974; David R. Dowty, Robert E. Wall and Stanley Peters, *Introduction to Montague Semantics*, D. Reidel, Dordrecht, 1981 (with further references to the literature).

[46] Cf. note 7 above.

[47] The extent to which Montague's approach is an extension of his master's methods has not been fully appreciated in the literature.

[48] Saarinen, "Backwards-Looking Operators in Tense Logic and in Natural Language".

[49] This chapter began its life as a contribution to a collection of papers on the work of Donald Davidson, to be edited by Bruce Vermazen and Merrill B. Hintikka, but it soon grew far too long to be acceptable for that purpose. I have not tried to eliminate all the signs of its early history, however. Much of the work that has gone into it was supported by a John Simon Guggenheim Memorial Foundation Fellowship for 1979–80.

GTS BIBLIOGRAPHY

In this bibliography we have tried to cover not only GTS, but a number of related developments as well. The reason is that GTS is in part a way of spelling out ideas that have long been implicit in logical and mathematical literature. However, some of these developments are so multifaceted that we have not aimed at completeness; instead we have sought to provide samples that would help a reader gain entry into the literature. This is indicated in the relevant sections below.

We would like to thank the following people for providing us with information: E.M. Barth, Jon Barwise, Lauri Carlson, Solomon Feferman, Margaret Gilbert, Mike Hand, Maaret Karttunen, David Lewis, Kuno Lorenz, Paul Lorenzen, David Over, Veikko Rantala, Neil Tennant, and Wilbur Walkoe. They are not responsible for any errors.

ABBREVIATIONS USED

AML	*Annals of Mathematical Logic*
AMLG	*Archiv für mathematische Logik und Grundlagenforschung*
APF	*Acta Philosophica Fennica*
FM	*Fundamenta Mathematicae*
IJM	*Israel Journal of Mathematics*
JMSJ	*Journal of the Mathematical Society of Japan*
JPL	*Journal of Philosophical Logic*
JSL	*Journal of Symbolic Logic*
LP	*Linguistics and Philosophy*
NDJFL	*Notre Dame Journal of Formal Logic*
ZMLGM	*Zeitschrift für mathematische Logik und Grundlagen der Mathematik*

I GAME-THEORETICAL SEMANTICS
(Including Critical and Related Discussions)

Barwise, Jon: 1979, "On Branching Quantifiers in English", *JPL* 8, 47-80.

Bresnan, Joan, editor: 1982, *The Mental Representation of Grammatical Relations*, The MIT Press, Cambridge, Mass.

Carlson, Lauri: 1975, "Peliteoreettista Semantiikkaa", MA Thesis, University of Helsinki (unpublished).

Carlson, Lauri: 1981, "Aspect and Quantification", in Philip J. Tedeschi and Annie Zaenen, editors, *Syntax and Semantics, Volume 14, Tense and Aspect*, Academic Press, New York, pp. 31-64.

Carlson, Lauri: 1982, "Plural Quantifiers and Informational Independence", *APF* 35, 163-74.

Carlson, Lauri: 1983, *Dialogue Games: An Approach to Discourse Analysis*, D. Reidel, Dordrecht.

Carlson, Lauri, and Alice ter Meulen: 1979, "Informational Independence in Intensional Contexts", in Esa Saarinen et al., editors, *Essays in Honour of Jaakko Hintikka*, D. Reidel, Dordrecht, pp. 61-72.

Chomsky, Noam: 1980, *Rules and Representations*, Columbia University Press, New York.

Dahl, Osten: 1977, "Games and Models", in Osten Dahl, editor, *Logic, Pragmatics and Grammar*, Studentlitteratur, Lund, pp. 147-99.

Davis, Lawrence: 1976, "The Rules of the Game: A Review of Hintikka's Proposals for Game Theory Semantics", in J. Stillings, editor, *U/Mass Occasional Papers in Linguistics*, Vol. 2, pp. 21-50.

Fauconnier, G.: 1975, "Do Quantifiers Branch?" *Linguistic Inquiry* 6, 555-78.

Higginbotham, James: 1982, "Comments on Hintikka's Paper" (Hintikka (1982a)), *NDJFL* 23, 263-71.

Hintikka, Jaakko: 1968, "Language-Games for Quantifiers", in Nicholas Rescher, editor, *Studies in Logical Theory* (American Philosophical Quarterly Monograph Series, No. 2), Basil Blackwell, Oxford, pp. 46-72. [Reprinted in Hintikka (1973a) with revisions.]

Hintikka, Jaakko: 1973a, *Logic, Language-Games, and Information: Kantian Themes in the Philosophy of Logic*, Clarendon Press, Oxford.

Hintikka, Jaakko: 1973b, "Quantifiers, Language-Games, and Transcendental Arguments", in Hintikka (1973a), pp. 98-122.

Hintikka, Jaakko: 1973c, "Quantifiers vs. Quantification Theory", *Dialectica* 27, 329-58. [Also in *Linguistic Inquiry* 5 (1974), 153-77; and in Saarinen (1979b).]

Hintikka, Jaakko: 1975a, "A Counterexample to Tarski-type Truth-Definitions As Applied to Natural Languages", in Asa Kasher, editor, *Language in Focus: Foundations, Methods and Systems: Essays in Memory of Yehoshua Bar-Hillel*, D. Reidel, Dordrecht, pp. 107-12. [Also in *Philosophia* 5 (1975), 204-12].

Hintikka, Jaakko: 1975b, "Impossible Possible Worlds Vindicated", *JPL* 4, 475-84. [Reprinted and extended in Saarinen (1979b).]

Hintikka, Jaakko: 1975c, "On the Limitations of Generative Grammar", in (no editor given) *Proceedings of the Scandinavian Seminar on Philosophy of Language, Uppsala, Sweden, 8-9 November 1974*, Philosophical Society and the Department of Philosophy, University of Uppsala, Uppsala, Sweden, pp. 1-92.

Hintikka, Jaakko: 1976a, "Language-Games", in Jaakko Hintikka et al., editors, *Essays on Wittgenstein in Honour of G.H. von Wright* (APF 28, nos. 1-3), North-Holland, Amsterdam, pp. 105-25. [Reprinted in Saarinen (1979b) with minor changes.]

Hintikka, Jaakko: 1976b, "Partially Ordered Quantifiers vs. Partially Ordered Ideas", *Dialectica* 30, 89-99.

Hintikka, Jaakko: 1976c, "The Prospects of Convention T", *Dialectica* 30, 61-66.

Hintikka, Jaakko: 1976d, "Quantifiers in Logic and Quantifiers in Natural Languages", in Stefan Körner, editor, *Philosophy of Logic*, Basil Blackwell, Oxford, pp. 208-32. [Reprinted in Saarinen (1979b).]

Hintikka, Jaakko: 1976e, *The Semantics of Questions and the Questions of Semantics: Case Studies in the Interrelations of Logic, Semantics, and Syntax* (APF 28, no. 4), North-Holland, Ámsterdam.

Hintikka, Jaakko: 1977a, "Quantifiers in Natural Languages: Some Logical Problems II", *LP* 1, 153-72. [Reprinted in Saarinen (1979b).]

Hintikka, Jaakko: 1977b, "The Ross Paradox as Evidence for the Reality of Semantical Games", *The Monist* 60, 370-79. [Reprinted in Saarinen (1979b) with some changes.]

Hintikka, Jaakko: 1979a, "'Is', Semantical Games, and Semantical Relativity", *JPL* 8, 433-68. [Reprinted in Hintikka and Kulas (1983) with minor changes.]

Hintikka, Jaakko: 1979b, "Quantifiers in Natural Languages: Some Logical Problems I", in Jaakko Hintikka, Ilkka Niiniluoto and Esa Saarinen, editors, *Essays on Mathematical and Philosophical Logic*, D. Reidel, Dordrecht, pp. 295-314. [Reprinted in Saarinen (1979b).]

Hintikka, Jaakko: 1979c, "Rejoinder to Peacocke" (Peacocke (1979)), in Saarinen (1979b), pp. 135-51.

Hintikka, Jaakko: 1980, "On the *Any*-Thesis and the Methodology of Linguistics", *LP* 4, 101-22. [Reprinted in Hintikka and Kulas (1983) with minor changes.]

Hintikka, Jaakko: 1981a, "Kant on Existence, Predication and the Ontological Argument", *Dialectica* 35, 127-46.

Hintikka, Jaakko: 1981b, "Semantics: A Revolt against Frege", in G. Fløistad and G.H. von Wright, editors, *Contemporary Philosophy: A New Survey, Vol. 1: Philosophy of Language/Philosophy of Logic*, Martinus Nijhoff, The Hague, pp. 57–82.

Hintikka, Jaakko: 1981c, "Theories of Truth and Learnable Languages", in Stig Kanger and Sven Ohman, editors, *Philosophy and Grammar: Papers on the Occasion of the Quincentennial of Uppsala University*, D. Reidel, Dordrecht, pp. 37–57. [Reprinted with minor changes and expanded in Hintikka and Kulas (1983).]

Hintikka, Jaakko: 1982a, "Game-Theoretical Semantics: Insights and Prospects", *NDJFL* 23, 219–41. [Reprinted in Hintikka and Kulas (1983) with minor changes.]

Hintikka, Jaakko: 1982b, "On Games, Questions, and Strange Quantifiers", in Tom Pauli, editor, *Philosophical Essays Dedicated to Lennart Aqvist on His Fiftieth Birthday*, Philosophical Society and the Department of Philosophy, University of Uppsala, Uppsala, Sweden, pp. 159–69.

Hintikka, Jaakko: 1982c, "Questions with Outside Quantifiers", in Robinson Schneider, Kevin Tuite, and Robert Chametzky, editors, *Papers from the Parasession on Nondeclaratives*, Chicago Linguistics Society, Chicago, pp. 83–92.

Hintikka, Jaakko: 1982d, "Semantical Games and Transcendental Arguments", in E.M. Barth and J.L. Martens, editors, *Argumentation: Approaches to Theory Formation*, Benjamins, Amsterdam, pp. 77–91. [Reprinted in Hintikka and Kulas (1983) with a number of changes.]

Hintikka, Jaakko: 1982e, "Temporal Discourse and Semantical Games", *LP* 5, 3–22. [Reprinted in Hintikka and Kulas (1983) with minor changes.]

Hintikka, Jaakko: 1982f, "Transcendental Arguments Revived", in André Mercier and Maja Svilar, editors, *Philosophers on Their Own Work*, Vol. 5, Peter Lang, Bern, pp. 119–33.

Hintikka, Jaakko: 1983, "Semantical Games, the Alleged Ambiguity of 'Is', and Aristotelian Categories", *Synthese* 54, 443-68. [Reprinted in Hintikka and Kulas (1983) with some changes.]

Hintikka, Jaakko: Forthcoming, "A Hundred Years Later: The Rise and Fall of Frege's Influence in Language Theory", *Synthese*.

Hintikka, Jaakko, and Lauri Carlson: 1977, "Pronouns of Laziness in Game-Theoretical Semantics", *Theoretical Linguistics* 4, 1-29.

Hintikka, Jaakko, and Lauri Carlson: 1979, "Conditionals, Generic Quantifiers, and Other Applications of Sub-games", in Avishai Margalit, editor, *Meaning and Use*, D. Reidel, Dordrecht, pp. 57-92. [Reprinted in Saarinen (1979b).]

Hintikka, Jaakko, and Jack Kulas: 1982, "Russell Vindicated: Towards a General Theory of Definite Descriptions", *Journal of Semantics* 1, 387-97.

Hintikka, Jaakko, and Jack Kulas: 1983, *The Game of Language: Studies in Game-Theoretical Semantics and Its Applications*, D. Reidel, Dordrecht.

Hintikka, Jaakko, and Jack Kulas: Forthcoming, "Different Uses of the Definite Article", *Communication and Cognition*.

Hintikka, Jaakko, and Esa Saarinen: 1975, "Semantical Games and the Bach-Peters Paradox", *Theoretical Linguistics* 2, 1-20. [Reprinted in Saarinen (1979b).]

Kulas, Jack: 1982, *The Logic and Semantics of Definite Descriptions*, Ph.D. Dissertation, Florida State University (unpublished).

McCawley, James D.: 1981, *Everything That Linguists Have Always Wanted to Know about Logic (But Were Ashamed to Ask)*, University of Chicago Press, Chicago [especially pp. 447-56].

Over, David E.: 1981a, "Game Theoretical Semantics and

Entailment", *Studia Logica* 40, 67-74.

Over, David E.: 1981b, "Review of *Game-Theoretical Se-mantics*, edited by Esa Saarinen", *Mind* 90, 309-11.

Peacocke, Christopher: 1979, "Game-Theoretical Semantics, Quantifiers and Truth: Comments on Professor Hin-tikka's Paper" (Hintikka (1977a, 1979b)), in Saarinen (1979b), pp. 119-34.

Qvarnstrøm, Bengt-Olof: 1977, "On the Concept of Formal-ization and Partially Ordered Quantifiers", *LP* 1, 307-19.

Rantala, Veikko: 1981, "Knowing a Contradiction", in W.K. Essler and W. Becker, editors, *Konzepte der Dialektik*, Vittorio Klostermann, Frankfurt am Main, pp. 191-98.

Rantala, Veikko: Forthcoming, "Logic and Methodology in Finland Since 1940 (1)", *Ruch Filozoficzny*.

Saarinen, Esa: 1977, "Game-Theoretical Semantics", *The Monist* 60, 406-18.

Saarinen, Esa: 1978, "Intentional Identity Interpreted: A Case Study of the Relations among Quantifiers, Pro-nouns, and Propositional Attitudes", *LP* 2, 151-223.

Saarinen, Esa: 1979a, "Backwards-Looking Operators in Tense Logic and in Natural Language", in Jaakko Hintikka, Ilkka Niiniluoto, and Esa Saarinen, editors, *Essays on Mathematical and Philosophical Logic*, D. Reidel, Dordrecht, pp. 341-67.

Saarinen, Esa: 1979b, *Game-Theoretical Semantics: Essays on Semantics by Hintikka, Carlson, Peacocke, Rantala, and Saarinen*, D. Reidel, Dordrecht.

Saarinen, Esa: 1982, "How to Frege a Russell-Kaplan", *Nous* 16, 253-76.

Saarinen, Esa, Risto Hilpinen, Ilkka Niiniluoto, and Merrill Provence Hintikka, editors: 1979, *Essays in Honour of Jaakko Hintikka: On the Occasion of His Fiftieth Birth-day on January 12, 1979*, D. Reidel, Dordrecht.

Scott, Dana: 1968, "A Game-Theoretic Interpretation of Logical Formulae", McCarthy Seminar, Stanford University, July 1968 (unpublished).

Stenius, E.: 1976, "Comments on Jaakko Hintikka's Paper 'Quantifiers vs. Quantification Theory'", *Dialectica* 30, 67–88.

Tennant, Neil: 1979, "Language Games and Intuitionism", *Synthese* 42, 297–314.

II GAME-THEORETICAL IDEAS IN LOGIC, FOUNDATIONS OF MATHEMATICS, AND LINGUISTICS

II (i) Partially Ordered Quantifiers and Other Operators (Partial Bibliography)

Barwise, Jon: 1976, "Some Applications of Henkin Quantifiers", *IJM* 25, 47–63.

Barwise, Jon: 1979, "On Branching Quantifiers in English", *JPL* 8, 47–80.

Barwise, Jon, and Robin Cooper: 1981, "Generalized Quantifiers and Natural Languages", *LP* 4, 159–220.

Bentham, Johan van: Forthcoming, "Higher-Order Logic", in F. Guenthner and D. Gabbay, editors, *Handbook of Philosophical Logic I*, D. Reidel, Dordrecht.

Carlson, Lauri, and Alice ter Meulen: 1979, "Informational Independence in Intensional Contexts", in Esa Saarinen et al., editors, *Essays in Honour of Jaakko Hintikka*, D. Reidel, Dordrecht, pp. 61–72.

Enderton, H.B.: 1970, "Finite Partially-Ordered Quantifiers", *ZMLGM* 16, 393–97.

Engdahl, Elisabet: Forthcoming, *The Syntax and Semantics of Constitutive Questions*, D. Reidel, Dordrecht. [Branching operators in questions are discussed.]

Fauconnier, G.: 1975, "Do Quantifiers Branch?" *Linguistic Inquiry* 6, 555–78.

Gabbay, D., and J.M.E. Moravcsik: 1974, "Branching Quantifiers, English and Montague Grammar", *Theoretical Linguistics* 1, 139–57.

Guenthner, F., and J. Hoepelman: 1974, "A Note on the Representation of 'Branching Quantifiers'", *Theoretical Linguistics* 1, 285–89.

Hartig, K.: 1965, "Uber einen Quantifikator mit zwei Wirkungsbereichen", in (no editor given), *Colloquium on the Foundations of Mathematics, Mathematical Machines and Their Applications (Tihany, Hungary, 1962)*, Budapest/Paris, pp. 31–36.

Henkin, L.: 1961, "Some Remarks on Infinitely Long Formulas", in (no editor given) *Infinitistic Methods: Proceedings of the Symposium on the Foundations of Mathematics* (Warsaw, 2–9 September 1959), Pergamon Press, New York, and Polish Scientific Publishers, Warsaw, pp. 167–83.

Herre, H.: 1974, *Entscheidungsprobleme für Theorien in Logiken mit veralgemeinerten Quantoren*, Dissertation zur Erlangung des akademischen Grades doctor Scientiae naturalis, Humboldt-Universität zu Berlin.

Hintikka, Jaakko: 1973, "Quantifiers vs. Quantification Theory", *Dialectica* 27, 329–58. [Also in *Linguistic Inquiry* 5 (1974), 153–77.]

Hintikka, Jaakko: 1976, "Partially Ordered Quantifiers vs. Partially Ordered Ideas", *Dialectica* 30, 89–99.

Hintikka, Jaakko: 1982, "Questions with Outside Quantifiers", in Robinson Schneider, Kevin Tuite, and Robert Chametzky, editors, *Papers from the Parasession on Nondeclaratives*, Chicago Linguistics Society, Chicago, pp.83–92.

Issel, W.: 1969, "Semantische Untersuchungen über Quantoren I", *ZMLGM* 15, 353–58.

Krynicki, Michał: 1979, "On the Expressive Power of a Language Using the Henkin Quantifier", in Jaakko Hintikka, I. Niiniluoto, and E. Saarinen, editors, *Essays on Mathematical and Philosophical Logic*, D. Reidel, Dordrecht, pp. 259–65.

Krynicki, Michał, and Alistair H. Lachlan: 1979, "On the Semantics of the Henkin Quantifier", *JSL* 44, 184–200.

Qvarnström, Bengt-Olof: 1977, "On the Concept of Formalization and Partially Ordered Quantifiers", *LP* 1, 307–19.

Stenius, E.: 1976, "Comments on Jaakko Hintikka's Paper 'Quantifiers vs. Quantification Theory'", *Dialectica* 30, 67–88.

Walkoe, W., Jr.: 1970, "Finite Partially Ordered Quantification", *JSL* 35, 535–55.

Walkoe, W., Jr.: 1976, "A Small Step Backwards", *American Mathematical Monthly* 83, 338–44.

Walkoe, W., Jr., and H. Jerome Keisler: 1973, "The Diversity of Quantifier Prefixes", *JSL* 38, 79–85.

II (ii) Generalized Quantifiers, the Semantics of Quantifiers, and Quantifier Ordering (Partial Bibliography)

Barwise, Jon, and Robin Cooper: 1981, "Generalized Quantifiers and Natural Languages", *LP* 4, 159–220.

Bruce, K.: 1978, "Ideal Models and Some Not So Ideal Problems in the Theory of $L(Q)$", *JSL* 43, 304–21.

Dowty, David, Stanley Peters, and Robert Wall: 1981, *Introduction to Montague Semantics*, D. Reidel, Dordrecht.

Ioup, G.: 1975, "Some Universals for Quantifier Scope", in J.P. Kimball editor, *Syntax and Semantics*, Vol. 4,

Academic Press, New York, pp. 37-58.

Keisler, H.J.: 1970, "Logic with the Quantifier 'There Exist Uncountably Many'", *AML* 1, 1-93.

Magidor, M., and J. Malitz: 1977, "Compact Extensions of *L(Q)* (Part 1a)", *AML* 11, 217-61.

Montague, Richard: 1974, *Formal Philosophy: Selected Papers of Richard Montague*, edited by Richmond Thomason, Yale University Press, New Haven, Conn.

Partee, Barbara Hall, editor: 1976, *Montague Grammar*, Academic Press, New York.

II (iii) Infinitely Deep Languages

Hintikka, Jaakko: 1980, "Leibniz on Plenitude, Relations, and the 'Reign of Law'", in Simo Knuuttila, editor, *Reforging the Great Chain of Being*, D. Reidel, Dordrecht, pp. 259-86.

Hintikka, Jaakko, and Veikko Rantala: 1976, "A New Approach to Infinitary Languages", *AML* 10, 95-115.

Karttunen, Maaret: 1979a, "Infinitary Languages $N_{\infty\lambda}$ and Generalized Partial Isomorphisms", in Jaakko Hintikka, I. Niiniluoto, and E. Saarinen, editors, *Essays on Mathematical and Philosophical Logic*, D. Reidel, Dordrecht, pp. 153-68.

Karttunen, Maaret: 1979b, "Model Theory of Infinitely Deep Languages", mimeographed thesis (in Finnish), University of Helsinki.

Karttunen, Maaret: 1981, "Model Theoretic Results for Infinitely Deep Languages", in H. Herre, editor, *Workshop on Extended Model Theory*, Akademie der Wissenschaften der DDR, Institut für Mathematik, Berlin, preprint, pp. 66-101.

Oikkonen, J.: 1978, "Second Order Definability, Game

Quantifiers and Related Expressions", *Societas Scientiarum Fennica, Commentationes Physico-Mathematicae* 48, 39–101.

Oikkonen, J.: 1979, "A Generalization of the Infinitely Deep Languages of Hintikka and Rantala", in E. Saarinen, R. Hilpinen, I, Niiniluoto, and M. Provence Hintikka, editors, *Essays in Honour of Jaakko Hintikka*, D. Reidel, Dordrecht, pp. 101–12.

Oikkonen, J.: Forthcoming, "On the Expressive Power of Game Sentences".

Rantala, Veikko: 1979, "Game-Theoretical Semantics and Back-and-Forth", in J. Hintikka, I. Niiniluoto, and E. Saarinen, editors, *Essays on Mathematical and Philosophical Logic*, D. Reidel, Dordrecht, pp. 119–31.

Rantala, Veikko: 1981, "Infinitely Deep Game Sentences and Interpolation", in I. Pörn, editor, *Essays in Philosophical Analysis* (APF 32), North-Holland, Amsterdam, pp. 211–19.

Rantala, Veikko: Forthcoming, "Constituents", in R.J. Bogdan, editor, *Jaakko Hintikka* (Profiles series, Vol. 3), D. Reidel, Dordrecht.

Väänänen, J.: Forthcoming, "Game Formulae and Their Generalizations".

II (iv) Game Quantifiers
(Partial Bibliography)

Aczel, P.: 1975, "Quantifiers, Games and Inductive Definitions", in Stig Kanger, editor, *Proceedings of the 3rd Scandinavian Logic Symposium*, North-Holland, Amsterdam, pp. 1–14.

Barwise, Jon: 1975, *Admissible Sets and Structures*, Springer-Verlag, Berlin. [See especially pp. 242–54].

Barwise, Jon, editor: 1977, *Handbook of Mathematical*

Logic, North-Holland, Amsterdam.

Barwise, Jon: 1978, "Monotone Quantifiers and Admissible Sets", in J. Fenstad, R. Grandy, and G. Sacks, editors, *Generalized Recursion Theory II*, North-Holland, Amsterdam, pp. 1–38.

Barwise, Jon, and Y.N. Moschovakis: 1978, "Global Inductive Definability", *JSL* 43, 521–34.

Moschovakis, Y.N.: 1971, "The Game Quantifier", *Proceedings of the American Mathematical Society* 31, 245–50.

Moschovakis, Y.N.: 1974, *Elementary Induction in Abstract Structures*, North-Holland, Amsterdam.

Oikkonen, J.: 1978, "Second Order Definability, Game, Quantifiers and Related Expressions", *Societas Scientiarum Fennica, Commentationes Physico-Mathematicae* 48, 39–101.

Svenonius, Lars: 1965, "On the Denumerable Models of Theories with Extra Predicates", in J.W. Addison, Leon Henkin, and Alfred Tarski, editors, *The Theory of Models*, North-Holland, Amsterdam, pp. 376–89.

II (v) Functional Interpretations
(Partial Bibliography)

Beeson, Michael: 1978, "A Type-free Gödel Interpretation", *JSL* 43, 213–27.

Diller, Justus: 1968, "Zur Berechenbarkeit primitiv-rekursiver Funktionale endlicher Typen", in H.A. Schmidt and K. Schütte, editors, *Contributions to Mathematical Logic*, North-Holland, Amsterdam, pp. 109–20.

Diller, Justus: 1979, "Functional Interpretations of Heyting's Arithmetic in All Finite Types", *Nieuw Archief voor Wiskunde* 27, 70–97.

Diller, Justus: 1980, "Modified Realization and the

Formulae-as-Type Notion", in J.P. Seldin and J.R. Hindley, editors, *To H.B. Curry: Essays on Combinatory Logic, Lambda Calculus, and Formalism*, Academic Press, New York, pp. 491-501.

Diller, Justus, and W. Nahm: 1974, "Eine Variante zur Dialectica-Interpretation der Heyting-Arithmetik endlicher Typen", *AMLG* 16, 49-66.

Diller, Justus, and Kurt Schütte: 1971, "Simultane Rekursionen in der Theorie der Funktionale endlicher Typen", *AMLG* 14, 69-74.

Diller, Justus, and H. Vogel: 1975, "Intensionale Funktionalinterpretation der Analysis", in J. Diller and G.H. Müller, editors, *Proof Theory Symposium Kiel 1974*, *Lecture Notes in Mathematics* 500, Springer-Verlag, Berlin, pp. 56-72.

Dragalin, A.G.: 1968, "The Computation of Primitive Recursive Terms of Finite Type, and Primitive Recursive Realization", Zap. Naucn. sem. Leningrad. Otdel. Mat. Inst. Steklov (*LOMI*) 8, 32-45.

Girard, J.-Y.: 1971, "Une extension de l'interpretation de Gödel à l'analyse, et son application à l'élimination des coupures dans l'analyse et la théorie des types", in J. E. Fenstad, editor, *Proceedings of the Second Scandinavian Logic Symposium*, North-Holland, Amsterdam, pp. 63-92.

Girard, J.-Y.: 1972, "Interprétation fonctionnele et élimination des coupures de l'arithmétique d'ordre supérieur", Thèse de doctorat d'état, Université Paris VII.

Girard, J.-Y.: 1977, "Functional Interpretation and Kripke Models", in R.E. Butts and Jaakko Hintikka, editors, *Logic, Foundations of Mathematics and Computability Theory* (Part One of the Proceedings of the Fifth International Congress of Logic, Methodology, and Philosophy of Science), D. Reidel, Dordrecht, pp. 33-57.

Gödel, Kurt: 1958, "Uber eine bisher noch nicht benützte

Erweiterung des finiten Standpunktes", *Dialectica* 12, 280-87.

Gödel, Kurt: 1980, "On a Hitherto Unexploited Extension of the Finitary Standpoint", Wilfrid Hodges and Bruce Watson, translators, *JPL* 9, 133-42. [Translation of Gödel (1958).]

Goodman, Nicolas D.: 1976, "The Theory of the Gödel Functionals", *JSL* 41, 574-82.

Grzegorczyk, A.: 1964, "Recursive Objects in All Finite Types", *FM* 54, 73-93.

Hanatani, Y.: 1966, "Démonstration de l´δ-non-contradiction de l'arithmétique", *Annals of the Japan Association of the Philosophy of Science* 3, 105-14.

Hanatani, Y.: 1975, "Calculatability of the Primitive Recursive Functionals of Finite Type over the Natural Numbers", in J. Diller and G.H. Müller, editors, *Lecture Notes in Mathematics* 500, Springer-Verlag, Berlin, pp. 152-63.

Hinata, S.: 1967, "Calculability of Primitive Recursive Functionals of Finite Type", *Sci. Rep. Tokyo Kyoiku Daigaku*, Sect. A, 9, 218-35.

Hindley, J.R., B. Lercher, and J.P. Seldin: 1972, *Introduction to Combinatory Logic*, London Math. Soc. Lecture Note Series 7, Cambridge University Press, Cambridge.

Hintikka, Jaakko, and Jack Kulas: 1983, "Semantical Games, Subgames, and Functional Interpretations", in Jaakko Hintikka and Jack Kulas, *The Game of Language*, D. Reidel, Dordrecht, pp. 47-76

Howard, W.A.: 1969, "Functional Interpretation of Bar Induction by Bar Recursion", *Compositio Math.* 20, 107-24.

Howard, W.A.: 1970, "Assignment of Ordinals to Terms for Primitive Recursive Functionals of Finite Type", in A. Kino, J. Myhill, and R.E. Vesley, editors, *Intuitionism*

and Proof Theory: Proceedings of the Summer Confer-
ence at Buffalo, 1968, North-Holland, Amsterdam, pp.
443-58.

Kreisel, Georg: 1959, "Interpretation of Analysis by Means
of Constructive Functionals of Finite Type", in A.
Heyting, editor, *Constructivity in Mathematics*, North-
Holland, Amsterdam, pp. 101-28.

Kreisel, Georg: 1965, "Mathematical Logic", in T.L. Saaty,
editor, *Lectures on Modern Mathematics III*, John Wiley,
New York, pp. 95-195.

Kreisel, Georg: 1968, "A Survey of Proof Theory", *JSL*
33, 321-88.

Kreisel, Georg: 1971, "A Survey of Proof Theory II", in
J.E. Fenstad, editor, *Proceedings of the Second
Scandinavian Logic Symposium*, North-Holland,
Amsterdam, pp. 109-70.

Luckhardt, H.: 1973, *Extensional Gödel Functional Inter-
pretation: A Consistency Proof of Classical Analysis*,
Lecture Notes in Mathematics 306, Springer-Verlag,
Berlin.

Rath, P.: 1978, *Eine verallgemeinerte Funktionalinterpretation der Heyting-Arithmetik endlicher Typen*,
Dissertation, Münster.

Sanchis, L.E.: 1967, "Functionals Defined by Recursion",
NDJFL 8, 161-74.

Scott, Dana: 1968, "A Game-Theoretic Interpretation of
Logical Formulae", McCarthy Seminar, Stanford University, July 1968 (unpublished).

Shoenfield, Joseph R.: 1967, *Mathematical Logic*, Addison-
Wesley, Reading, Mass.

Spector, Clifford: 1962, "Provably Recursive Functionals of
Analysis: A Consistency Proof of Analysis by an
Extension of Principles Formulated in Current
Intuitionistic Mathematics", in J.C.E. Dekker, editor,
Recursive Function Theory: Proceedings of the

Symposium   on   Pure   Mathematics   V,   American
Mathematical Society, Providence, R.I., pp. 1-27.

Stein, M.: 1978, "Interpretationen der Heyting-Arithmetik
endlicher Typen", *AMLG* 19, 175-89.

Stein, M.: 1980, "Interpretations of Heyting's Arithmetic -
an Analysis by Means of a Language with Set Symbols",
AML 19, 1-31.

Stenlund, S.: 1972, *Combinators, λ-Terms, and Proof
Theory,* D. Reidel, Dordrecht.

Tait, W.W.: 1965, "Infinitely Long Terms of Transfinite
Type", in J.N. Crossley and M.A.E. Dummett, editors,
Formal Systems and Recursive Functions, North-
Holland, Amsterdam, pp. 176-85.

Tait, W.W.: 1967, "Intensional Interpretations of Functionals of Finite Type I", *JSL 32,* 198-212.

Tait, W.W.: 1971, "Normal Form Theorem for Barrecursive
Functions of Finite Type", in J.E. Fenstad, editor,
*Proceedings of the Second Scandinavian Logic Sym-
posium,* North-Holland, Amsterdam, pp. 353-67.

Troelstra, A.S.: 1973, "Realizability and Functional Inter-
pretations", in A.S. Troelstra, editor, *Metamathematical
Investigations of Intuitionistic Arithmetic and Analysis,
Lecture Notes in Mathematics* 344, Springer-Verlag,
Berlin, pp. 175-274.

Yasugi, M.: 1963, "Intuitionistic Analysis and Gödel's Interpretation", *JMSJ* 15, 101-12.

II (vi) Back-and-Forth Methods
and Ehrenfeucht Games (Partial Bibliography)

Barwise, Jon, and Solomon Feferman, editors: Forthcoming (probably 1983), *Model-Theoretic Logics,* Springer-
Verlag, Berlin. [This book has a large bibliography
compiled by Dana Scott on the uses of games and back-

and-forth methods in logic.]

Ebbinghaus, H.-D., Jörg Flum, and W. Thomas: 1978, *Einführung in die Mathematische Logik*, Wissenschaftliche Buchgesellschaft, Darmstadt [See especially pp. 253-55 on "Ehrenfeucht Games".]

Ehrenfeucht, A.: 1957, "Applications of Games to Some Problems of Mathematical Logic", *Bulletin de l'Academie Polonaise des Sciences* 5, 35-37.

Ehrenfeucht, A.: 1961, "An Application of Games to the Completeness Problem for Formal Theories", *FM* 49, 129-41.

Feferman, S.: 1957, "Some Recent Work on Ehrenfeucht and Fraïssé", *Summaries of Talks Presented at the Summer Inst. of Symbolic Logic, Cornell*, pp. 201-209.

Flum, Jörg: 1977, "Distributive Normal Form", in S. Miettinen and J. Väänänen, editors, *Proceedings of the Symposiums on Mathematical Logic in Oulu 1974 and Helsinki 1975*, Helsinki, pp. 71-76.

Hintikka, Jaakko: 1965, "Distributive Normal Forms in First-Order Logic", in J.N. Crossley and M.A.E. Dummett, editors, *Formal Systems and Recursive Functions*, North-Holland, Amsterdam, pp. 48-91.

Rantala, Veikko: 1979, "Game-Theoretical Semantics and Back-and-Forth", in Jaakko Hintikka, I. Niiniluoto, and E. Saarinen, editors, *Essays on Mathematical and Philosophical Logic*, D. Reidel, Dordrecht, pp. 119-51.

Tenney, Richard L.: 1972, "Some Decidable Pairing Functions", *Notices of the Amer. Math. Soc.* 19, A-26-A-27.

Tenney, Richard L.: 1975, "Second Order Ehrenfeucht Games and Decidability of the Second Order Theory of an Equivalence Relation", *Journal of the Australian Mathematical Society* 20 (Series A), 323-31.

II (vii) Distributive Normal Forms

Chang, C.C., and H.J. Keisler: 1973, *Model Theory*, North-Holland, Amsterdam.

Cunningham, E.: 1975, "Chain Models: Applications of Consistency Properties and Back-and-Forth Techniques in Infinite-Quantifier Languages", in D.W. Kueker, editor, *Infinitary Logic: In Memoriam Carol Karp, Lecture Notes in Mathematics* 492, Springer-Verlag, Berlin, pp. 125-42.

Ehrenfeucht, A.: 1957, "Applications of Games to Some Problems of Mathematical Logic", *Bulletin de l'Academie Polonaise des Sciences* 5, 35-37.

Ehrenfeucht, A.: 1961, "An Application of Games to the Completeness Problem for Formalized Theories", *FM* 49, 129-41.

Feferman, S.: 1957, "Some Recent Work on Ehrenfeucht and Fraïssé", *Summaries of Talks Presented at the Summer Institute of Symbolic Logic, Cornell*, pp. 201-209.

Flum, Jörg: 1977, "Distributive Normal Forms", in S. Miettinen and J. Väänänen, editors, *Proceedings of the Symposiums on Mathematical Logic in Oulu 1974 and in Helsinki 1975*, Helsinki, pp. 71-76.

Fraïssé, R.: 1955, "Sur quelques classifications des relations, baisees sur des isomorphismes restreints", *Publ. Sci. de l'Universite d' Alger, Serie A (Mathematiques)*, Part I:2, 16-60; Part II:2, 273-95.

Hanf, W.: 1965, "Model-Theoretic Methods in the Study of Elementary Logic", in J.W. Addison et al., editors, *The Theory of Models*, North-Holland, Amsterdam, pp. 132-45.

Hintikka, Jaakko: 1953, "Distributive Normal Forms in the Calculus of Predicates", *APF* 6, 1-72.

Hintikka, Jaakko: 1964, "Distributive Normal Forms and

Deductive Interpolation", *ZMLGM* 10, 185–91.

Hintikka, Jaakko: 1965, "Distributive Normal Forms in First-Order Logic", in J.N. Crossley and M.A.E. Dummett, editors, *Formal Systems and Recursive Functions: Proceedings of the Eighth Logic Colloquium, Oxford, July 1963*, North-Holland, Amsterdam, pp. 47–90. [Reprinted with changes as Chapter XI in J. Hintikka, *Logic, Language-Games, and Information: Kantian Themes in the Philosophy of Logic*, Oxford University Press, Oxford, 1973, pp. 242–86].

Hintikka, Jaakko: 1970, "Surface Information and Depth Information", in J. Hintikka and P. Suppes, editors, *Information and Inference*, D. Reidel, Dordrecht, pp. 263–97.

Hintikka, Jaakko: 1972, "Constituents and Finite Identifiability", *JPL* 1, 45–52.

Hintikka, Jaakko: 1973, "Surface Semantics: Definition and Its Motivation", in H. Leblanc, editor, *Truth, Syntax and Modality*, North-Holland, Amsterdam, pp. 128–47.

Hintikka, Jaakko, and Ilkka Niiniluoto: 1973, "On the Surface Semantics of Quantificational Proof Procedures", *Ajatus* (Yearbook of the Philosophical Society of Finland) 35, 197–215.

Hintikka, Jaakko, and Veikko Rantala: 1975, "Systematizing Definability Theory", in S. Kanger, editor, *Proceedings of the Third Scandinavian Logic Symposium*, North-Holland, Amsterdam, pp. 40–62.

Hintikka, Jaakko, and Veikko Rantala: 1976, "A New Approach to Infinitary Languages", *AML* 10, 95–115.

Hintikka, Jaakko, and Raimo Tuomela: 1970, "Towards a General Theory of Auxiliary Concepts and Definability in First-Order Theories", in J. Hintikka and P. Suppes, editors, *Information and Inference*, D. Reidel, Dordrecht, pp. 298–330.

Karp, C.R.: 1965, "Finite-Quantifier Equivalence", in J.W. Addison et al., editors, *The Theory of Models*,

North-Holland, Amsterdam, pp. 407-12.

Oglesby, F.C.: 1963, "An Examination of a Decision Procedure", *Memoirs of the American Mathematical Society* 44.

Rantala, Veikko: 1973, *On the Theory of Definability in First-Order Logic*, Reports from the Institute of Philosophy, University of Helsinki, No. 2.

Rantala, Veikko: 1975, "Urn Models: A New Kind of Non-Standard Model for First-Order Logic", *JPL* 4, 125-42.

Rantala, Veikko: 1977, *Aspects of Definability* (*APF* 29, nos. 2-3), North-Holland, Amsterdam.

Scott, Dana: 1965, "Logic with Denumerably Long Formulas and Finite Strings of Quantifiers", in J.W. Addison et al., editors, *The Theory of Models*, North-Holland, Amsterdam, pp. 329-41.

Scott, Dana: 1979, "A Note on Distributive Normal Forms", in Esa Saarinen et al., editors, *Essays in Honour of Jaakko Hintikka*, D. Reidel, Dordrecht, pp. 75-90.

II (viii) Axioms of Determinateness
(Partial Bibliography)

Fenstad, J.E.: 1971, "The Axiom of Determinateness", in J.E. Fenstad, editor, *Proceedings of the Second Scandinavian Logic Symposium*, North-Holland, Amsterdam, pp. 41-61.

Freidman, Harvey: 1971, "Higher Set Theory and Mathematical Practice", *AML* 2, 326-57.

Martin, Donald A.: 1970, "Measurable Cardinals and Analytic Games", *FM* 66, 287-91.

Martin, Donald A.: 1975, "Borel Determinacy", *Annals of Mathematics* 102, 363-71.

Martin, Donald A.: 1977, "Descriptive Set Theory: Projective Sets", in Jon Barwise, editor, *Handbook of Mathematical Logic*, North-Holland, Amsterdam, pp. 783-815. [See especially pp. 807-14].

Moschovakis, Y.N.: 1980, *Descriptive Set Theory*, North-Holland, Amsterdam. [See especially chapter 6].

Mycielski, J.: 1964, "On the Axiom of Determinateness", *FM* 53, 205-24.

Mycielski, J., and H. Steinhaus: 1962, "A Mathematical Axiom Contradicting the Axiom of Choice", *Bulletin de l'Academie Polonaise des Sciences*, Series III, 10, 1-3.

Paris, J.B.: 1972, "ZF $\vdash \Sigma_4^0$ Determinateness", *JSL* 37, 661-67

II (ix) Urn Models

Hintikka, Jaakko: 1975, "Impossible Possible Worlds Vindicated", *JPL* 4, 475-84.

Olin, Philip: 1978, "Urn Models and Categoricity", *JPL* 7, 331-45.

Rantala, Veikko: 1975, "Urn Models: A New Kind of Non-Standard Model for First-Order Logic", *JPL* 4, 455-74.

Rantala, Veikko: 1977, *Aspects of Definability* (*APF* 29, nos. 2-3), North-Holland, Amsterdam.

III DIALOGUE GAMES
(Partial Bibliography)

Carlson, Lauri: 1983, *Dialogue Games: An Approach to Discourse Analysis*, D. Reidel, Dordrecht.

Carlson, Lauri: Forthcoming (probably 1983), "Focus and Dialogue Games", in Lucia Vaina and Jaakko Hintikka, editors, *Cognitive Constraints on Communication*, D.

Reidel, Dordrecht, pp. 295-333.

Hintikka, Jaakko: Forthcoming (probably 1983), "Rules, Utilities, and Strategies in Dialogical Games", in Lucia Vaina and Jaakko Hintikka, editors, *Cognitive Constraints on Communication*, D. Reidel, Dordrecht, pp. 277-94.

Hintikka, Jaakko, and Merrill B. Hintikka: 1982, "Sherlock Holmes Confronts Modern Logic: Towards a Theory of Information-Seeking through Questioning", in E.M. Barth and J.L. Martens, editors, *Argumentation: Approaches to Theory Formation*, Benjamins, Amsterdam, pp. 55-76

IV OTHER GAME-THEORETICAL APPROACHES

IV (i) Lorenzen and Lorenz
(Partial Bibliography)

Lorenz, Kuno: 1968, "Dialogspiele als semantische Grundlage von Logikkalkülen", *AMLG* 11, 32-55, 73-100. [Reprinted in Lorenzen and Lorenz (1978).]

Lorenz, Kuno: 1972, "Der dialogische Wahrheitsbegriff", *Neue Hefte für Philosophie* 2/3 (Dialog als Methode), 111-23.

Lorenz, Kuno: 1973, "Rules versus Theorems: A New Approach for the Mediation between Intuitionistic and Two-Valued Logic", *JPL* 2, 352-69.

Lorenz, Kuno: 1980a, "Dialogic Logic", in W. Marchiszewski, editor, *Dictionary of Logics As Applied in the Study of Language: Concepts - Methods - Theories*, Den Haag.

Lorenz, Kuno: 1980b, "Main Ideas of Dialogic Logic", in *Studies in Logic, Grammar and Rhetoric I*, Warschauer Universität, Białystock, pp. 17-34.

Lorenz, Kuno: 1982, "On the Criteria for the Choice of the
    Rules of Dialogic Logic", in E.M. Barth and J.L. Mar-
    tens, editors, *Argumentation: Approaches to Theory
    Formation*, Benjamins, Amsterdam, pp. 145–57.

Lorenzen, Paul: 1960, "Logik und Agon", in *Atti del XII
    Congresso di Filosofia* (Venezia, 12–18 1958), Sansoni
    Editore, Firenze, pp. 187–94. [Reprinted in Lorenzen
    and Lorenz (1978).]

Lorenzen, Paul: 1961, "Ein dialogisches Konstruktivitäts-
    kriterium", in (no editor given), *Infinitistic Methods:
    Proceedings of the Symposium on the Foundations of
    Mathematics* (Warsaw, 2–9 September 1959), Pergamon
    Press, New York, and Polish Scientific Publishers,
    Warsaw,, pp. 193–200. [Reprinted in Lorenzen and
    Lorenz (1978).]

Lorenzen, Paul, and Kuno Lorenz: 1978, *Dialogische Logik*,
    Wissenschaftliche Buchgesellschaft, Darmstadt.

Stegmüller, Wolfgang: 1977, "Remarks on the Completeness
    of Logical Systems Relative to the Validity-Concepts of
    P. Lorenzen and K. Lorenz", in Wolfgang Stegmüller,
    Collected Papers, Vol. 2, D. Reidel, Dordrecht, pp.
    241–77. [Originally in *NDJFL* 5 (1964), 81–112.]

IV (ii) Others (Partial Bibliography)

Barth, E.M.: Forthcoming (probably 1983), "Towards a
    Praxis-Oriented Theory of Argumentation", in M.
    Dascal, editor, *Dialogue*.

Barth, E.M., and E.C.W. Krabbe: 1982, *From Axiom to
    Dialogue – Philosophical Study of Logics and Argumen-
    tation*, Walter de Gruyter, Berlin.

Barth, E.M., and J.L. Martens: 1977, "Argumentum Ad
    Hominem: From Chaos to Formal Dialectics. The Dialog-
    ical Tableau Method As a Tool in the Theory of Fal-
    lacy", *Logique et Analyse* 20, no. 2.

Barth, E.M., and T.C. Potts: 1974, *The Logic of the Articles in Traditional Philosophy. A Contribution to the Study of Conceptual Structures*, D. Reidel, Dordrecht.

Dahl, Osten: 1977, "Games and Models", in Osten Dahl, editor, *Logic, Pragmatics and Grammar*, Studentlitteratur, Lund, pp. 147-99.

Gilbert, Margaret: 1974, "About Conventions", *Second-Order* 3, 71-89.

Gilbert, Margaret: 1981, "Game Theory and Convention", *Synthese* 46, 41-93.

Gilbert, Margaret: 1983, "Agreements, Conventions, and Language", *Synthese* 54, 374-407.

Gilbert, Margaret: Forthcoming (probably 1983), "Notes on the Concept of a Social Convention", *New Literary History*.

Giles, Robin: 1973, "Physics and Logic", lecture notes.

Giles, Robin: 1974, "A Non-Classical Logic for Physics", *Studia Logica* 33, 397-415.

Giles, Robin: 1976a, "Comment" (on Dana Scott's paper "Does Many-Valued Logic Have Any Use?"), in Stephan Körner, editor, *Philosophy of Logic*, Basil Blackwell, Oxford, pp. 92-95.

Giles, Robin: 1976b, "A Logic for Subjective Belief", in W.L. Harper and C.A. Hooker, editors, *Foundations of Probability Theory, Statistical Inference, and Statistical Theories of Science, Vol. I, Foundations and Philosophy of Epistemic Applications of Probability Theory*, D. Reidel, Dordrecht, pp. 41-72.

Giles, Robin: 1976c, "A Pragmatic Approach to the Formalization of Empirical Theories", in M. Przelecki, K. Szaniawski, and R. Wojcicki, editors, *Formal Methods in the Methodology of Empirical Sciences*, D. Reidel, Dordrecht, pp. 113-35.

Hilpinen, Risto: 1982, "On C.S. Peirce's Theory of the

Proposition: Peirce As a Precursor of Game-Theoretical Semantics", *The Monist* 65, 182-88.

Krabbe, E.C.W.: 1978, "The Adequacy of Material Dialogue-Games", *NDJFL* 29, 321-30.

Krabbe, E.C.W.: 1982, *Studies in Dialogical Logic*, Dissertation, Rijksuniversiteit te Groningen.

Lewis, David: 1969, *Convention: A Philosophical Study*, Harvard University Press, Cambridge, Mass.

Lewis, David: 1972, "Utilitarianism and Truthfulness", *Australasian Journal of Philosophy* 50, 17-19.

Lewis, David: 1975, "Languages and Language", in Keith Gunderson, editor, *Minnesota Studies in the Philosophy of Science*, Vol. 7, University of Minnesota Press, Minneapolis, pp. 3-35.

Scott, Dana: 1968, "A Game-Theoretic Interpretation of Logical Formulae", McCarthy Seminar, Stanford University, July 1968 (unpublished).

Scott, Dana: 1976, "Does Many-Valued Logic Have Any Use?" in Stephan Körner, editor, *Philosophy of Logic*, Basil Blackwell, Oxford, pp. 64-79.

Stenius, Erik: 1967, "Mood and Language-Game", *Synthese* 17, 254-74.

Tennant, Neil: 1981, "Formal Games and Forms for Games", *LP* 4, 311-20.

INDEX OF NAMES

Ackrill, J.L. 228n
Andrews, P. 27n
Apelt, O. 228n
Aristotle 23, 30n, 33, 173, 179-81, 186, 194, 218-21, 223-27, 228n
Arbib, M. 292n
Austin, J.L. 226

Bach, E. 152, 199n, 200n
Baker, C.L. 199n
Bartsch, R. 199n
Barwise, J. 28n, 88, 196n, 272
Bayes 256n
Benveniste, E. 228n
Bernays, P. 183
Blum, A. 278-79
Bonitz, H. 228n
Bresnan, J. 30n, 197n, 222-24

Carden, G. 29n
Carlson, L. 26, 28n, 31n, 42, 45n, 65, 72, 92, 110n, 126-27, 136n, 154, 157-59, 159n, 160n, 167-68, 171-72, 228n, 255n, 256n, 271, 290n, 291n
Carnap, R. 291n
Chomsky, N. 14, 18, 21, 111n, 162, 172, 186, 244-54, 255n, 257n, 280
Culicover, P. 287n
Curme, G. O. 196n

David, M. 27n
Davidson, D. 21, 117, 135n, 162, 172, 259-60, 262, 264, 272, 274, 277, 279-80, 285, 288n, 289n
Davison, A. 109
De Morgan, A. 22, 161, 186, 208
Diller, J. 60, 76n
Dowty, D. 126, 292n
Dummett, M. 35, 37, 39-41, 288n, 291n

Fenstad, J.E. 44n
Fillmore, C. 89, 255n
Fodor, J.A. 198n
Frede, M. 198n, 207-8
Frege, G. 15-16, 20-22, 162, 171-72, 175-79, 183, 185-87
    190-91, 194, 195n, 216, 219, 261-62, 268, 274-76,
    286-87, 289n

Gale, D. 27n
Geach, P. 24, 111n, 168, 198n
Girard, J.-Y. 45n
Gödel, K. 2, 7, 41, 45n, 57-62, 75n, 92, 201
Gomperz, T. 228n
Grice, P. 199n

Hegel 180
Heijenoort, J. van 186, 195n
Hemingway, E. 270
Henkin, L. 7, 37, 49, 292n
Heyting, A. 60-61
Higginbotham, J. 69-70
Hilbert, D. 183
Hilpinen, R. 255n
Hintikka, J. 9, 24, 26, 28n, 29n, 30n, 31n, 34, 37,
    39-42, 42n, 43n, 44n, 45n, 47, 50, 64-65, 69-70, 76n,
    77, 88, 92, 99-100, 110n, 111n, 122, 126, 130, 135n,
    136n, 137, 154, 157-59, 159n, 160n, 167-68, 171-72,
    187-89, 192-93, 195n, 199n, 201, 215, 228n, 231-34, 240
    255n, 256n, 257n, 264, 266, 271-72, 274, 277-78, 290n,
    291n, 292n
Hintikka, M.B. 41-42, 44n, 136n, 175, 279

Jackendoff, R. 273

Kahn, C. 179, 194, 228n, 255n
Kamp, H. 133
Kant, I. 26, 33, 34, 38, 39, 41
Kaplan, D. 133
Karttunen, L. 24, 76n, 149, 199n
Katz, J.J. 185-86
Klagge, J. 277-78
Klima, E. 89-91, 100, 197n, 255n
Knuuttila, S. 30n
Kreisel, G. 27n, 75n
Krynicki, M. 28n

Kulas, J. 29n, 31n, 64, 136n, 137, 160n
Kuno, S. 29n

Lachlan, A.H. 28n
Lakoff, G. 21, 29n, 162, 172, 198n
Laplace 191
Leibniz 8, 35, 180
LePore, E. 111n
Lorenz, K. 39, 76n
Lorenzen, P. 26n, 39–41, 62
Luce, R.D. 43n, 196n
Lyons, J. 159n

Maier, H. 228n
Mates, B. 160n, 180
Meulen, A. ter 28n
Mill, J.S. 22, 208
Montague, R. 14, 183, 216, 221, 284–85, 292n
Morgenstern, O. 75n
Mostowski, A. 27n, 75n
Mycielski, J. 44n

Neumann, J. von 75n
Newton, I. 94

Ockham 228n
Owen, G.E.L. 198n

Partee, B.H. 89, 152, 197n, 255n, 288n, 289n
Peano, G. 162
Peirce C.S. 255n
Pelletier, F.J. 199n, 229n
Perlmutter, D. 224
Peters, S. 288n, 292n
Plato 208, 219
Prawitz, D. 35, 37, 39–40
Provence, D. 255n

Quine, W.V.O. 21, 162, 172

Raiffa, H. 43n, 196n
Ramsey, F. 159n
Rantala, V. 9, 187, 272
Reichenbach, H. 121
Reinhart, T. 14

Richards, B. 136n
Ritchie, R. 288n
Ross, J. 228n
Russell, B. 15-16, 20-22, 137-42, 152, 161-62, 172,
    175-76, 183, 187, 190-91, 194, 208, 216, 219-20, 269-70

Saarinen, E. 45n, 75n, 133-34, 135n, 196n, 227n, 255n,
    267-68, 286
Schachter, P. 89, 197n, 255n
Spector, C. 76n
Stegmüller, W. 44n
Scott, D. 2, 45n, 60, 62, 186
Steinhaus, H. 44n
Stewart, F.M. 27n
Stockwell, R. 89, 197n, 255n
Stoy, J.E. 199n
Strawson, P.F. 39, 137, 148

Taiminen, L. 195n
Tarski, A. 3, 19-20, 215, 259-60, 277-78, 288n, 292n
Tichy, P. 121
Trendelenburg, A. 228n

Venneman, T. 199n

Walkoe, W.J. 28n, 50, 76n, 110n
Wall, R. 292n
Weisler, S. 200n, 254n
Wexler, K. 287n
Whitehead, A.N. 162
Whorf, B. 185
Wittgenstein, L. 21, 26, 33-34, 39, 152, 196n, 201, 259,
    261
Wolfe, T. 267

Ziff, P. 183

INDEX OF SUBJECTS

"a(n)", see indefinite article
acceptability, see well-formedness
accidental predication, see predication
actuality operators, see indexical time reference
activities that connect language and the world 201, 279-80
adjectives
    attributively used 170
    nonpredicatively used 174
    predicatively used 168, 174
"after" 129, 131
"ago" 132
"all" 78, 223
"almost all" 25
alternativeness relation 9, 267, 276
ambiguity 14, 21, 115, 128 161, 172, 183-84, 192, 208,
      279; *see also* semantical relativity
    and deixis 159n
    eliminated in ordinary discourse 118
    lexical 193
    of sentences with multiple verbs 122
    scope 116-17
anaphora 13, 29n, 71, 73, 76n, 150, 152, 274
    as a basically semantical phenomenon 157-59
    discourse 74
anaphoric
    back reference to time points 134, 269
    cross reference 70, 271
    pronouns 13, 64-65, 69, 73, 150, 152
        in game rules, qualifications for, 166-67, 204, 232,
        256n
    relation, see head-anaphor relation
"and" 12, 166-67
antecedence relation, see head-anaphor relation
"any" 17, 78, 85, 87, 90-92, 94, 97-99, 131, 163, 166-69,
      212, 236, 241, 246,
    as a universal quantifier 11, 77, 99, 104-7, 109, 168,
      186, 231

323

as an apparent existential quantifier 11, 15, 98–99, 109
    plural uses of, 25
    reason for wide scope of, 85
    semantical interaction of, with environment 265–66,
        277–78, 280
any-thesis 17–18, 100, 130–31, 233–35
    apparent counterexamples to, 235–43
    Chomsky's criticisms of, (with replies to Chomsky)
        243–54
    consequence that the set of English sentences is not
        recursively enumerable 243, 256n
    criticisms of, 100
argumentation
    language games of, 40
    theory of, 38–40
Aristotelian logic, break from 227
Aristotle's doctrine of categories, see categories
"as long as" 129
assertability, conditions of 61
atomic sentences 2, 4, 16, 114, 163, 170, 173, 177, 196n,
      201, 205, 271
    as end-points of semantical games 191
    functional-lexical approach to the treatment of, 16, 197n
    passive constructions in, 16
    prepositional constructions in, 16
    problems for game-theoretical semantics with, 164
    semantical interpretation of different functional struc-
        tures in, 16
    truth defined for 3
auxiliaries, grammatical theory of 208

back-and-forth methods 2
backwards-looking operators 133–35, 265, 267, 269, 276
    not syntactically marked in natural languages 135, 268
    return-ticket operators 267
backwards pronominalization 14
"before" 129
being
    being qua, science of 220
    frameworks for the logic of, 22
    verbs for, 218
belief sentences, negative 96–100, 105
"bottomless" languages 272
branching quantifiers 2, 7–8, 13, 35–37, 47–50, 58–59, 73,
      76n, 101, 110n. 187, 203, 232, 282

in natural languages 37, 88, 238, 266, 272, 281
irreducibility of, 58, 73, 88, 274
negation of, 88
reduction to linear form 49, 88
truth-definition for, 20
with nonstandard quantifiers 273-74
branching time structure 114

categories
Aristotle's doctrine of, 29n, 194, 218-22, 224, 226-27, 232
as logical types 220-21, 226
grammatical 221
change and motion, Aristotle's difficulty with 227
charity, principle of 49
choice, axiom of 72
Chomsky's *Aspects* theory 14
classical logic 6, 7, 41
classical (invariant) models 203
commanding, syntactic relation of 151
comparatives 187
compositionality 19, 115, 121-22, 127, 133, 196n, 259-87, 289n
failure of, in formal languages 271-72
Montague grammar's commitment to, 20, 285
computable functions, see recursive functions
conditionals
conditionality of, 6, 52, 63, 66
Gödel's interpretation of, 57, 59, 61
higher-order translations as interpretations of, 57
use of subgames in the interpretation of, 6
using modal notions to interpret, 51
conjunction 12, 70
constructivism 61-62
context
and restrictions to recursive strategies 7
-dependence, semantical 19, 266-67, 270-71, 278, 286
-independence, semantical 19,
-independence thesis 262-63, 265, 269, 275, 277
meaning varies with, 19
resolving ambiguiities 191
continuity, epsilon-delta definition of 1
continuum hypothesis 50
conversational
assumptions 189

expectations 117, 189
   principles 122–23, 152, 190, 199n
coreference 154
count nouns 224–25
   in Finnish 225
cyclic principle 29n, 233, 263

decision problem for second-order logic 7, 37, 50
deep structure 89
   semantics, rejection of, 265
defensibility, conditions of 61
definability, Rantala's theory of 9
definite article 206, 223
   anaphoric use of, 15, 24, 137–39, 141, 146, 148–50,
         152–53, 156–59, 269–70
      and optimal strategies for Myself 149
      as a semantical phenomenon 148–50
      as semantically basic use 137
      "in" formal languages 142–43
      similar to pronouns, see pronouns
   counterepithetic uses of, 146
   epithetic uses of, 145–46, 148
   generic use of, 137
      as variant of anaphoric use 159n
   Russellian use of 139–42, 269–70
      as variant of anaphoric use 159n
definite descriptions 137–160, 274
   Mates-type uses of, 154–55
   of laziness 157
   Russell's theory of, 137–41, 269
      existence requirement 138
      uniqueness requirement 138
   Strawson's thesis about, 148
   treatment of in game-theoretical semantics 139–56
deixis 159n
derivational constraints 29n
descending-chain condition 62
determinacy thesis 264–66, 275
determinateness, axioms or assumptions of, 4, 44n, 62–63,
      93
deviance 67
dialogical games 25, 40, 42
   Lorenzen, 26n, 39, 41
discourse semantics 25–26, 126
   game-theoretical, 143

disjunction 12, 70
distributive-collective distinction 116-17
doxastic possibility 124
Duhemian preference 184
Dummett-Prawitz proof procedures 41

"each" 78, 85-86, 90-91, 131, 163, 166
economy principle for rule application 122-25
Ehrenfeucht games 2
entities, classes of 209
epistemic
    logic 40, 105, 188-90, 193, 199n
    notions 232
    operators 14, 24
ε-calculus 183
essential predication, see predication
events
    and nominalization processes 227
    as basic particulars 227
    Davidsonian ontology of, 116-18
"ever" 234, 241
ever-thesis 234-35
"every" 17, 78, 84-87, 90-91, 118, 131, 163, 166, 205,
    212, 223, 236, 246
excluded middle, law of 44n, 59, 62-63, 93
    in game-theoretical semantics 4
    in game theory 4
exclusion
    phenomena 151-52
    rules for quantifiers 153
existence, reasoning about 33
existential instantiation 38
existential presuppositions, Aristotle's 180
existential quantifier as Myself's move 36, 70, 168
extensionality 274-75
extensive form of a game 5

falsity, see truth
"few" 25, 206, 273
"first philosophy" (Aristotle) 220
form
    in relation to modern idea of relation 227
    -matter distinction (Aristotle) 223, 226-27
fragment (of a language) boundaries 214-25
free relative clauses and indirect questions 192, 200n

Fregean conception of a logical system 186, 195n
Fregean semantics 184, 216
Frege Principle, see compositionality
Frege-Russell ambiguity thesis, see "is", ambiguity of
Frege's second principle (a word has meaning only in context) 261-62
Frege's trichotomy, see "is", ambiguity of
functional interpretations 56, 232
   and game-theoretical semantics 2, 6, 60, 92, 203
   and intuitionism 60-61
   and natural language phenomena 64
   foundational studies, using 60, 62
   motivation for, 60, 62
   of first-order arithmetic 2, 41, 45n
   of first-order languages 6, 7, 41, 45n, 59
functional-lexical approach, see atomic sentences
functionals, see "higher-order languages, functions in"
   classification of, 62
fuzzy logic 109

game quantifiers 2, 232, 271-72
game rules
   (G. A) 3-4, 202
   (G. a(n)) 10, 20, 108, 143-44, 146, 165, 170-71, 232
   (G. after) 131
   (G. ago) 132
   (G. anaphoric the) 141-49, 151, 153-56, 158
   (G. and) 166, 168, 233, 242, 256n
   (G. any) 11, 15, 103, 108, 165, 231, 233, 242-43, 251, 256n
   (G. before) 129-30
   (G. both) 108
   (G. E) 3, 201, 204-5
   (G. E$_{ex}$) 153
   (G. each) 11, 131, 165, 231
   (G. either) 108
   (G. ever) 234
   (G. every) 11, 15, 81, 84, 108, 165, 205, 231, 233, 251-52
   (G. fut) 125
   (G. gen) 160n
   (G. genitive) 143, 154
   (G. if) 15, 77, 81, 92, 167
   (G. knows whether) 77, 102
   (G. many) 108

(G. neg) 108
(G. neg + believes) 78, 96-97, 99
(G. no) 78, 144
(G. not) 120, 168, 243
(G. now) 132
(G. only) 78, 105, 107-8
(G. or) 166, 233, 242-43
(G. past) 108, 114-16, 118, 120-25
(G. past perf) 108, 124-25
(G. phrasal and) 167
(G. phrasal or) 168
(G. pred) 168, 174
(G. pres perf) 120, 125, 129
(G. rarely) 128
(G. repeatedly) 128
(G. Russellian the) 140
(G. several) 108
(G. some) 10, 12-14, 22, 29n, 69, 84, 108, 114, 164,
    203, 205, 208, 211, 216, 232, 252
(G. the) 108
(G. U) 3, 202
(G. U$_{ex}$) 153
(G. when) 128
(G. &) 3, 202
(G. v) 3, 56, 202
(G. ~) 3, 202
coordination of joint application of different, 126
coordination of simultaneous application of several, 115,
    122-27, 235
for modal operators 14
for negation 56
for pronouns 65-66
for propositional connectives 11, 14, 16, 56
for quantifiers 12-13, 16
inverses of, as rules of sentence generation 233, 252-53
stopping rule 170
with parallel translation rules 176
games
determinate 4
infinite 8, 197n, 271-72
material 44n
mathematical theory of, 34, 201
two-person (zero-sum) 3-4, 11, 27n, 34, 47, 113, 163,
    201, 231
with perfect information 7, 176

game-theoretical conceptualizations
  logicians' use of, 2, 8, 232, 255n
game-theoretical semantics (GTS)
  and intuitionism 61-62
  and the Frege trichotomy 162-70
  applications to natural language 9, 23, 71, 203, 206, 232
    translations into logical notation as by-product 71, 176, 206
  Aristotle's doctrine of categories reconstructed in, 218-21
  as truth-conditional semantics 4, 196n
  explanations in, 18, 250
  failures of invariance in 264
  for formal languages 2, 5, 23, 47, 152-53, 203
  interpretation of conditionals in, 6, 51-59, 71, 77, 93
  paradigm problem of, 1
  parallelism holds but compositionality fails in, 265
  Peirce as a precursor of 255n
  philosophical implications of, 42n
  regimented formalism for, 183
  relation to logic and the foundations of mathematics 47, 60
  treatment of anaphora in, 65
  treatment of descriptions in, 139-159
  treatment of quantifiers in, 1
  true Kantian approach 34
  use of, in philosophical analysis 23
generative
  explanations in syntax 18
  grammar 247-50, 263
    and recursive methods 243-44
    and semantics 244
  history of a sentence 12
  semantics 29n, 198n
genitive case 72, 76n, 154, 160n, 175
genus-species, in Aristotle 228n
"given" 1
Gödel's functional interpretations, see functional interpretations
grammaticality
  as a key concept in linguistics 244
  modification of the goal of language theory with respect to, (by Chomsky) 248-49

head-anaphor relation 146-50
Henkin quantifiers, see branching quantifiers
hide and seek 39
hierarchical structures in natural languages, suitable for
    semantical theories 215
higher-order languages (logics), 70, 73
    functions in, 6, 51, 72
    translations of first-order languages into, effected by
        game-theoretical semantics 5-6, 47, 50, 60
    variables 56
"homonymous" (Aristotle) 220
hypostatization of use as meaning, see meaning

I (set of individuals) 140-45, 147, 149, 152, 158
    inductively defined 155
"if" 17, 166, 235
if-then statements 54
"ill-definedness" of language (Chomsky) 249, 252, 254
imperfect tense 284
imperfections of natural language (Chomsky) 18
INDEF(inite) 90
indefinite article 163, 166-68, 170
    as a proclitic variant of the numeral "one" (Perlmutter's
        hypothesis) 224
    as apparent universal quantifier 158, 271
    as existential quantifier 67, 159, 168, 171, 271
    generic uses of, 182-83
    wide scope over negation 87
indefinite pronoun
    as existential pronoun 71
independent choices, minimization of in game rules 123-25
INDET(erminate) 90
indexical time reference 132-33, 286
indirect questions and free relative clauses 192, 200n
individuals "available" to players 64-65, 69, 155, 159
individuals, category of, in logic 186-87
"indivisible concepts" (Aristotle) 219
inferences in natural language 180-83
infinite analysis, Leibniz's idea of 8
infinitely deep logics 8, 63, 203, 271
information
    concept of 36
    sets 9, 36, 43n, 236
informational
    dependence 8, 36, 236, 238, 266

independence 9, 25, 36, 38, 176, 203, 238-39, 266, 281
information-seeking dialogues 41
inside-out principle 262, 264, 268, 272, 276, 289n
inside-out semantical analysis 19, 121, 133, 196n, 262-63
intensional
    contexts 266, 274-76
    logics 9, 24, 267
    operators 9, 51
interpreted languages 2, 11, 163, 201
interpretive semantics 265
intonation 111
intuitionism 60
intuitionistic
    arithmetic of higher types 61
    logic and mathematics 41, 61, 63
    logic, based on game-theoretical ideas (Lorenzen) 62
    predicate logic (Heyting's) 60
intuitions
    of grammaticality 186, 243
    semantical 185-86, 189, 199n
invariance thesis 263-65, 276
"is"
    ambiguity of, 15-16, 20, 21-22, 161, 169-70, 172-73,
        175-80, 185-87, 189-91, 193-94, 195n, 196n, 207-8,
        216, 219-20
        codified in quantificational languages 21, 162, 207-8
        "first serious advance in logic since the Greeks"
            (Russell) 161
        not discussed by philosophers before Frege 22, 179,
            208
    De Morgan's trichotomy 161
    of class inclusion (general implication) 15, 20, 161,
        171-72, 207
    of existence 15, 161-62, 171-72, 183, 207, 217
    of identity 15, 20, 161-62, 170-72, 174, 179-81, 183,
        191, 193-94, 207, 216-17
    of predication 15, 20, 161-62, 170-72, 175, 179-80, 183,
        191, 193-94, 195n, 207, 216-17
    treatment of, in GTS 173-76, 181, 189-90, 205-6
"it is not the case that" 101-2

"knows" 192-93
knowing how, skill sense of, 189
knowledge-acquiring activity 39
"knows" + direct object 192

"knows" + wh-clause 192
"knows whether" 102, 105
    nonrecursivity of, 105

lambda calculus, Scott semantics for, 186
language and reality, links between 39
language games (Wittgenstein's) 26, 33-34, 39, 201, 279
"language of thought" theories 185
learnability, language 259, 262, 264, 280
    Davidson's use of the concept to support a Tarski-type
        approach to semantics 259-60
    formal conditions on, as studied by mathematical
        linguists 259
    presupposes meaning of a whole determinable from a
        finite number of its parts 260
    Wittgenstein's use of the concept in his semantical
        investigations 259
left-to-right ordering 69, 118
    of verbs 122
linguistics
    dominance of generative methods in, 249-50
    methodology of, 16, 243
logical form, as underlying meaning 184; see also
    semantical relativity
logical omniscience, the problem of 9
logical system, modern conception of, see Fregean
    conception of a logical system

"many" 25, 206, 273
many-dimensional tense logics 133-34
many-sorted quantification 12, 16, 22, 212, 215
mass terms 187, 224-26
    in Finnish 225
mathematics
    Kant's views on, 26, 33-34
    reasoning in, 33-34
maximal genera 210-14, 216-17, 219
    nouns that correlate with, 213
    predicative correlates of, 210-13
    superpredicates correlated with, see superpredicates
meaning
    as truth conditions 149; see also semantics, truth
        conditional
    in context, see Frege's second principle
    in isolation 261

theories of, see semantics
use reified into, 261, 286-87
megiste gene (Plato's) 210, 219
"memory" of time moments 133-34, 267, 269, 286
methodological precepts 256n
"miraculous translation", of natural language into formal language 175, 279
Montague grammar 14, 20, 183, 206, 215-16, 221-22, 284-85
"most" 206, 273
motion, see change

natural language
and formal logic 65, 109, 153
nonlogical character of, 109
neg
as a contradictory forming operation 77, 93, 99, 106, 167
as a sentence-initial constituent 89, 97-98, 100
as a syntactic operation 93, 96, 103, 106
operating on an ungrammatical string 78-79, 96-97, 99, 106
negation 12, 17, 25, 29n, 56, 77-111, 232, 242
idiomatic 87
importance of ordering principles in semantics of, 91, 108-9
Klima-type treatment of, 89-91, 100
nonrecursivity of, 82, 87-89, 92, 100, 102, 109
regular 95, 98
term 95-96
negation formation
how competent speakers perform, 83
incompleteness of effective, purely syntactic rules for, 82, 87-89, 92, 100, 110n, 267
in formal languages 89, 101
natural rules for, 89, 267
semantical character of, 82
"no" 212
no-counterexample interpretation 54
nonatomic sentences 206
truth defined for, 3, 163
nonclassical logic 6, 41
nonidentifiability of transformational grammars 288
nonintuitionistic procedures 63
nonrecursive (noncomputable) functions needed for values of variables in classical logic 6

nonrecursive strategy 49
nonstandard interpretation
    of first-order logic 7
    of higher-order logic 7
nonstandard quantifiers 25, 119-20, 135n, 206, 273
normal form of a game 5, 27n, 51, 75n
"normal sentence", perceptual distance from, 257n
"not" 17, 96, 235
"now" 132-33
N-rules 79, 88, 90, 101, 110n
    (N. and) 79
    (N. atomic) 80
    (N. every) 79
    (N. if) 80
    (N. no) 79, 86
    (N. or) 80
    (N. some) 79, 86
    (N. some)* 86
    derivations using, 80-81, 83-86, 90
    for "a(n)" 79
    for "any" 79
    for "each" 79
    modified 85-86, 90
    need for context sensitivity in, 86
    problem with preserving scope relations 82-83, 85
numerical quantifiers 116, 119

one-sorted quantification 22
"only" 105-7
    nonrecursivity of, 107
"or" 12, 166-67
order of verbs matches order of time elements 123, 126,
    283-84
ordering principles 14, 15, 25, 29n, 65, 90, 92, 94, 108,
    197n, 198n, 232, 234, 237, 246
    (O. any) 14, 17, 19, 98, 233, 235-40, 243, 251, 256n
    (O. comm) 14, 20, 232
    (O. each) 14, 233
    (O. every) 233, 251
    (O. LR) 14, 119, 232
    general 14, 232-33
    special 14, 232-33
    tenses and other quantifiers 114, 118, 121, 133, 135
outside-in semantical analysis 19, 121-22, 196n, 267, 271,
    279, 284

paradoxes, semantical and set-theoretical 215, 272
parallelism of syntax and semantics 109; *see also*, SPS
   principle
parallelism thesis 263-65
"parameterized dependency" thesis 252
parameterized version of the autonomy of syntax, see
   syntax
partially ordered quantifiers, see "branching quantifiers"
Peirce, C. S., as a precursor of GTS 255n
philosophy of logic 34, 40
philosophy of mathematics 7
possible-worlds semantics 9, 274-76
pragmatics 41, 188
predication, accidental and essential 173, 179, 220
prepositional phrases 16, 210
primary and secondary occurrences of descriptions
   (Russell) 140
  insufficiency of distinction 140
primative predicates 23
Principia Mathematica 162
principles vs. rules in semantical explanations 89, 94-95,
   104, 108-9
probability theory 153
pronouns, 15, 68; *see also*, anaphora
  anaphoric use of, similar to anaphoric use of definite
    article 25, 156-59
  and variables, see variables
  apparent assymetries with definite articles, 153-55
  of laziness 24, 68, 157
  referential mechanism for, 157-59
  with quantifier phrases as heads 24, 157-59
proof
  activities of formal, 40
  as attempt to construct a counterexample 44n, 61
  methods of, 35
  -theoretical methods 41
  theory 60
proper names, role in game rules 160n
psycholinguistics 20, 282; *see also* realism

quantification theory 34
  with(out) replacement 153
quantifiers
  exclusive interpretation of, 152-54
  inclusive interpretation of, 153

post-Aux occurrences of, 85, 91-92
pre-Aux occurences of 86, 91
sortal 16
quantifier phrases
as antecedents of anaphoric pronouns 73
Bresnan's analysis of, 222-25
plural 12, 88-89
singular 12, 73, 88
syntactical analysis of, 221-225
quantifier ranges 232
different wh-words associated with different, 209
dynamically restricted in treatment of descriptions, in game-theoretical semantics 139
gathered from syntactical clues 16
"manufactured" in ordinary discourse 225-26
widest, see maximal genera
question-answer dialogues 127
questioning logics 41
questioning as a method for acquiring information 41-42
questions
any- 240
assimilated to yes-no questions 241
express apparent disbelief or surprise 240-41
desiderata of, 187, 190, 193-94, 241
direct 187
iterated 274
multiple 24, 189, 199n, 254, 274
relation of, to answers 74
wh- 24, 187, 240-41
preference for universal reading of, 189
treatment in GTS 189
two-barrelled character of, 135n, 188-90, 199n
uniqueness presuppositions with, 189
question words 30

readings, number of 21
realism
methodological 20
psycholinguistic 20, 249-50, 279, 282-85, 287
recursive functions
restricting players' strategies to, 6-7, 45n, 49, 56-59, 63, 283
recursive strategies 6-7, 50-51
"reference time" (Reichenbach) 121, 134, 286
reflexive pronouns 154

"related word" notion, in parameterized version of
    autonomy of syntax thesis 251
relation, Aristotle's category of, 219-20
relative clauses 13, 22
    formation rules for, 253, 257n
relative pronouns 210
relativized quantification 213
relativity, see semantical, and see Whorfian
replacement, quantification theory with(out), 153
role swapping 12, 66, 68, 93
rule ordering
    in formal languages 13
    in natural languages 13-14
    underdetermination of, in GTS 14, 115

scope
    absence of indicators of, in natural languages 15, 19
    extends arbitrarily far in natural language 270
    in formal languages 15
second-order
    languages (logics) 6, 7, 37, 45n, 51, 56, 281
    quantifiers 12
seeking and finding
    activities of, 33, 38, 40-41
    language games of, 34
semantical games, 201
    as games of seeking and finding 34, 36, 39-40
    attempts at verification 10, 11, 25, 34, 113, 165, 201,
        231
    defined 3
    determinateness of, 57
    finiteness of, 4, 11, 202
    infinitely long 63
    rule ordering in, 14
    rules for, see "game rules"
    rules of semantical analysis 4, 8, 176
semantical interpretability and syntactical well-formedness
    18
semantical relativity 185
    of ambiguity 178-79, 189-90, 217
    of logical form 183-84, 196n
semantical representation
    frameworks for, 21, 172, 178, 184, 203, 207-8, 250
    inadequacy of first-order logic for, of natural language
        25

semantics
    canonical notation for, 21, 162, 175, 195n, 278
    central concepts of, 21
    for formal languages 13, 15
    for natural languages 13, 15
    logical 34-35
    methodology for, 21
    model-theoretical 125
    possible-worlds 9, 274-76
    referential system of (atomic sentences), 206
    standard (Henkin's sense of) 37, 292n
    structural subsystem of (nonatomic sentences), 206
    truth-conditional, 4, 35, 259-60, 277
        Davidson's attempt to find a "foundation" for in
            language learnability, 259
        new paradigm needed for, 280
    verification theories of, 35
sense, Frege's notion of, 276
sense perception 33
    Kant's views on 34, 38
sentence components with isolable meanings 19
set theory 4, 93, 283
"several" 25, 206
simple past tense 118, 120-21, 282
    "incompleteness" of, 121
simple (primitive) predicates, different classes of 217-18
"since" 129
Skolem functions 1-2, 5-6, 8, 232, 281-83
"some" (and cognates) 13, 23, 84-85, 87, 90-91, 114, 118,
        163, 166, 203, 211, 223
    plural uses of, 25
    reason for wide scope of, 85
some-any suppletion rule 90-91
sorts, see entities, classes of
SPS principle 95, 97, 103-5
    consequences of, 95-101, 103, 106
strategies 27
    as functions 6, 47, 70, 156
    in games 163
    pure 27
    "remembered" 64, 66, 69, 145, 159
stress, emphatic 111n, 277
    effect on scope relations 278
subcategorization of verbs 120
subdomains of quantifiers (sorts) 11-12, 22, 194

subgames 50-51, 56, 59, 93, 176, 203
    use of, for treating anaphora 24, 155-56, 158-59
    use of, for treating conditionals 6, 59, 63, 66-69, 92
    use of, for treating discourse semantics 25, 74, 126-27,
        143, 147
    use of, in natural language 63-64, 73
subordinate clauses 118, 133, 263
substance in Aristotle's metaphysics 220, 223
supergames 74, 126
superpredicates 214
surface structure 89, 265
syllogistic, traditional 180-83
    as a calculus of equations, 182-83
syncategorematic 228n
syntactic domains 29n
syntactical acceptability, see well-formedness
syntactical structure and logical form
    and rule ordering 14
syntax, thesis of the autonomy of, 250-51
    parameterized version of, 251

Tarski's T-schema 19-20, 277-79, 288n
    meant to capture "pretheoretical" truth 278-79
temporal
    adverbs 114, 115, 119, 125, 127-29, 132
    connectives 129
    language 24, 114-15
        semantics of, 113
tenses; see also temporal language
    construed as quantifiers 116
    interaction with "other quantifiers" 116-21, 131, 134
"that" 22, 141, 212
"the", see definite article
theoretical insight vs. particular examples 243
τὸ εἶναι 30, 179-80, 220
"tomorrow" 132-33
trace 12
transcategorial theory of "is" 217
transcategorematic words 214-15, 219, 226, 228n
    metalogical and metasemantical function of, 215
transcendental deduction 34-35, 38, 41
transfinite ordinals 62
transformations
    meaning preserving 89
translation of natural language into first-order logic

175, 203-4, 206, 247 (Chomsky's idea), 250, 279
truth
    logical 38
    material 38, 61
    mathematical 61
truth definition
    for a language must be in another language 215
    game-theoretical 3, 4, 8-9, 12, 36, 44n, 47, 163-64,
        201, 203
        as the existence of a winning strategy 4, 202, 231
    Tarski-type 2-4, 7-8, 19-20, 196n, 202, 259-60, 265,
        271-72, 279, 285, 288n, 292n
truth or falsity of sentences 2
two-dimensional tense logics 133, 268
    counterexamples to, 134
type-theoretical ascent
    to save compositionality 20, 284-85
    using subgames 56

ungrammaticality 67
universalizability in ethics and psycholinguistics 282
universal quantifier as Nature's move 36, 70, 168
    the point of using, 139
"universals (true)" (Aristotle) 219
"until" 129
urn models 9, 187, 203
use reified into meaning, see meaning

variables
    absence of, in natural language 10
    pronouns unlike bound, of quantification theory, 24-25,
        65, 152
verification and falsification
    as sequences of questions 41
    epistemic element in, 40

"we can find" 1
well-formedness 18
    and meaningfulness, not coextensive 233-34, 253
    explanations of, 18
    not a recursive notion 18
"what" 22, 194
"when" 22, 141, 163
"where" 22, 141, 163, 209, 213
"whether" 102-5

"which" 141, 163, 212
"while" 129
"who" 22, 113, 141, 163, 194, 204, 209, 213
Whorfian relativity 185
wh-quantifiers 194
wh-words 10, 12, 22-23, 209-17
    and relative pronouns 210
    correlation with maximal genera, see maximal genera
    correlation with quantifier ranges, see quantifier ranges
    two-barrelled character of, in their interrogative use
        135n

"yesterday" 132

SYNTHESE LANGUAGE LIBRARY

Texts and Studies in Linguistics and Philosophy

Managing Editors:

JAAKKO HINTIKKA (Florida State University)
STANLEY PETERS (The University of Texas at Austin)

Editors:

EMMON BACH (University of Massachusetts at Amherst), JOAN BRESNAN
(Massachusetts Institute of Technology), JOHN LYONS (University of Sussex),
JULIUS M. E. MORAVCSIK (Stanford University), PATRICK SUPPES (Stanford
University), DANA SCOTT (Oxford University).

1. Henry Hiż (ed.), *Questions*. 1978.
2. William S. Cooper, *Foundations of Logico-Linguistics. A Unified Theory of Information, Language, and Logic*. 1978.
3. Avishai Margalit (ed.), *Meaning and Use*. 1979.
4. F. Guenthner and S. J. Schmidt (eds.), *Formal Semantics and Pragmatics for Natural Languages*. 1978.
5. Esa Saarinen (ed.), *Game-Theoretical Semantics*. 1978.
6. F. J. Pelletier (ed.), *Mass Terms: Some Philosophical Problems*. 1979.
7. David R. Dowty, *Word Meaning and Montague Grammar. The Semantics of Verbs and Times in Generative Semantics and in Montague's PTQ*. 1979.
8. Alice F. Freed, *The Semantics of English Aspectual Complementation*. 1979.
9. James McCloskey, *Transformational Syntax and Model Theoretic Semantics: A Case Study in Modern Irish*. 1979.
10. John R. Searle, Ferenc Kiefer, and Manfred Bierwisch (eds.), *Speech Act Theory and Pragmatics*. 1980.
11. David R. Dowty, Robert E. Wall, and Stanley Peters, *Introduction to Montague Semantics*. 1981.
12. Frank Heny (ed.), *Ambiguities in Intensional Contexts*. 1981.
13. Wolfgang Klein and Willem Levelt (eds.), *Crossing the Boundaries in Linguistics: Studies Presented to Manfred Bierwisch*. 1981.
14. Zellig S. Harris, *Papers on Syntax*, edited by Henry Hiż. 1981.
15. Pauline Jacobson and Geoffrey K. Pullum (eds.), *The Nature of Syntactic Representation*. 1982.
16. Stanley Peters and Esa Saarinen (eds.), *Processes, Beliefs, and Questions*. 1982.
17. Lauri Carlson, *Dialogue Games. An Approach to Discourse Analysis*. 1983.
18. Lucia Vaina and Jaakko Hintikka (eds.), *Cognitive Constraints on Communication*. 1983.
19. Frank Heny and Barry Richards (eds.), *Linguistic Categories: Auxiliaries and Related Puzzles. Volume One: Categories*. 1983.
20. Frank Heny and Barry Richards (eds.), *Linguistic Categories: Auxiliaries and Related Puzzles. Volume Two: The Scope, Order, and Distribution of English Auxiliary Verbs*. 1983.
21. Robin Cooper, *Quantification and Syntactic Theory*. 1983.